MEXICO'S ONCE AND FUTURE REVOLUTION

MEXICO'S ONCE AND FUTURE REVOLUTION

*Social Upheaval and
the Challenge of
Rule since the Late
Nineteenth Century*

GILBERT M. JOSEPH AND
JÜRGEN BUCHENAU

Duke University Press Durham and London 2013

Designed by Heather Hensley
Typeset in Arno Pro by Tseng Information Systems, Inc.

Library of Congress Cataloging-in-Publication Data
Joseph, G. M. (Gilbert Michael), 1947–
Mexico's once and future revolution : social upheaval and the
challenge of rule since the late nineteenth century / Gilbert M.
Joseph and Jürgen Buchenau.
pages   cm
Includes bibliographical references and index.
ISBN 978-0-8223-5517-5 (cloth : alk. paper)
ISBN 978-0-8223-5532-8 (pbk. : alk. paper)
1. Mexico — History — Revolution, 1910–1920. 2. Mexico —
History — Revolution, 1910–1920 — Influence. 3. Mexico —
Politics and government — 20th century. 4. Mexico — Politics and
government — 21st century. I. Buchenau, Jürgen, 1964– II. Title.
F1234.J835 2012
972.08′2 — dc23
2013010104

PUBLISHED WITH THE ASSISTANCE OF THE FREDERICK W. HILLES
PUBLICATION FUND OF YALE UNIVERSITY.

DEDICATED TO THE MEMORY OF PATRICIA PESSAR

Contents

Acknowledgments

We have incurred many debts in the preparation of this volume. Thanks go to Emilia Viotti da Costa for suggesting the need for a concise and accessible interpretive volume on the Mexican Revolution and its consequences, and for encouraging the project in its formative stages. The scholarship of many colleagues in the field of modern Mexican history, across several academic generations, has inspired what appears in these pages. Indeed our teaching and writing on the origins, process, and legacy of the revolution have been enriched by decades of engagement with friends who often doubled as sounding boards and debating partners. We hope they will recognize the impact their ideas have registered on us. Several colleagues have been particularly stimulating interlocutors over the decades: the late Friedrich Katz, Alan Knight, the late Daniel Nugent, Adolfo Gilly, Bill Beezley, John Womack, Tim Henderson, Allen Wells, Ben Fallaw, Mary Kay Vaughan, Florencia Mallon, Steve Stern, the late Paul Vanderwood, Seth Fein, Pablo Piccato, Alejandra García Quintanilla, Daniela Spenser, Thomas Benjamin, Linda Hall, Mark Wasserman, Marjorie Becker, the late Bill Roseberry, Greg Grandin, Eric Van Young, John Hart, Romana Falcón, Javier Garciadiego, Paul Eiss, Barry Carr, Eric Zolov, Anne Rubenstein, Jolie Olcott, Ray Craib, Rick López, Mark Overmyer Velázquez, Louise Walker, Bill Schell, Gregory Crider, and last, but by no means least, the late Hernán Menéndez Rodríguez. Scores of students at Yale, UNC Chapel Hill, and

UNC Charlotte have patiently listened and talked back as we worked out kinks in the broader interpretation and individual chapters that appear here. Patricia Pessar dialogued with Gil Joseph for decades about themes of power and culture, and here, as in so many areas of his life, her partnership was without peer. She passed away as this book went into production, and we dedicate the volume to her memory.

We are also grateful to the anonymous readers at Duke University Press for their timely and insightful comments. Special thanks go to Sarah Beckhart and Micah Landau for their research assistance at important junctures. And, once again, Valerie Millholland proved her mettle as an indispensable editor and friend, helping this project along when life's challenges made its fruition seem distant.

Finally, this volume benefited from the generous financial assistance of the National Endowment for the Humanities, Yale University, and the University of North Carolina at Charlotte.

The tragedy of the Revolution was the moral impossibility of not supporting it and the material impossibility of achieving through it the regeneration of Mexico that would justify so much violence and destruction.

— MARTÍN LUIS GUZMÁN, *EL ÁGUILA Y LA SERPIENTE*

Introduction
REVOLUTION AND THE NEGOTIATION
OF RULE IN MODERN MEXICO

1

The Mexican Revolution is the defining event of modern Mexican history. The long, bloody, chaotic struggle began on November 20, 1910, as a rebellion against President Porfirio Díaz, the nation's authoritarian ruler since 1876, who was then eighty years old. Trouble had been brewing for several years. In 1908, Díaz had declared that, owing to his tutelage, Mexico was at last ready for democracy and that, accordingly, he would not seek a sixth presidential term. But when Francisco I. Madero, the scion of a wealthy northeastern Mexican family, took the dictator at his word and launched an energetic campaign that threatened to land him in the presidential palace, Don Porfirio ordered his arrest and prepared for a standard round of election fixing. This time, however, Díaz had badly miscalculated. Radical activists had been stirring up opposition to his faltering project of modernization for years. At the time of the elections, in mid-1910, an economic downturn and the dictator's increasing repression prepared Mexicans across the social spectrum to repudiate the regime. Thus, when Madero called for a national rebellion in November 1910, his call was seconded by a broad cross section of Mexican society, including members of the nation's burgeoning middle sectors and disaffected regional elites, as well as long-suffering workers and peasants. By mid-1911 Don Porfirio's federal army had been defeated in a far-flung guerrilla struggle with local Maderista bands. But Madero, proclaimed by many as Mexico's "Apostle of Democracy," quickly lost control of the diverse, hastily assembled revolutionary coalition. A decade of violence ensued as a bewildering array of interests clashed. This tumultuous process—dubbed a "fiesta of bullets" by one of its participants[1]—finally spent its fury, at a demographic cost that some have estimated as high as two million of the nation's more than fifteen million inhabitants. The revolutionary winners eventually institutionalized a new political regime, whose aptly named official party, the Institutional Revolutionary Party (PRI), ruled Mexico for the next seven decades, a remarkable stretch by Latin American and global standards.

This volume attempts to make sense of what it all meant. Luis Cabrera, perhaps the greatest intellectual of the Mexican Revolution, declared, "La revolución es la revolución," contending that the fundamental purpose of revolutions is "transcendent," for they "seek to change the laws, customs, and the existing social structure in order to establish a more just order."[2] As we shall see, the revolution certainly brought change, but the question of whether the postrevolutionary arrangement was more "just" continues to be hotly debated. Even the appropriate case of the initial letter in *revolution* is a matter of some dispute. We have chosen lowercase to distinguish what began as a multifaceted, distinctly local process from the institutional regime's subsequent appropriation, simplification, and mythification of that process—after which the PRI always rendered *revolution* in the uppercase—*la Revolución*—or "the Revolution." But as we will also see, this official political-cultural construct did not go unchallenged; indeed, a multitude of actors and interests within and outside the government continued to claim and negotiate the meaning of Mexico's social upheaval and its legacy. Thus the revolution has always served both regime projects and counterhegemonic impulses. We contend that it is precisely the durability and flexibility of "revolutionary" traditions and symbols, through which both the state and its opponents have sought to legitimate themselves, that differentiates the Mexican Revolution from other twentieth-century social movements.

Mexico's Once and Future Revolution traces the coming, process, consolidation, and consequences of the Mexican Revolution from an array of perspectives, including those of politicians, artists, and students; ideologues on the Left and the Right; rural campesinos and urban workers; the well-heeled, the dispossessed, and a multitude of people in between; and women as well as men. At the same time, we seek to contextualize these perspectives over a long duration, that of Mexico's "long twentieth century," from the origins of Porfirio Díaz's liberal oligarchic regime in 1876 through the neoliberalism of the present day. To study the history of the revolution and its legacies, therefore, is to reckon with the complex forces that contested and represented the processes that shaped modern Mexico and to glimpse Mexico's modernization as a nation and polity.

The timing of this volume could not be better, given the fanfare generated by the centennial celebrations of the epic revolution of 1910. Throughout Mexico and internationally, the centennial triggered a veritable cottage industry of commemorative events and has begun to generate a harvest of scholarly production in a field of study that was already quite robust. Long before the huge digital clocks strategically placed in the nation's major town squares began their dramatic countdown to the revolution's *centenario*—November 20, 2010—few branches of Latin American historiography had developed with such a degree of methodological sophistication and thematic richness as the study of the Mexican Revolution. Certainly no branch of Mexican historiography has more effectively utilized a regional and local approach and an array of analytic and hermeneutic techniques to probe central questions and test conventional national-level interpretations. Over the past several decades, historians have debated a host of "big questions" about the nation's revolution: Did its causation owe more to endogamous or exogenous factors? Does it make sense to regard it as a xenophobic "war of national liberation," as one historian has termed it?[3] To what extent did U.S. political and economic interests condition the contours of struggle and influence its outcomes? Should the epic revolution be singled out as the culminating moment of historical struggle in Mexican history, or did its denouement more properly signal a betrayal of revolutionary ideals and the ultimate triumph of a new (not so revolutionary) state over the people? In a related, comparatively informed discussion, the historian Alan Knight has asked whether the Mexican Revolution was "bourgeois," "nationalist," or just a "great rebellion"—that is, a nontranscendent, largely political event hijacked by the winners to shore up new or residual class interests.[4]

And do the "high politics" of the factionalized struggle (as critical as they were in establishing winners and losers and setting the terms for "the Revolution's" institutional consolidation) provide only a partial history of the first great upheaval of the twentieth century? Do they really map onto the messy local equations of the Mexican revolutionary process, what Knight refers to as the internal "logic of the revolution"?[5] Significantly, representations in Mexican popular culture have come to refer to the factional struggle as *la bola*, which conjures up images of a mass of intertwined humanity or of a great boulder that rolls across the landscape, gathering force, veering in one direction, then the other.[6] This careening bola moves arbitrarily, brings death and destruction, and turns normalcy into chaos. While the whimsy of revolution is no doubt exaggerated in this popular depiction, it usefully evokes a revolution that was far from the phased and sequential affair that master narratives suggest.

In the past ten years, historians have also become increasingly preoccupied by the extent to which the Mexican Revolution was a revolution for women, both during and after the military phase. In what ways were the gender, class, and ethnic conditions of women transformed, positively and negatively, by the revolutionary process and its aftermath? To what extent did the social workers, educators, and eugenicists affiliated with the new "revolutionary state" use gender as a category in reshaping the domestic sphere and "modernizing" patriarchy?[7]

And what blend of social reform, political coercion and incorporation, and cultural hegemony accounts for the longevity — seventy-one years of rule — by the Institutional Revolutionary Party and its predecessors? Does the PRI's celebrated characterization as Latin America's "perfect dictatorship" (in the words of the Peruvian Nobel laureate Mario Vargas Llosa)[8] owe mostly to the regime's capacity to promote — at least until the Tlatelolco Massacre in October 1968 — an encompassing and reassuring discourse or myth of national belonging and inclusion, amid annual growth of 6 percent fueled by import substitution industrialization (the so-called economic miracle)? Or does it more properly index the official party's shrewd articulation of local and national institutions of patronage and clientelism (the PRI's *caciquismo revolucionario*), which, underpinned a "soft authoritarianism" beneath a democratic façade that could alternately co-opt or repress, as circumstances dictated?[9]

Finally, is the Mexican Revolution — either as an institutional structure or as a legacy of ideas, symbols, and expectations — definitively "frozen," "dead," or "over"?[10] To what extent does it still "have legs" — a question that problematizes both the residual strength of the PRI's elaborate twentieth-century cultural project as well as the continuing relevance of popular revolutionary symbols and social memory for diverse segments of society that were shaped by that project but took issue with the authoritarianism that underwrote it? In the wake of the demise of Mexico's institutional revolutionary state in a neoliberal moment of narco-induced political crisis that many also regard as distinctly *postnational*, does the revolution have any real significance? If so, what meanings can Mexicans within the country or residing across international borders recover and claim for it?

This recounting of a succession of historical debates merely scratches the surface of the past and present vitality that distinguishes Mexican revolutionary studies. *Mexico's Once and Future Revolution* is steeped in this provocative literature and, within the parameters of a short and accessible interpretive volume, engages either explicitly or implicitly with most of these "big questions." Yet it does so as it wrestles with what we regard to be perhaps the fundamental problematique in Mexican history: the continuing tension between grassroots political processes and cultures and the ongoing (and nationally and internationally conditioned) process of nation-state formation. Thirty years ago Friedrich Katz thoughtfully captured the terms of a paradox that historians and social scientists must continue to address in their work. Mexico is the only country in the Americas where "every major social transformation has been inextricably linked to popular [mostly] rural upheavals."[11] In fact three times within a century, in the independence insurgency of the 1810s, in the wars of Liberal reform of the 1850s and 1860s, and again in the 1910 revolution—that is, during Mexico's three much heralded "cycles of violence"—social and political movements emerged that destroyed the existing state and most of the military establishment, then set up a new state and army. Nevertheless, in each of the three cycles, the changes in the countryside and in the poorer sectors of urban society that these popular movements ultimately wrought were rather modest. Armies that began as largely campesino-based forces soon became the guarantors of an increasingly oppressive social order, which, in time, was itself challenged and eventually toppled. For example, the devastating Wars of Independence ushered in a weak central state in which powerful regional warlords held sway with the help of peasant-based armies. First and foremost among these warlords was the iconic nineteenth-century caudillo, Antonio López de Santa Anna, who governed Mexico with a combination of indifference and brutality on eleven occasions for a grand total of five years and could not stop the United States from annexing half of the national territory during his heyday (1828–53). Likewise both the Liberal Reforma and its Conservative enemies drew on campesino support and then turned to elite allies: the Liberals to the U.S. government and a growing national bourgeoisie, and the Conservatives to the Church hierarchy and Emperor Napoleon III of France. The ultimate outcome of this conflict was the thirty-four-year dictatorship of Porfirio Díaz.

Why have Mexico's embattled power holders repeatedly called upon campesinos and other subordinate groups, and why have the latter so often followed? Perhaps more important, what have been the political and cultural terms of engagement between dominant elites and subordinate classes, and how were they negotiated? These, Katz suggested, remain among the most enduring and tantalizing questions with which students of the Mexican past grapple — and they lie at the heart of this volume.

In 1986, almost fifteen years after his amiable challenge to fellow historians to produce "microhistories" of modern Mexico,[12] Luis González y González, the nation's most distinguished twentieth-century historian, could take satisfaction in the state of the new genre. Practitioners were legion, and the value of a regional or subnational approach to Mexican (and Latin American) studies was undisputed. Observed Don Luis, "We no longer have to prove the truth of the tongue-twisting *muchos Méxicos*. . . . It is a fundamental truth."[13] *Mexico's Once and Future Revolution* builds on two generations of regional scholarship that includes our own monographic studies of the Northwest and Southeast. It analyzes the reciprocal engagement of social movements and forms of domination during particularly consequential junctures, as well as over longer periods of time — in other words, before, during, and after "the Revolution." Integrating multiple timescales, such an approach enables us to gain a clearer understanding of what actually changed over the course of Mexico's long twentieth century, as well as to identify the agents and agencies of social and political transformation. By interpreting contributions from recent scholarship that illuminate the continuities and discontinuities of power as well as the experience of popular resistance, we show the ways in which popular involvement in the arenas through which the state advanced its official projects resulted in some measure of negotiation from below.

In one important respect, our volume contributes to an emerging watershed in the field: the international and transnational history of the Mexican Revolution. As Alan Knight has powerfully argued, Mexico's epic revolution was "one of those relatively rare episodes in history when the mass of the people profoundly influenced events." At the same time, "the necessary precursor of the *étatiste* 'revolution'" (the "high politics") that followed in the 1920s and 1930s,[14] was never closed to external influences and participation. Indeed, the glittering notion of popular revolutionary promise—and the commitment of a new state (at some junctures more intensely than others) to social well-being and betterment—fueled the ideas and actions of many progressive international travelers. Beginning with the military struggle and gathering momentum in the 1920s and 1930s, these transnational activists, writers, and artists often played the role of "citizen diplomats," spreading the message of what they understood to be the revolution, or to live the political and personal ideals they nurtured in its name.[15] Although the revolutionary state rather quickly moved to the center, displaying relatively little inclination to exercise a "world historical" role in the manner of the Soviets or, later, the Chinese and the Cubans, the Mexican Revolution still had profound international consequences. Not only did agrarian activists affiliated with the revolution's losing radical and populist factions fan out to other regions, there to create intriguing social laboratories of revolutionary reform (e.g., former Zapatista Felipe Carrillo Puerto in Yucatán), but observers from other nations, including internationalists like the Peruvian Víctor Haya de la Torre and the Nicaraguan Augusto César Sandino, traveled to their home countries to organize resistance against oligarchic rule. One cross-border sojourner, India's M. N. Roy, traveled to revolutionary Mexico after being exiled from the United States by President Woodrow Wilson. He helped found the Mexican Communist Party before moving on to Europe and Asia to work with the Third Communist International. Still other radical intellectuals, artists, and cultural workers extended the revolutionary impulse across borders. Best known, of course, is the muralist Diego Rivera, who pioneered expressive forms of public and plastic art that would galvanize popular mobilization beyond Mexico (including African American and left-wing artists in the United States during the New Deal and after).

Although the ideology of the incipient revolutionary state builders (especially the so-called Sonoran Dynasty, headed by Alvaro Obregón and Plutarco Elías Calles, from 1920 to 1934) was rather moderate, the revolutionary struggle—codified in the highly nationalist Constitution of 1917 that qualified capitalist property relations—riveted the attention of powerful U.S. elites. Throughout the 1920s and 1930s, Washington's posture toward Mexico alternated between threat and accommodation, which no doubt played a role in tempering the pace of reform of the new regime. At the same time, however latent before the high tide of reform during the presidency of Lázaro Cárdenas (1934–40), the revolution's social, agrarian, and nationalist promise made it impossible for the United States to reflexively adhere to the economic and political assumptions and practices that had previously guided nearly a half century of unrestrained dollar and gunboat diplomacy in Latin America. Recent works have conjured up the transnational webs and bohemian communities of nomadic U.S. intellectuals and activists who operated with equal facility in Mexico City and New York. Such transnational subjects involved themselves in the new revolutionary state's cultural initiatives and several, like the journalist Anita Brenner, played important roles in fashioning the state's new formulations of the popular national character (*mexicanidad*), which turned in part on a mainstreamed notion of mixed-race identity (*mestizaje*). Other public intellectuals and progressive scholars, such as Carleton Beals, Frank Tannenbaum, and Ernest Gruening, helped to advance formidable radical critiques of private property and American interventionism. In the process, these border-crossing citizen diplomats penetrated (and "stretched") the highest rungs of U.S. political culture in the 1920s and early 1930s and, in a manner of speaking, constituted the Mexican origins of the New Deal.[16] Other scholarly contributions similarly underscore the international reach of the Mexican Revolution, emphasizing the hemispheric Latin American intelligentsia that thrust the revolution's statist notions of social property and sovereignty onto the world stage. They show that even as bellicose U.S. business interests were applying strong pressure on their government to demand the revocation of the Constitution of 1917 and overthrow the Constitutionalist regime, President Carranza himself went on the offensive, charging Mexico's unofficial envoy to the 1919 Paris Peace Conference to "have the ideas of the new Mexican Constitution [including Article 27's agrarian notion of 'social property'] incorporated as a principle of international law." In the middle decades of the twentieth century, international jurists like the Chilean legal theorist Alejandro Alvarez would draw upon Mexico's revolutionary charter to formulate what they referred to as

"American international law," a corpus that featured respect for national sovereignty and state-sanctioned social, ethnic, and agrarian rights. Many of these social democratic principles, which challenged sacrosanct U.S. assumptions underwritten by Lockean constructions of liberalism, were subsequently enshrined in the 1948 United Nations Declaration of Human Rights. In the interim nearly every Latin American nation had adopted a constitutional charter similar to, if not modeled on, Mexico's revolutionary constitution.[17]

It would be hazardous, of course, to make great claims about the Mexican Revolution's impact on the rest of Latin America or the world, comparing it in the same breath with the Cuban Revolution later in the twentieth century. Its influence on the American Popular Revolutionary Alliance (APRA) in Peru in the 1920s, the original Sandinistas in Nicaragua in the 1920s and 1930s, or the National Revolutionary Movement in Bolivia in the early 1950s pales by comparison to the Cuban Revolution's inspiration of Latin American New Left regimes and social movements in Guatemala, Nicaragua, El Salvador, and various South American nations. No Mexican hero cult like Che Guevara's ever emerged to provide iconic images for the banners and dorm rooms of the international student and Left movement in 1968. Perhaps Mexico's most influential revolutionary export over the long term was revolutionary indigenism, dating from the 1920s and 1930s. Mesoamerican and Andean nations sent delegates to the Cardenista-era *indigenista* congresses, like the one in Pátzcuaro in 1938, and modeled their indigenista institutions on Mexican models, such as those of the Departamento de Asuntos Indígenas and the Instituto Nacional Indigenista. For all of their paternalistic and corporatist shortcomings, these Mexican institutions afforded indigenous leaders a modicum of participation in the state, a strategy that would resonate elsewhere in the hemisphere. Although whatever vitality resided in Mexico's state-led *indigenismo* was clearly spent by the onset of neoliberalism in the 1980s, as we shall see, a new grassroots Mexican model would beckon in the mid-1990s with the dramatic proclamation of the Zapatista movement of Chiapas (the Ejercito Zapatista de Liberación Nacional). To a degree the PRI had never contemplated, and taking advantage of the latest electronic technologies, the EZLN cultivated international and South-South linkages and registered an impact on indigenous social movements in Central and South America.

Thus an emerging international and transnational history informs this

volume's discussions of Mexican foreign relations and the complex manner in which the external and internal were interwoven during the epic
revolution and in the decades that followed. Until recently—perhaps as
late as the early 1990s—state propagandists, critical intellectuals, and professional scholars alike discussed the cultural affairs of Mexico in terms
of a bounded nationalism celebrated for its authenticity and idiosyncrasy
and epitomized by amorphous concepts such as *lo mexicano* (the Mexican way) or *mexicanidad*. Part official construct, part popular narrative,
these concepts emerged in the 1920s as organizing motifs for a society
devastated by revolutionary turmoil and in search of a unifying, modern
identity. But as recent scholarship and this volume seek to demonstrate,
one must vigorously interrogate cultural-political constructs like lo mexicano or mexicanidad and their claims for exceptionalism. For starters, a
multitude of state, market, and local actors and interests that *transcended*
national boundaries shaped, resisted, and ultimately negotiated these constructs. Moreover they came to serve oppositional impulses as well as the
PRI's official political and cultural project.[18]

THE BOOK'S STRUCTURE

Mexico's Once and Future Revolution is organized around seven consequential periods of Mexican revolutionary history. Following chapters devoted
to these eras, the concluding chapter reprises the volume's conceptual
argument and brings the revolution's relevance and legacies up-to-date.
Every revolution has an ancien régime, and chapter 1 examines the backdrop of Mexico's epic revolution in terms of the structural and triggering causes embedded in the dictatorship of Porfirio Díaz. At the outset
of the chapter, we briefly contextualize the Porfiriato in the earlier history of mid-nineteenth-century Mexico. Specifically Díaz's regime was the
result of the development of Mexican Liberalism, first unleashed by the
watershed of legislative reforms presided over by the Liberal leader Benito
Juárez in the 1850s. This Era of Reform triggered Conservative reaction,
which over the next decade drove both the War of the Reform (1858–61)
and the French Intervention (1862–67)—and ultimately the war to lib-
erate Mexico from French occupation. Collectively this decade of turbu-
lence constitutes Mexico's second celebrated cycle of violence. We argue
that both Juárez's Liberal Reform and the French-supported empire of
Maximilian of Hapsburg introduced new modernizing notions of capital-

ist property and the role of the central state that would pave the way for Díaz's "Order and Progress" regime after 1876. While this regime finally produced a stable government after a half century of political instability, civil war, and foreign intervention, its mixture of modernization and repression created the social and political conditions that led to Madero's call to revolution in November 1910.

Chapter 2 seeks to explain the military victory and subsequent demise of Francisco Madero's unwieldy revolutionary coalition. More broadly, the chapter analyzes the failure of Mexico's first experiment in liberal democracy during a fifteen-month administration that saw President Madero besieged by forces on both the Left and the Right. The failure of Madero's brand of nineteenth-century Liberalism paved the way for General Victoriano Huerta's brutal neo-Porfirian dictatorship.

In turn, this dictatorship unleashed the revolution's bloodiest phase, which first pitted the revolutionaries against Huerta and then, each other, and devastated the nation. Chapter 3 evokes the chaos of this "fiesta of bullets" and chronicles the ultimate triumph of Venustiano Carranza and Alvaro Obregón's middle-class Constitutionalist faction over Pancho Villa and Emiliano Zapata's more humble agrarian Conventionists. The victors went on to promulgate what was then the world's most progressive constitution, in 1917, but Carranza's ensuing moderate presidency (1917–20) made little headway in implementing it amid the daunting challenges of political and economic reconstruction.

Chapter 5 examines more thoroughgoing efforts at reform and reconstruction after the violent decade. It conceives of state and nation building under the Sonoran presidents Obregón and Calles as a negotiated and contested process in which both an embryonic revolutionary state and popular grassroots movements played essential roles in triggering and later resolving conflicts regarding education, health, and religious practice. As the revolution began to institutionalize itself under the new National Revolutionary Party (PNR) in 1929, it invented the myth of the "revolutionary family," a fictive consensus that united in death martyred heroes (Madero, Zapata, Villa, Carranza, and Obregón) who not long before had been bitter adversaries in life. Meantime, amid the gathering Great Depression, Calles, after 1928 the regime's formidable *jefe máximo*, increasingly turned away from land redistribution and other reform initiatives called for in the revolutionary Constitution of 1917.

Chapter 6 privileges the brief revival of social revolution under Mexico's iconic populist president, Lázaro Cárdenas. It seeks to explain the phenomenon of Cardenismo as a response to the growth of popular radicalism during the period when Calles ruled from behind the scenes as jefe máximo. The reciprocal relationship between the initiatives of the Cardenista state (e.g., unprecedented agrarian reform and the nationalization of the foreign oil industry) and their reception at the grassroots and among powerful domestic and international elites, is critical to an understanding of both the reach and the limits of structural change in the ideologically polarized climate of the 1930s. Cárdenas's greatest legacy may well be the corporatist political arrangement he set in place, which centered on the capacity of his new Party of the Mexican Revolution (PRM), established in 1938, to vertically incorporate, legitimate, and control through patronage the nation's peasants, workers, and other organized sectors. In the progressive and combative climate of the mid-1930s, corporatism provided channels for Cardenistas to mobilize and redress the grievances of campesinos and workers. But after a center-right candidate focusing on national economic development emerged victorious in the 1940 elections (with Cárdenas's blessing), the capacity of the corporatist state to demobilize and defang radical initiatives became increasingly manifest.

In chapter 7 we examine the conclusion of the process of institutionalization, fittingly marked by the creation of the eponymous (and oxymoronic) Institutional Revolutionary Party (1946). The fully formed PRI represented a retooling of Cárdenas's PRM to better serve the oligarchy of state bureaucrats, industrialists, financiers, and international investors that drove the administration of President Miguel Alemán (1946–52). We dissect the PRI's capacity to claim the legacy of "the Revolution" and mediate social conflict in its name, while alternately co-opting or crushing dissenting elements. The PRI's vaunted—if exaggerated—hegemony was abetted by the so-called Mexican Miracle, fueled by the strategy of import substitution industrialization that consistently produced high annual rates of economic growth. The Miracle also facilitated the emergence of Mexico City as a postwar megalopolis, a mecca of mass consumer culture that included transnational ideas and lifestyles underpinning the rise of the Mexican counterculture and worker, peasant, and student protest movements of the late 1950s and 1960s. When these waves of protest culminated in mass demonstrations in the nation's capital on the eve of Mexico's hosting of the 1968 Olympic Games, the state responded with violence, killing several hundred students and civilian protesters in Tlatelolco Square on a single afternoon. This seminal moment unmasked the PRI regime as repressive and *anti*revolutionary.

Chapter 8 examines the legacies of the Mexican Revolution from Tlatelolco until the PRI's unexpected electoral defeat in 2000. In addition to accounting for the genesis and political impact of the student massacre, we analyze the neopopulist—and excessively corrupt—regimes of Luis Echeverría and José López Portillo (1970–82), which attempted to restate the official party's claims to embody the revolution. These claims were dealt a death blow by the 1982 debt crisis, which brought IMF-dictated austerity to the already reeling working classes and introduced the neoliberal economic reforms that would soon abolish the nationalist, agrarian, and social welfare provisions of the 1917 revolutionary constitution. The devastating earthquakes that razed poor and middle-class barrios throughout Mexico City in 1985 further discredited the indifference and corruption of the PRI. Less than a decade later, on January 1, 1994, the Zapatista rebellion in Chiapas, which broke out on the very day that the neoliberal North American Free Trade Agreement took effect, signaled the end of PRI dominance while simultaneously demonstrating the continuing power of revolutionary symbols to contest state oppression. Six years later, in the next presidential election, Vicente Fox and his conservative Partido Acción Nacional (PAN) swept the PRI from power after seven decades of unbroken rule.

In the volume's conclusion, we examine the revolution's legacies and paradoxes in the new millennium. We take advantage of the epic revolution's 2010 centennial to glance backward and forward, assessing enduring continuities and introducing new social movements and political phenomena, such as the PRI's return to power in the presidential election of 2012.

We are free, truly free, when we don't need to rent our arms to anybody
in order to be able to lift a piece of bread to our mouths.

— RICARDO FLORES MAGÓN, SPEECH, MAY 31, 1914

PORFIRIAN MODERNIZATION AND ITS COSTS | 2

The long reign of General Porfirio Díaz is more accessible to our present-day sensibilities than the chaotic age of Santa Anna (1824–53), with its endless sagas of opera bouffe caudillos, foreign interventions, and caste warfare. Indeed, the so-called Porfiriato (1876–1911) is often cast as Mexico's version of the Gilded Age, the political-economic regime that ushered in "modern Mexico." The period is more accessible to us because it exhibits many of the characteristics of the nation at the turn of the twenty-first century, namely, a relatively strong and stable central state and the opening up of the economy to robust foreign investment. But the Porfiriato is also similar to the present moment in its privileging of economic growth and modernization over meaningful social reform. The costs of this nineteenth-century "Order and Progress" model of economic growth would be steep, culminating in the epic revolution of 1910.

Important changes in the global economy that gathered force in the second half of the nineteenth century would play a key role in shaking Mexico out of the political and economic doldrums that had plagued the young republic since independence. This transformation accompanied the second phase of the Industrial Revolution, which not only witnessed the geographic spread of industrialization but also integrated primary commodity producers like Mexico more tightly into the burgeoning Atlantic industrial economy. The great industrial powers prized Mexican tropical agricultural commodities like rubber and henequen from the southern states, industrial ores and metals from the North, and, of course, oil from the Gulf.

THE BEGINNINGS OF MODERNIZATION, 1848–1876

We might pick up the story in the aftermath of the Mexican-American War (1846–48), when Mexicans pondered the effects of their nation's catastrophic invasion and defeat by the U.S. Army, which resulted in the loss of more than half of Mexico's territory. This national humiliation prompted the emergence of a coalition of Liberals who believed that the only way to survive U.S. expansionism was to adopt much of the socioeconomic and political philosophy of its northern neighbor. In 1854, the year after General Santa Anna sold off northern Sonora to the United States, the Plan of Ayutla engineered the defeat and exile of the Conservative caudillo. Juan Alvarez, the Liberal general who spearheaded the Ayutla rebellion, soon disappeared from the spotlight, leaving a group of idealistic young civilians that included the Oaxacan Benito Juárez to reorganize Mexico's political and economic structure.

Thus began the Liberal Reform (1855–57), a period when Juárez and his associates experimented with many of the recipes for modernization that would become guiding principles during the Porfiriato. Most important, the Liberals sought to turn a country in which the Roman Catholic Church held half of the arable land and a small landed oligarchy much of the rest into a nation of property owners. They also desired to erode the influence of the Church, which enjoyed a virtual monopoly over the educational system and also served as the country's primary moneylender and real estate broker.

With the political allies of the Church, the Conservative Party, discredited through their association with Santa Anna, the Liberals passed a series of laws culminating in the 1857 Constitution, which proclaimed Mexico a democratic, secular republic. Among the more progressive provisions, the constitution abolished slavery, debt servitude, and the death penalty. As a precursor of the revolutionary Constitution of 1917, it was most notable for Article 27, which forbade the Church — or any other "corporation" — from acquiring or managing land or real estate. Foreshadowed in the earlier Lerdo Law (1856), this provision allowed the government to expropriate Church lands and sell them to private investors. In a nation rent by factional strife, foreign intervention, and prolonged economic crisis since the devastating Wars of Independence (1810–21), the new constitution presaged the kind of orderly, capitalist transition that was a prerequisite for the flow of foreign investment needed to develop infrastructure, exploit the country's vast natural resources, and thereby stave off the threat of further U.S. annexations.

Predictably, however, neither the Church nor the Conservatives accepted the new order. In 1858 they rose up against Juárez's Liberal government, and the ensuing War of the Reform (1858–61) added another bitter chapter to a history of rebellions, civil wars, and foreign interventions. As both sides found out, the conflict over the Reform Laws ran deeper than a disagreement within the elite over landownership and the role of the Church. Indeed, many indigenous villages that owned land as communal property viewed the Lerdo Law as a threat to their existence, since Article 27 could be interpreted as an attack on collective landownership. Other campesinos defended the Church because ecclesiastical officials had allowed peasants to farm on Church-owned property—lands that now faced expropriation and transfer to private owners. For their part, the Liberals also counted on widespread popular support owing to the new constitution's progressive if theoretical provisions dealing with debt servitude and forced labor. Finally, in 1861 Juárez and the Liberals emerged victorious from three years of brutal war that claimed tens of thousands of lives and left the economy prostrate.

At that very moment, foreign powers once again entered the scene. Britain, France, and Spain signed an agreement that they would enforce the collection of Mexico's massive foreign debt—much of it incurred during the recent war—by military occupation. While British and Spanish forces intended only to seize the customhouses, Emperor Napoleon III of France had the broader ambition of converting Mexico into the heart of a tropical empire. In 1862 French troops invaded. Briefly repelled at the first Battle of Puebla on May 5, a date celebrated to this day as Cinco de Mayo, the French troops went on to occupy Mexico City in alliance with the Conservatives. Two years later this alliance installed a young Austrian noble, Maximilian of Habsburg, as emperor.

Maximilian's empire would prove important for Mexico's subsequent history for three reasons. First and most important, Maximilian, like his Liberal adversaries, was a modernizer (indeed, he himself was a crypto-Liberal and a Mason), and his regime introduced an array of modern

French and Austrian ideas, values, legal codes, and practices. His advisers, the so-called *imperialistas*, closely followed French political thought, and collectively the European occupiers made their presence felt in cuisine as well as music and other forms of art. Second, the imperialistas' association with a foreign occupying army ultimately destroyed the Conservative Party as a political element, allowing Juárez's Liberals to claim the mantle of sole defenders of the Mexican nation. Third, the empire set the stage for a long-standing collaboration between the Liberals and the United States. Juárez's faction received diplomatic, economic, and military aid from the United States, which played an important role in their final victory over Maximilian and the Conservatives. Victorious in the Civil War, the U.S. government made it clear to the French that its occupation violated the Monroe Doctrine, which stipulated that the United States would resist any European efforts at colonization in the Americas. With Maximilian's government failing and the Liberals steadily increasing their military pressure, Napoleon III withdrew his troops in 1866–67. In June 1867 Maximilian's government fell to the Juarista forces, led, among others, by a young brigadier general, Porfirio Díaz. Fifty thousand Mexican lives had been lost fighting the French, and Mexico's existence as an independent republic remained as fragile as ever. Resolved to send a signal to European powers that further invasions would not be tolerated, Juárez ordered the execution of Emperor Maximilian and his leading Conservative generals. Thereafter, however, he mitigated reprisals against Conservative elite clans, many of whom managed to work their way back into positions of power in the decades ahead (e.g., the Cantón family in Yucatán).

Juárez's new government set the nation on a course toward a long period of relative political stability. On both sides of the Rio Grande, Juárez continues to enjoy a reputation as Mexico's Abraham Lincoln, the contemporary he approximated as a symbol of nationalism and republicanism, and even in dress. (Although as a five-foot-two Zapotec Indian, he cut a rather different image in his black frock coat and stove pipe hat!) Foreshadowing Mexico's subsequent political tradition, Juárez put together a powerful political machine. In the wake of so much social and economic dislocation and forced to contend with an unbroken tradition of regionalized cacique politics, Juárez reasoned that a strong central regime was essential to Mexico's future development.

Thus began the Restored Republic (1867–76) under the leadership of

Juárez and his successor, Sebastián Lerdo de Tejada—indeed, the beginning of Mexico's modern history. The Restored Republic expanded the state's presence in a variety of key sectors, establishing clear precedents on which the Porfiriato would build. It standardized a patchwork of tax and tariff schedules; it began to improve the nation's woeful transportation and communications facilities, most notably completing the stretch of railroad between Mexico City and the main port of Veracruz; it established the office of *jefe político*, or political boss; and it increased the state's capacity for public security, forming a federal rural constabulary (the *rurales*) to police the roads. All of these measures served to make Mexico more attractive to foreign investors. Simultaneously the Restored Republic established more professionalized diplomatic relations and cultivated a less antagonistic posture with the now-chastened Catholic Church, formerly the Conservatives' main ally. Finally, the Restored Republic began to reorganize the educational system, emphasizing mathematics, science, and "pragmatic knowledge" over the humanities. In sum, the Restored Republic paved the way for a more muscular centralized state, albeit one clothed in the guise of liberal federalism.

In 1876 General Díaz, a hero of the Liberals' first great victory over the French on Cinco de Mayo (1862), who had failed to reach power earlier in two elections and one unsuccessful coup d'état, finally succeeded in deposing Lerdo. The slogan of Díaz's coup was "Effective Suffrage and No Reelection," a pointed reference to the Juarista machine, which had engineered the reelections of Juárez (1867 and 1871) and Lerdo (1876) in violation of the 1857 Constitution. It was a slogan that would come back to haunt him several decades later.

The watchwords of Díaz's modernizing regime became "Order and Progress," *progress* representing the transcendental goal of modernity, and *order* the means to get there. Previously the Liberal Party's traditional slogan had been "Liberty, Order, and Progress." Much like the French Third Republic of the late nineteenth century, the Díaz regime fused the Liberal belief in material progress with the Conservative emphasis on political order of the authoritarian variety. Stability trumped individual and civil freedoms, which was a bitter pill for orthodox Liberals to swallow. During parts of five different decades, Díaz would rule Mexico by co-optation when possible and by coercion when necessary—an incredible feat, considering the whistle-stop presidencies of the first fifty years of the Mexican

republic. Santa Anna had occupied the presidential chair on eleven different occasions. By contrast, Díaz would step aside after one presidential
term in 1880 to honor his promise of no reelection, but then return in 1884
to a post he would not relinquish until 1911.

Viewed from the perspective of the tumultuous revolution that followed, the Porfiriato represents Mexico's old regime: the calm before
the revolutionary deluge. Yet its contradictions, inequities, and structural
violence ultimately rendered the dictatorship vulnerable to popular challenges. These weaknesses constituted the background causes of revolution. And in the three years or so (1908–10) that constituted the regime's
denouement, we can identify more immediate precipitants, the triggering
causes of the revolution.

In analyzing the causes, we might conceive of Don Porfirio's regime in
two phases. In the first phase, from 1876 to about 1905, we can gauge the
regime's political and economic accomplishments against a period of prosperity and economic boom. Indeed, foreign observers considered the Díaz
regime a model for Latin American export-led development and modernization. Contemporaries marveled at Mexico's enduring political stability and daunting economic expansion, particularly the opening up of
the mineral-rich northern frontier. By contrast, during the second phase,
from about 1905 until the outbreak of the revolution in November 1910, the
regime's contradictions stand out in bold relief in a period of economic
downturn. The Porfirian political-economic model began to fray, then unravel, in the face of financial panic, poor harvests due to climatic changes,
a nationwide shortage of credit, increasing opposition from elites and a
pinched middle class, a decline in real wages, urban labor militancy, and
a rising incidence of banditry and revolt in a rural sector increasingly bur-
dened by debt and stagnation.

THE FIRST PHASE OF THE PORFIRIATO, 1876–1905

Díaz's accomplishments during the first quarter century of his regime de-
serve to be recounted, not least because they came to constitute a standard of comparison against which his performance after 1905 could only
suffer. First, given what occurred during Mexico's first fifty years of existence as an independent nation, it is hard to minimize Don Porfirio's feat
of checking strong centrifugal tendencies and bringing peace to a country devastated by decades of war and ideological partisanship. Díaz skill-

fully struck bargains with local power holders, offering them *pan o palo*, bread or the stick. Regional caciques (strongmen) could be incorporated into his regime, rewarded with political and military posts, or expunged from the political landscape. At least until his final term in office, Díaz deftly alternated competing elite clans in power; even if they did not immediately occupy office and the economic perquisites that incumbency conferred, they might expect that their time would come. Refusing cooptation into — let alone rebellion against — the system became unthinkable. In one celebrated instance, when one rebellious local chief was taken into custody and the federal commanding officer cabled Don Porfirio for instructions, he tersely replied, "Mátalos en caliente" (Kill them immediately).[1] Not for nothing, then, have many historians credited Díaz as the predecessor of the PRI's more elaborately institutionalized strategy of cooptation and coercion.

Equally impressively, Díaz presided over financial solvency. For the first time since independence, Mexico balanced its budget in the 1880s. Foreign debts were renegotiated at a reasonable rate of interest (from 20 to 4 percent) by now more obliging and respectful foreign governments and financial houses. There was no more need for the great powers to invade Mexico and ransack the customhouses; foreign claims were paid off without recourse to gunboat diplomacy.

This solvency became possible by the reactivation of the productive forces of the nation and the export economy — in truth, for the first time since the silver boom in the Bourbon period of the late eighteenth century. Foreign capital and technology helped restore the silver mines, U.S. investments unlocked the vast copper deposits of the northwestern state of Sonora, and foreign investment in oil and plantation crops (cotton, rubber, henequen, and coffee) also soared. Simultaneously Mexico experienced a veritable revolution in infrastructure and communications; here too foreign capital played a leading role. Rail, road, and telegraph capacity expanded geometrically. The rail net, for example, grew from four hundred to nineteen thousand miles; and telegraph companies strung forty-five thousand miles of new cables. New ports were built and old ones deepened. The most strategic transportation routes led to the northern border, to get goods to U.S. markets and finish the "pacification" of "savage tribes" in the name of progress and civilization. In the process of establishing vital export zones of mines, ranches, and irrigated agriculture, the Porfirians activated Mexico's regional peripheries, and the nation's vast northern frontier expanses became what we've come to know as "the border."

Not surprisingly, foreign statesmen and diplomats treated Díaz and his associates with great respect and as a model for other Latin American governments. In the early 1900s U.S. President Theodore Roosevelt—he of the "big stick" approach to foreign relations—even asked Díaz and his secretary of foreign relations, Ignacio Mariscal, to help him mediate the perennial wars and conflicts among the Central American countries.

If one were to play devil's advocate, one might say that by the Latin American standards of the day, Porfirio Díaz was perhaps a superior brand of benevolent despot and that some formula of efficient, centralized rule was inevitable after the chaos of midcentury. Had Díaz not consolidated his particular regime, it is possible, even likely, that the lesser caudillos he (and Juárez) neutralized would have continued to tear the republic to pieces.

As it was, Don Porfirio maintained stability and quelled dissent by means of an elaborate, multitiered mechanism of social control and violence. The paramount layer of force at the regime's disposal was the reinforced national line regiments of the federal army (los federales). Díaz also strengthened the rurales, the federal rural constabulary created by Juárez. At the state level, the regime was able to call upon the state police and militias, which in turn were supported locally by the jefes políticos and private, hacienda-based forces (guardias blancas), which not only enforced social relations on estates but hunted down runaway peons. Private security detectives and gun thugs in the mining camps and factories further enforced the Porfirian social regime. Finally, Díaz and his northern governors established working relationships with the Texas, New Mexico, and Arizona Rangers to crack down on disturbances on the border. In 1906, for example, 275 Arizona Rangers were individually sworn in as "Mexican volunteers" and helped to crush the miners' strike at Colonel Greene's Cananea Consolidated Copper Company in Cananea, Sonora. Díaz and his subordinates were so proud and convinced of the efficiency of this security apparatus that one of them was said to have bragged, "A blonde gringuita in a tight-fitting dress could walk from (northwestern) Tijuana to (southeastern) Yucatán and not have one hair on her head touched."[2]

President Díaz and his oligarchic clique of ministers and technocrats—

the self-proclaimed *científicos*, or scientists — were also proud of the modernization that Mexico experienced in this period. In many ways, the científicos were the heirs of Maximilian's imperialistas, a fact that demonstrated the fusion of Mexican liberalism and French thought. The fashionable centers of the major cities were lit, paved, and sanitized with modern sewage systems. Mexico City and certain regional capitals like Guadalajara, Puebla, and Mérida, Yucatán, had amenities for the *gente decente* that ranked with those of the world's leading cities. Maximilian's advisers had modeled Mexico City's Paseo de la Reforma after European grand boulevards such as the Champs d'Élysée in Paris. In turn, the Porfirian elite of Yucatán patterned Mérida's Paseo Montejo after La Reforma. Indeed, imported elegance and ideas, particularly from France, were all the rage among the Porfirian elite. Mexico City featured French-owned department stores such as El Palacio de Hierro that evoked comparisons to the *grands magasins* of Paris. Likewise most of the científicos subscribed to the pseudo-scientific French positivist notions of the day that exalted Western Europe and its peoples as the pinnacle of progress. As Anglo-American capital poured in, the elites combined this French cultural influence with British, German, and North American models. The científicos blended Comtean positivism with Herbert Spencer's social Darwinism, which denigrated Indians and mixed races; the German Böker family built a posh new hardware store in Mexico City widely dubbed "the Sears of Mexico"; and Mexicans who could afford it took up bicycle riding and baseball and drank imported beers (figure 2.1). The historian Lesley Byrd Simpson effectively evokes the fin de siècle elite mentality:

> Elegant carriages drawn by high-stepping thoroughbreds . . . paraded up and down the Paseo on Sundays, but the crowds of léperos [beggars] and country Indians who had offended good taste . . . were kept out of sight. The ladies discarded the graceful Spanish mantilla for [millinery] from Paris; their sons were sent to France for an education and came back pattering the lingo of the *boulevardier* and scoffing at the barbarism of their own country. The best people went in for building houses in the villainous style of the Second Empire. I was shown through one of them by its proud owner. . . . It was a museum piece of velvet draperies, pier glasses, marble tables, gilt, dazzling chandeliers, spindly chairs. . . . "Isn't it beautiful!" she exclaimed, "they don't build

FIGURE 2.1 Early twentieth-century promotion for North American Schaefer beer in Mérida, Yucatán, featuring a local elite woman in folkloric regional dress. Archivo Pedro A. Guerra, Mérida, Yucatán.

houses like this anymore. *There is nothing Mexican in it!*" Happy days were here again, and Don Porfirio would live forever.[3]

If Mexico was a gilded age for the creole aristocracy, it was equally so for foreign investors. Not surprisingly, Díaz was lionized abroad; foreigners knew he was a very vain man, and they heaped it on. Witness the following paean by U.S. Secretary of State Elihu Root in 1907:

If I were a poet I should write eulogies; if I were a musician I should compose triumphal marches; if I were a Mexican I should feel that the steadfast loyalty of a lifetime would not be too much to give in return for the blessings that he has brought to my country. But as I am neither poet, musician, nor Mexican, but only an American who loves justice and liberty, and hopes to see their reign among mankind progress and strengthen and become perpetual, I look to Porfirio Díaz, the President of Mexico, as one of the great men to be held up for the hero-worship of mankind.[4]

THE SECOND PHASE OF THE PORFIRIATO, CA. 1905–1910

And yet the social cost of what foreigners liked to refer to as the "Pax Porfiriana" ultimately proved too dear for most Mexicans. The regime's contradictions became especially patent during the second phase of the Porfirato, 1905–10, in which we can identify both the structural and triggering causes of the revolution of 1910.

Two significant statistics speak volumes about the yawning gap between rich and poor. First, the average life expectancy was thirty years in 1910, a shocking comment on the high level of infant mortality at the end of the Porfiriato (30 percent of live births). Second, in 1910 real wages in the agricultural sector were a quarter of what they had been a century before, at the end of the colonial period. Thus while prices had increased significantly, wages were up only slightly, if at all. As impressed as they were by the gaudy indicators of elite wealth, travelers frequently commented on the poor standard of living among urban and rural workers.

A survey of specific groups along the late Porfirian social pyramid bears this out. Regional variation aside, the conditions of hacienda workers, tied to the estates by debt, had deteriorated badly. Centuries, even decades back, the protection and paternalism bestowed by a *hacendado* had infused status as a resident worker, or *acasillado*, with distinct advantages. Now, however, the perquisites of the acasillado, such as housing, medical care, and the amount of the initial advance that bound the worker to the hacienda, had deteriorated, along with his wage. On the tropical southern plantations of Yucatán, Chiapas, and the Valle Nacional of Oaxaca, the harsh labor conditions, coupled with the workers' immobility, triggered indictments of "slavery" by social critics such as the U.S. muckraking journalist John Kenneth Turner. There is little doubt that paternalism on export-driven estates had become increasingly tepid over the course of the Porfiriato: in boom times, planters maximized their profit margins; in times of bust, debt-ridden hacendados passed down their losses to their dependent laborers.

The plight of independent peasants had also worsened. Throughout the Porfiriato, the assault on corporately held village lands, begun by the Liberals at midcentury, escalated, particularly in areas of intensified cash crop production. In the southern states of Morelos and Yucatán, for example, sugar and henequen plantations engulfed entire villages. In Morelos one of the sugar kings provided simple advice to peasants: "Let them farm in a flower pot."[5] In the northern state of Chihuahua, rural military colonists, who for generations had fought Indians on behalf of the Spanish and then the Mexican authorities, saw their landed patrimonies declining in the face of expanding ranches, mines, and railroads and skyrocketing property taxes. Even though free villages had contested their land and labor with the haciendas across the centuries in a process that had witnessed both victories and defeats, the late Porfiriato marked a particularly low ebb in this contest.

The condition of urban workers was similarly precarious. After 1905 they too suffered a drop in real wages and a marked deterioration in working conditions. With the influx of foreign capital, foreign personnel displaced many skilled workers and foremen; increasingly Mexicans heard English spoken in the mines, factories, and railroad yards, and they were obliged to accept lower pay than foreign workers. Denied the legal right to organize and strike, workers mobilized and struck anyway, only to face brutal repression — witness the bloody strikes at the Cananea copper mine (Sonora, 1906) and the Río Blanco textile mills (Veracruz, 1907). Not surprisingly, Mexican workers came to refer to their nation as "mother to gringos and stepmother to Mexicans."

At the very bottom of the social pyramid were the *léperos* (literally, lepers), the members of the urban lumpenproletariat, a floating population of beggars, the jobless, and underemployed street people. Swept off the street by the authorities empowered to make arrests by vagrancy laws, the léperos were preyed upon by unscrupulous Porfirian labor contractors. Hooked after a few drinks, they awakened from their hangovers en route to Yucatán's henequen plantations or the lumber camps in Chiapas, from which many never returned.

In other words, there was no shortage of grievances at the broad base of the social pyramid. Yet harsh oppression and perceived injustice do not a revolution create. The aggrieved must have room to maneuver; otherwise they will be forced to brood on the sidelines. For example, the Yucatecan henequen plantations, which were marked by one of the most oppressive regional labor regimes during the late Porfiriato, demonstrated low potential for revolutionary mobilization. They had to contend with a harsh work regimen, a diverse labor force made up of ethnic and linguistic strangers, a multitiered security apparatus, restricted mobility, and isolation from potential allies in the peasant villages, let alone in surrounding urban areas. It is little wonder, then, that the revolution came last to remote and oppressive southeastern plantation societies like Yucatán.

By contrast, the revolution came first to those areas that experienced the greatest amount of social change during the Porfiriato. On the other end of the spectrum, the copper miners of Cananea, Sonora, numbered among the highest-paid workers in the entire nation. Most of these miners had come to the Northwest from elsewhere in the republic, attracted by the relatively high wages. Aware that their North American coworkers enjoyed even higher pay for the same work, the Cananea miners displayed a high level of social and political mobilization, and it was no coincidence that, in 1906, they set off the first large-scale labor protest that heralded the crisis of the Porfiriato. Not surprisingly, Sonora would prove to be the breeding ground of the most enduring clique of revolutionaries, which included several participants and observers of the Cananea strike. Ironically, in 1915 one of them, Salvador Alvarado, would belatedly bring the revolution to Yucatán as an externally imposed governor of the state.

Perhaps more significant in the revolutionary equation is the role of the middle and upper classes, which typically provide the catalysts and early leaders of social revolutions. Fidel Castro was the son of a Spanish-born landowner in Cuba; many of the Nicaraguan Sandinistas hailed from the educated urban middle class; and the Iranian mullahs were similarly middle-sector actors. All of them had the requisite "tactical power," the room to maneuver politically and economically; moreover their defection (and that of others of their ilk) from the Old Regime deprived it of legitimacy—a crucial factor in the outbreak of the insurrectionary phase of a revolution.

The Mexican middle sectors had numerous reasons for dissatisfaction with the late Porfirian regime. Although the size of the middle class had grown dramatically during the economically dynamic Porfiriato, it had borne the brunt of an inequitable tax structure, one that placed unreasonable taxes on small businesses and properties. The middle class often had little ready access to credit, which, like the tax structure, was controlled by the ruling oligarchy. This created obstacles to middle-class advancement in good times and particularly victimized it during the economic shocks after 1905, when unemployment soared and financial panic led to numerous foreclosures on debt-ridden businesses and properties.

The newly expanded middle class, particularly a rising generation of university-trained professionals, also saw its advancement stymied in the political arena. After 1900 Díaz tended to rely on a trusted network of clients and cronies, a veritable "gerontocracy" of cabinet ministers, jefes políticos (district prefects), municipal presidents, judges, state governors, and military officers grown old in office with their patron. In these circumstances, an asphyxiating *empleomanía* remained endemic, with a young and frustrated white-collar workforce that included many people with university degrees chasing a dwindling number of political appointments and opportunities.

Not surprisingly, some members of this intelligentsia under duress carried out an aesthetic and philosophical revolt against the ruling Positivism of the científico oligarchy. In the Ateneo de la Juventud (Atheneum of Youth), an association of writers and philosophers based in Mexico City and founded in 1909, middle-class thinkers railed against an official curriculum of science and practical knowledge that had kept the bulk of the population illiterate. In their own literary production, they championed a subversive aesthetic that revalued romantic poetry, philosophy, and the humanities. Many of these Ateneistas, most notably Martín Luis Guzmán and José Vasconcelos, would soon fuel the ranks of the revolutionary factions, where they advised often unlettered revolutionary chieftains and drafted their proclamations. Along with this group, a few intellectuals close to the científicos began to criticize the Porfiriato. For example, in 1909, the year of the Ateneo's founding, Andrés Molina Enríquez published *Los grandes problemas nacionales* (The great national problems). The book assailed the hacienda as a feudal institution that impeded Mexico's economic and social development and posited that citizens of mixed-race ancestry (*mestizos*), and not the creoles of pure Spanish descent, were the true Mexicans. After the outbreak of the revolution, Molina also called for land reform, advocating the parceling out of hacienda land to individual campesinos.

Like urban workers, Mexico's middle sectors were vulnerable to displacement by foreigners. Many merchants and artisans lost out to more efficient foreign competitors; similarly, local accountants and managers became expendable as foreign firms brought their own professionals with them. In the rural sector, the venerable (and profitable) profession of muleteer could not compete with the new foreign-owned railroads in long-distance hauling. Thus, like urban workers, middle-class Mexicans feared that they—like their nation as a whole—were losing ground to foreigners. It is not coincidental that the revolutionary slogan *México para los mexicanos* (Mexico for the Mexicans) emerged from the middle class. At the same time, the members of that class, particularly the intelligentsia, were profoundly influenced by North American technology and values and would carry on a love-hate relationship with North American culture in their capacity as agents of the new postrevolutionary state.

At the radical fringe of the middle sectors, the Flores Magón brothers from the southern state of Oaxaca espoused a brand of anarchosyndicalism that borrowed from radical thinkers such as the Russian anarchists Peter Kropotkin and Emma Goldman. The Flores Magóns founded an opposition party, the Partido Liberal Mexicano, affiliated with the U.S.-based Industrial Workers of the World, as well as a newspaper, *La Regeneración*, which assailed both authoritarianism and capitalism as the interwoven legacies of an international system that favored the industrialists of Western Europe and North America.

Finally, as we near the top of the late Porfirian social pyramid, we come to the small upper class, which bore powerful grievances against the científico oligarchy favored by Díaz and foreign investors and would supply many influential opponents of the regime. In other words, here we must distinguish between a rather small upper-class elite and a truly privileged segment of that elite who constituted an oligarchy. It was this exclusive club of super-planters and merchants who dominated the national and regional economies as well as the most important political positions and who advised Don Porfirio.

Many of the regime's elite opponents were large hacendados and merchants who represented notable families of some standing in regional society. In a variety of cases, their rural properties and businesses had become encumbered with debts, and they had few prospects of obtaining the level of credit needed to salvage them during and after the economic crisis of 1907–8. At worst, these elites could lose their estates and businesses via foreclosure to the científico oligarchs who controlled the sources of credit. More often, these elites were disgruntled because they were unable to *increase* their wealth and landholdings as rapidly as they would have liked. They saw themselves as underprivileged in comparison to powerful foreign interests and the well-connected oligarchs, many of whom they regarded as mere parvenus elevated by Díaz. For example, the Madero family of the northeastern state of Coahuila bitterly chafed at the preferential treatment Díaz gave to the Guggenheim mining and smelting interests and to other rivals in the fluctuating investment climate of the North. And the notable family of Venustiano Carranza, also of Coahuila, which owned large estates and had made inroads into the regional political system (Don Venustiano had been a senator), lost ground as the Porfirian regime hardened in its later years. Myriad other regional cases could be invoked, from Sonora and Chihuahua to Yucatán, as powerful local clans, used to taking their turns in the statehouse and disposing of healthy shares of the energized export economy, took a stand against the recently entrenched oligarchs who now blocked their paths.

These accumulated contradictions and discontents that pervaded late Porfirian society collectively constitute the *structural* determinants or background causes of the Mexican Revolution of 1910. They are necessary but not sufficient to account for the coming of the revolution. There was still a formidable repressive mechanism at the disposal of the oligarchic regime that had previously forestalled widespread protest and revolt. What were the immediate causes that unleashed the upheaval in November 1910?

PRELUDE TO REVOLUTION

If the background causes were largely socioeconomic in nature, the immediate triggers of the revolution were political events and other contingencies that eroded the legitimacy of the Porfirian regime in the eyes of the people and ultimately emboldened diverse groups to act. The best place to begin is Don Porfirio's decision to give the American journalist James Creelman a high-profile interview in March 1908. Published under the title "President Díaz, Hero of the Americas," Creelman's article in *Pearson's Magazine* presented a portrait of the venerable dictator that was embarrassingly hagiographical, not to mention offensively patronizing of

MAP 1 Mexico in the Epic Revolution: Cities, Railroads, and Major Battles

MAP 2 Mexico and Its States

the Mexican masses. Yet mixed in with Creelman's gushing tribute and simplistic analysis of late Porfirian society was a revelation that distinguished the interview from similar contemporary puff pieces. For Creelman quoted Don Porfirio as saying that the Mexican people, having been nurtured by his stern tutelage, were finally ready for democracy and that he planned to step down at the end of his term in 1910.

What was Díaz thinking? Some believed that, as he approached his eightieth birthday, Don Porfirio had become preoccupied with his legacy; ever vain, he wanted his people to love as well as fear him, and he truly was pondering retirement. Others speculated that by encouraging politicians to campaign in the 1910 election, Don Porfirio (increasingly referred to by pundits as "Don Perpétuo") merely hoped to smoke his most ambitious rivals out of the woodwork, the better to squash their challenges. At any rate, 1909 arrived and Díaz appeared to have either forgotten his conversation with Creelman or published it only for North American consumption.

Few political aspirants had taken the bait anyway. And with good reason, for Díaz had meanwhile undercut serious political competition within the regime. Most notably, the wily dictator had stymied the ambitions of General Bernardo Reyes, the progressive, modernizing governor of the northeastern state of Nuevo León, whom many regarded as a possible successor to Díaz. Reyes represented the hope of the anti-científico upper class and of many frustrated middle-class intellectuals. He seemed to be an ideal successor to Don Porfirio: a strong, younger leader who would maintain the formula of political stability and economic development but who also appeared able to remove some of the current model's bottlenecks. Thus General Reyes appeared to allow disgruntled elites and middle sectors a chance to share more fully in Mexico's modernization and not discriminate in favor of foreigners, to the detriment of Mexican entrepreneurs. Indeed, as governor of Nuevo León, Reyes had encouraged the development of Monterrey, Mexico's fastest growing industrial park, with domestic capital. In short, Reyes appeared to represent the possibility of *Porfirismo sin Porfirio y los científicos.*

That hope never materialized. Díaz skillfully removed Reyes from the scene with a diplomatic posting to Europe, a military mission to study the advances of the Prussian Army. Therefore, as it became increasingly clear that 1910 would produce no significant political change, let alone democratization, an unlikely hero came to the fore: Francisco I. Madero, a short, squeaky-voiced landowner from Coahuila. Madero was a spiritualist who occasionally consulted a Ouija board, and he was a scion of the powerful, dissident, northeastern Madero clan. Despite his spiritualist eccentricities and unremitting hostility to the científicos, he himself pursued scientific and modern approaches to the management of his mining interests and cattle and cotton estates. In fact he was a model hacendado, one who combined the latest agricultural technology, learned at Berkeley and the Sorbonne, with enlightened treatment of his workers, whom he provided with decent wages and working conditions, small food plots, health care, and basic education.

In late 1908, Madero published *The Presidential Succession in 1910*, a political and economic critique of the Porfirian regime. The book advocated moderate political reform and contained no social program. Invoking Díaz's old slogan of "Effective Suffrage and No Reelection," Madero essentially argued that political solutions — single-term presidencies, clean, democratic politics, and respect for the right of states and municipalities to elect their own leaders without federal interference — could solve Mexico's problems. He knew from whence he spoke: in 1904 and 1905 he had thrown his support behind candidates challenging the official slate in Coahuila, only to witness Díaz rig the final results.

Despite its moderate tone, Madero's book detonated a chain reaction. Gradually, inexorably, Madero became a consensus choice for a diverse array of groups opposed to Díaz and the científicos. Madero was more idealistic and naïve than a savvy political and military man like General Reyes, but his status as an outsider became for many one of his principal attractions. For Madero offered hope that had previously seemed all but foreclosed — and hope for even minimal political change became a heady elixir in the economically fragile, politically repressive environment of the late Porfiriato. Soon this hope would become the tinder for the revolutionary fuse.

At first, Madero (like Reyes before him) considered being only a vice-presidential candidate, but before he realized it, he was being swept up into something much larger than he bargained for. Shortly after the publication of his book, anti-reelection clubs sprung up across the nation. In April 1910 a national Anti-Reelectionist Party convention in Mexico City nominated Madero for president. Following his nomination, Madero embarked on a large-scale presidential campaign trip, the first such effort in Mexican history. At whistle-stops to promote his candidacy, first hundreds, then thousands greeted him. In short order, his anti-reelectionist banner for moderate reform began to galvanize a host of antiregime forces: embittered Reyistas, old-time Liberals who resented the loss of traditional individual freedoms and civil liberties, local leaders excluded from power by the Porfirian system, disfranchised landowners and merchants, cramped middle-class intellectuals, leaders of repressed labor syndicates and embattled peasant communities, and even some socialists and anarchosyndicalists who had earlier been persecuted heavily by the regime and gone into exile in the United States. In other words, Madero's fledgling party was attracting individuals and groups who had never been in the regime, as well as many intellectuals and elites who were now defecting from the regime, creating a demoralizing effect as they left.

At this crucial juncture, Don Porfirio, previously so shrewd in his political calculations, miscalculated badly. On June 13 he arrested Madero on trumped-up charges of sedition following a large and raucous campaign stop in Monterrey. Less than two weeks later, Madero sat out the elections in a prison in San Luis Potosí; thousands of his anti-reelectionist colleagues remained behind bars. Díaz then claimed reelection by an overwhelming majority—a preposterous assertion that fooled no one. Madero continued to languish in jail in September, as Mexico prepared to celebrate the centennial of its Declaration of Independence by Miguel Hidalgo, the beloved parish priest who struck the first blow against Spanish tyranny and was subsequently jailed and martyred for it. As Mexicans increasingly drew comparisons between Padre Hidalgo and the incarcerated Madero, the Díaz regime staged the biggest, most lavish independence celebration that the nation had ever seen. The celebrations lasted an entire month and included the commemoration of the dictator's eightieth birthday. No expense was spared to fete royalty and foreign dignitaries, even as the country suffered a particularly crippling drought and peasants starved due to shortages of corn and other staples. The bill for all this revelry easily surpassed Mexico's entire educational budget for 1910. Foreigners were mightily impressed by the party, but the early motion picture footage that captured Díaz's reenactment of Father Hidalgo's dramatic *grito* (shout of independence)—as well as the proceedings of his sixth presidential inauguration—reveal lifeless rituals marked by little popular celebration or joy.

In his jail cell, Madero was already plotting an insurrection for November 1910. Too late, Díaz began to sense how isolated he had become from the Mexican people. He allowed Madero to be released on bail, but in October his opponent boarded a northbound train incognito, slipped across the U.S. border, and continued his plotting in El Paso. Interestingly, Madero was given a wide berth to operate on North American soil, unlike much more radical insurgents influenced by socialist thought, such as the Flores Magón brothers. The Flores Magóns found themselves relentlessly harried by U.S. authorities when they went into North American exile, and Ricardo Flores Magón would sit out most of the Mexican Revolution and ultimately die in Leavenworth Prison in Kansas.

Why was Madero allowed to make final preparations for insurrection from U.S. soil while the U.S. government repeatedly incarcerated the anti-capitalist Magonistas for violating the neutrality and espionage laws? In part, of course, the U.S. government liked Madero's moderate message better than the Magonistas' radical one. It also appears likely that both the U.S. government and North American investors had reached a consensus that time had passed Don Porfirio by. Díaz was no longer able to guarantee either Order or Progress, and during the final years of the regime the dictator had tilted toward favoring the investment interests of the European powers, particularly the British in the oil sector. Realizing how supremely dependent Mexico had become on U.S. capital, Don Porfirio reportedly exclaimed what has become perhaps the signature phrase of beleaguered Mexican presidents ever since: "Poor Mexico, so far from heaven and so close to the United States."

Unfortunately for Díaz, these eleventh-hour efforts to diversify his nation's dependence only made him more expendable to the United States when he began to lose his grip in 1910. On November 20, 1910, with the tacit support of the U.S. state and business community, the Mexican Revolution broke out. The Porfirian regime fell barely six months later.

"What are you fighting for?"

"We are fighting . . . for *libertad*."

"What do you mean by *libertad?*"

"*Libertad* is when I can do what I want!"

— PANCHO VILLA SUPPORTER QUOTED IN JOHN REED, *INSURGENT MEXICO*

THE REVOLUTION COMES (AND GOES), 1910–1913 | 3

In late April 1911, President Díaz's undersecretary of education, Jorge Vera Estañol, wrote a letter to Foreign Secretary Francisco León de la Barra that issued a dire warning regarding Mexico's future. According to Vera Estañol, Don Porfirio faced not one, but two revolutions. One was a political revolution, whose protagonists were respectable upper- and middle-class leaders such as the northern *hacendados* Francisco Madero and Venustiano Carranza. The goal of this revolution, Vera Estañol declared, was democracy, the principle of free suffrage, and no reelection. The other revolution he labeled "anarchy." "Every day," Vera Estañol observed, "the newspapers carry news of new rebel bands being organized in different parts of the country. . . . They carry out pillage, they commit murders, . . . they take money and food in the cities and horses, arms, and other supplies in the countryside." The triumph of this other revolution, he believed, might usher in "a period of real barbarism in the midst of civilization."[1] Defeating this insurgency was therefore of the greatest importance, yet Vera Estañol believed it would require the co-optation of the political revolution by granting its participants some access to power.

Although Vera Estañol recognized the diverse social and political origins and stakes of the revolution, he greatly underestimated the complexity of the movement against Díaz. In a country with a difficult topography, rent with deep regional, cultural, class, and gender divisions, effective communication, let alone consensus among diverse groups of insurgents, would be exceedingly difficult to achieve. In short, in "many Mexicos" there would be many revolutions. As the Madero rebellion took shape, there was a variety of potential revolutionary projects, fueled by widely divergent types of insurgents who came from different settings and harbored different motives and goals. And some of these goals were not particularly revolutionary.

THE MADERISTA COALITION

All of these insurgent types found their way into the Maderista movement that played itself out between November 1910 and May 1911. They sustained its military operation by fueling the local and regional bands that composed it. Still, one hesitates to call this far-flung operation a revolutionary army.

The Maderista coalition included many nineteenth-century Liberals: the urban middle-class intellectuals and upper-class landowners and merchants who felt excluded from the Porfirian model and sought a political solution to Mexico's problems. These dissident elites demanded free and clean politics, which implied an end to the oligarchy's imposition of political bosses at the municipal and state levels, and an end to *continuismo* (perpetual reelection) at all levels, including the presidency. Many of them had previously supported the ambitions of General Bernardo Reyes for the presidency. These Liberals called for a real implementation of Juárez's Constitution of 1857 to restore their civil liberties and guarantee their political rights. Many of them criticized the Church for its long-term collusion with Díaz's oligarchy. They shared a national orientation, a nationwide prescription for Mexico's woes, albeit one that advocated only limited, politically oriented change. Still, their cause could strike a responsive chord in the remote villages and sierras throughout Mexico where grassroots (and often devoutly Catholic) populations resented the intrusion of Porfirian central authority, preferring the kind of decentralization and local authority that had reigned amid the chaos of the mid-nineteenth century. For them, the cry of *municipio libre*, a free municipality, meant the right to be left alone by the federal government.

The champion of these nineteenth-century Liberals was, of course, Madero, yet their ranks included other powerful northern hacendados like

Carranza (1859–1920) and José María Maytorena (1867–1948), as well as middle-class leaders. Both Carranza and Maytorena had joined the opposition because the Díaz machine had denied them political opportunities. Carranza opposed Don Porfirio after a failed attempt at accommodation. He came from a middle-class ranching family in the town of Cuatro Ciénegas in the state of Coahuila. After an excellent education in the schools of Saltillo (the state capital) and Mexico City, he returned to convert his family ranch into a thriving agribusiness. He entered politics in 1893, when he allied with Bernardo Reyes in opposition to the Coahuila governor, a corrupt Díaz crony. Successful in this endeavor, Carranza rapidly rose through the political ranks and gained election to the federal Senate in 1904. In 1909 he received Díaz's permission to run for governor, and he gained the support of the sitting governor as well as Madero's father, but in the end, Don Porfirio's influence blocked him from winning the election. Maytorena, by contrast, hailed from one of the most influential clans in the northwestern state of Sonora, a clan that had always opposed the Porfirian regime. In 1886 his father found his ambitions for the governorship frustrated by a triumvirate of Díaz protégés (including the eventual vice president Ramón Corral) who would go on to dominate Sonoran politics for twenty-five years. Over that time, the younger Maytorena gained notoriety as a thorn in the Porfirians' side, opposing the mass deportation of the Yaqui indigenous people to Yucatán, giving shelter to fugitive Yaquis, and (like Carranza) supporting Reyes. During the rebellion led by Madero, Sonora remained a sideshow, but Maytorena coordinated an effort to seize the federal garrisons in the state. Among his Sonoran associates were middle-class professionals and entrepreneurs, such as the future president Adolfo de la Huerta.

While they remained in the background in the 1910 Madero rebellion, middle-class leaders such as de la Huerta would figure among the victors and principal beneficiaries of the Mexican Revolution. We might call them twentieth-century Liberals in order to distinguish them from nineteenth-century, laissez-faire Liberals like Madero and Carranza. These actors could be found throughout the nation, with disproportionate representation in the northern states that bordered the United States. These states had been the foci of Porfirian boom and development in partnership with North American capital; they had also been the prime incubators of the dynamic new middle sectors. These northern reformers were more in tune with popular social grievances than the Maderos and Carranzas yet were more professional and disciplined than Zapata's and Villa's followers. Like Madero's traditional liberals, they possessed a national orientation and vision, but unlike them, they grasped early on that political reform alone would not solve Mexico's weighty structural problems. These men wanted to perfect the Porfiriato, not just politically but socially and economically as well. Significantly several of them (e.g., Sonora's Salvador Alvarado) often hyperbolically described themselves as "socialists," and most were ardent exponents of anticlericalism.

Mexico's other, more socially based revolution had diverse and predominantly rural roots. First of all, village-based campesinos participated in the 1910 rebellion. These people pressed urgent agrarian demands, and they fought to preserve or win back from the great haciendas their traditional village lands and time-honored way of life. Their existence was based on a society of free villages, where land was typically titled in the community and farmed by individual peasant families—an agrarian way of life that had been expressly targeted by Liberal land policies since the mid-nineteenth century. This struggle was locally and regionally based, with rather focused agrarian goals; campesinos remained rooted in the local soil for which they fought. These villagers felt they *had to fight*, although they did not want to fight. As one historian has put it, they were "country people who did not want to move and therefore got into a revolution."[2] These peasant villagers had neither larger national aspirations nor a desire to transcend their regional base. They were predominantly located in the old, indigenous core region, comprising the states of México, Morelos, Puebla, and Tlaxcala. But *agrarista* insurgents also populated other regions, including regional peripheries such as Yucatán and Chihuahua, where villagers struggled against similarly expansive capitalist interests.

The regional leader who came to symbolize the struggle of these peasant villagers was Emiliano Zapata (1879–1919). Of mixed Spanish and Nahua ancestry, Zapata's family had long supported Porfirio Díaz; unlike many of their neighbors, they owned their own land in the village of Anenecuilco, Morelos. But as he grew older, Zapata witnessed the encroachment of the neighboring sugar plantations onto the land of his community, and in 1906 he attended his first political meeting organized for the purpose of defending the village lands. In 1909 the inhabitants of Anenecuilco elected him president of their village council. In that capacity he vowed to defend the

FIGURE 3.1 Emiliano Zapata during his fight against the
dictator Victoriano Huerta. Fideicomiso Archivos Plutarco
Elías Calles y Fernando Torreblanca, Mexico City.

lands of his village, first through the judicial system by asserting the property rights laid out in old title deeds, and then by appealing to the governor of Morelos. Frustrated in these endeavors, Zapata and other agrarian
villagers finally took up arms in December 1910, one month after the beginning of the Madero revolt (figure 3.1).

Zapata's agrarians represented precisely those social sectors that José
Vera Estañol and the other Porfirians most feared. Witness, for example,
the following description of the Zapatista troops by the U.S.-born owner
of a hotel in the city of Cuernavaca:

[They were] a wild-looking body of men, undisciplined, half-clothed, mounted on half-starved broken down horses. Grotesque and obsolete weapons, long hidden away or recently seized in the pawnshops, were clasped in their hands, thrust through their belts, or slung across the queer old saddles of shapes never seen before.... There was about them the splendor of devotion to a cause, a look of all the homespun patriots who, from time immemorial, have left the plough in the furrow when there was need to fight.[3]

Another revolutionary type that fueled the Maderista rebellion consisted of telluric chiefs like Francisco ("Pancho") Villa (1878–1923) and their retinues. These social bandits were the least disciplined and most mobile revolutionaries: they were out for spoils and adventure, to be sure, but fundamentally their insurgent drive was rooted in hunger, poverty, and a low and demeaning social status—all exacerbated by the late Porfirian economic downturn. Unlike the agrarian villagers, these insurgents spoiled for a fight. They came to regard the revolution as an opportunity to settle scores with their betters and to raise themselves up socially and economically. Disproportionately from the vast, rugged expanses of the northern states of Chihuahua and Durango, they were a floating group of predominantly mestizo miners, cowboys, and mule-skinners, men who might work on a ranch for part of the year and in a mine or factory the rest of the time. A number of them had worked occasionally in the United States, although the recession had forced them back across the border in search of new possibilities. Wherever these mobile opportunists appeared, they tended to have a regional focus and a limited range of expectations.

Just as Zapata epitomized the village campesinos in revolt, Doroteo Arango, better known as Pancho Villa, was the archetype of the social bandit. Villa began his life as a humble peon in Durango, the son of sharecroppers working on the land of a wealthy clan. According to legend, when one of the members of this rich family raped his sister, he avenged her humiliation by murdering the offender, then took to the hills. Villa joined the revolutionary troops in Chihuahua under the leadership of Pascual Orozco (1882–1915), another bandit chief, yet one of higher social background and lower political principles than Villa. Of middle-class origin, Orozco was a petty trader and muleteer best known for his ruthless military tactics. Attracted by the anarchosyndicalist ideas of the Flores Magón brothers, he ran afoul of the law after reading anti-Díaz newspapers. In 1909 he began the illicit import of U.S. arms. Thus he rebelled against the Díaz regime even before Madero did, but pledged his support to Madero's Plan of San Luis Potosí. It was Orozco who soon provided the Mexican Revolution with one of its most famous quotes. Upon ambushing a federal contingent in early January 1911, he sent the uniforms of the dead soldiers to Don Porfirio with a note saying, "Here are the wrappers; send me more tamales!"[4] During the Madero rebellion, Villa served under his command, and historians credit Orozco with leadership in the most significant military victory over the *federales*: the capture of the border city of Ciudad Juárez on May 10, 1911.

It was Villa and his supporters, however, who would generate a longer-lasting legacy, in large part due to their refusal to make common cause with wealthy landowners such as Luis Terrazas, as Orozco did. To conceive of the Villistas as *social* bandits, of course, is not to depict them spotlessly as Robin Hoods, who stole from the rich and gave to the poor. Instead the social bandit label alludes to the popular magnetism of these leaders as vicarious executors of the rage of the poor and oppressed. In Villa's case, it is also to gesture to fundamental notions of social justice and reform that, as recent research has shown, would underwrite his later stint as a revolutionary governor of Chihuahua. The novelist Mariano Azuela, an erstwhile supporter of Villa, observed that "thinkers prepare . . . revolutions; bandits carry them out."[5] Azuela's observation speaks volumes about the Villista bands that provided Madero's rebellion with some of its best fighters, as well as about a host of other participants in the 1910 revolution.

It would be a mistake, however, to ignore the broader political goals of the Villistas, however regional they were in scope. As the epigraph to this chapter indicates, the humble northern revolutionaries sought to rid themselves of interference from the federal government, thereby regaining the relative autonomy they had known prior to the arrival of the railroad in the Porfirian era. For them, the principle of municipio libre meant freedom from the Porfirian prefects who oppressed them through their local cronies. Absent the *rurales* and other uniformed security forces who defended elite property rights, the Villistas believed they could settle their scores with the wealthy. Not surprisingly, Villa was an ardent admirer of Madero, despite the latter's upper-class background.

Finally, there were the cynical revolutionaries, the type that the novelist Carlos Fuentes aptly described in *The Death of Artemio Cruz*. Indeed many local caciques and powerful elites primarily participated in Maderismo to protect or extend their existing power domains (*cacicazgos*). These large landowners and local bosses resembled the cacique warlords of the mid-nineteenth century: they recognized the collapse of Porfirian central authority and moved into the resulting power vacuum as nominal Maderistas, mobilizing their peons, clients, and dependents in support of the rebellion. Such warlords often became the agents of big foreign and domestic interests, which were obliged periodically to pay them substantial sums to safeguard their properties and economic enterprises from the revolution's spiraling violence and chaos. These local power holders frequently switched sides, declaring themselves Porfiristas one moment and Maderistas the next. Later on, they would navigate amid several factions of revolutionaries warring against one another. They much more closely resembled Mafiosi gangster chieftains than revolutionaries. The prototype warlord was the Veracruzano chief Manuel Peláez, a large hacendado in the Gulf region who astutely shifted allegiances and parlayed the revolution into a lucrative protection racket at the expense of the British and American oil companies that operated within the boundaries of his expanding cacicazgo. But there was an array of lesser Peláezes, each operating regionally with no real agenda other than his own aggrandizement.

As a postscript to this analysis of the forces involved in the Maderista movement, we should remind ourselves of the ideological road not taken in the revolution of 1910. For there was indeed another group of much more radical revolutionaries who had already been severely weakened before hostilities broke out: the anticapitalist Magonistas. As we have seen, these radicals were staunch partisans of the international anarchist movement, which declared private property to be theft, denounced government of all stripes, and advocated "direct action" in place of political participation. In his own writings and in *La Regeneración*, Ricardo Flores Magón championed self-governing, self-reliant, socialistic communities and expressed his disdain for Madero's brand of anti-reelectionism. The Magonistas had attempted to organize urban workers and miners, mostly in the North, during the final years of the Porfiriato, and they turned out some dedicated fighters in 1910, especially in Baja California. Still, persecution of them was so intense on both sides of the Rio Grande that they registered little impact during the struggle against Díaz. However, some Magonista intellectuals would later resurface in the revolution, helping to ensure that radical ideas found their way into the Constitution of 1917. Together these disparate types and groups of insurgents fueled the initial phase of the Mexican Revolution of 1910 under Madero's nominal leadership.

THE REVOLUTION TRIUMPHS

One is struck by the easy victory of the Madero movement. Within a few short months, the Porfiriato crumbled, virtually beneath its own weight. So discredited was the regime late in 1910 that it suffered an avalanche of defections from within the elite and middle strata, which hastened defections from the army and police forces. Of course, the Maderista military operation also deserves a measure of credit: irregular Maderista detachments fought a skillful, highly dispersed guerrilla offensive against the federales, who won a series of engagements but lost the war. Although Madero was seriously lacking in military savvy, he was blessed with wily tacticians like Orozco in the North and Zapata in the South. By the time Orozco's troops approached Ciudad Juárez in May 1911, the Porfirians had realized that they were fighting a lost cause: demoralized from within, deserted by most of the Mexican people, and abandoned by their powerful northern ally, which turned a blind eye to arms smuggling along the border. After three days of siege, the federal garrison at Ciudad Juárez capitulated to the rebels, as thousands of El Paso residents watched the spectacle and shouted from their rooftops across the river.

Following the rebel capture of Ciudad Juárez, Díaz and the *científicos* called it quits. On May 21, 1911, in the Treaty of Ciudad Juárez, Díaz agreed to step down in return for Madero's acceptance of the nomination of Foreign Secretary Francisco León de la Barra as interim president until new elections could be held in October 1911. Don Porfirio is said to have remarked as he boarded a steamer into European exile, "Madero has unleashed a tiger; let's see if he can tame it."[6] Perhaps the Porfirians' strategy was to give ground now, wait for Mexico to fall into chaos, and then return to pick up the pieces. That, in effect, had been Santa Anna's gambit in a similarly chaotic period, following independence, and it had repeatedly returned him to power. As it turned out, Don Porfirio's doubts about Maderismo's staying power were warranted, though the old warhorse would never return to office. He went into exile and died in Paris in 1915 at the age of eighty-four.

Unfortunately for Madero's movement, it had won too quickly. As one scholar has quipped, "As with marriages, so with revolutions, the best take years to turn out well."[7] Hastily assembled, the Hydra-headed insurgency had toppled Díaz rather easily; there had not been enough clarification of common goals through struggle. The revolution of 1910 was not forged in the crucible of adversity, with years in the wilderness, like many other subsequent revolutions of the twentieth century whose participants paid heavy dues before they won power. We think of Mao Zedong's long and grueling march across China in the 1920s, mobilizing and learning from the Chinese peasantry as he went; or of Ho Chi Minh's years in exile, followed by generations of campaigns in Vietnam against the French and the Americans. We reflect on Vladimir I. Lenin's ceaseless plotting throughout the cities of Europe and the terrible disappointment of the failed Russian revolt of 1905, all of which was preceded by a century of social criticism of the czarist regime that helped to produce some consensus on basic points of ideology. Where Latin America is concerned, we recall Fidel Castro's failed revolt on the Moncada barracks and the rigorous apprenticeship his rebels endured in Cuba's Sierra Maestra, or the two decades of death and attrition experienced by the Sandinista Front in Nicaragua before its militants reached a modicum of ideological consensus, which enabled them to galvanize a successful popular insurrection against the Somozas.

In Mexico, on the other hand, Madero's disparate forces won a quick victory in the absence of any common, unifying ideology. Of course, despite the material transformations wrought by the modernizing Porfirian state, the Mexico of 1910 remained a country of deep contrasts and contradictions. There was little sense of shared commonalities, let alone broadly diffused notions of an imagined national community. In these circumstances, which differed markedly from those that obtained in revolutionary situations like Cuba and Nicaragua much later in the twentieth century, any ideological consensus among insurgents would have been extraordinarily difficult to achieve.

Moreover, there was no intellectual tradition in Mexico that paved the way for revolution. Mexico had nothing analogous to the French philosophes, the Russian social critics, or the generations of revolutionary Latin American intellectuals who bridged the nineteenth and twentieth centuries with their rich critiques of imperialism and exploitation. (Here one thinks of traditions anchored by such national icons as José Martí in Cuba, Carlos Mariátegui in Peru, Pablo Neruda in Chile, and Carlos Fonseca in Nicaragua.) As one astute U.S. observer of the revolution remarked, "The Mexican Revolution was anonymous. It was essentially the work of the common people. No organized party presided at its birth. No great intellectuals prescribed its program, formulated its doctrine, outlined its objectives. . . . There [was] no Lenin in Mexico."[8]

Popular culture of the period evokes the absence of a clear ideology in the 1910 rebellion. Witness, for example, the short, popular Maderista jingle that exhorted support for the movement's leader:

Poco trabajo
Mucho dinero
Pulque barato
Viva Madero!

We don't want much work
We do want a lot of money
And if there's cheap *pulque*
Long live Madero![9]

One gets a similar (albeit elite) reading on the absence of clear aims, consensus, and sophistication from a joke from the period. Madero, the so-called Apostle of Democracy, is riding triumphantly down the Paseo de la Reforma with his troops, in the wake of Don Porfirio's departure. Two campesinos, clad in the traditional white pajamas, stand amid the throngs that line both sides of the broad avenue. As Madero passes, the crowd erupts: "Viva Madero! Viva Democracia!" One campesino turns to the other and says, "Sí, long live our Liberator, Señor Madero. But who is this Democracia?" His companion replies, "Well, it must be Señora Madero."[10] Related by the grandson of a regional journalist prominent during the early revolutionary years, this nugget of family lore captures the feelings of class and racial superiority that urban intellectuals displayed toward campesinos. At the same time, it evokes the yawning ideological and cultural divide between city and countryside that rendered revolutionary mobilization so problematical during the first, violent decade.

FROM REVOLUTION TO COUNTERREVOLUTION, 1911–1913

Yet it was not just the absence of a clear ideology or consensus tempered over time that weakened Madero's revolutionary movement from the outset. The so-called Apostle of Democracy made some grievous blunders almost as soon as Díaz acknowledged defeat. In the Treaty of Ciudad Juárez, Madero agreed to preserve the old Porfirian officer corps, now led by General Victoriano Huerta, as well as to honor existing judicial and executive appointments. During his five-month tenure, Interim President de la Barra arranged the political survival of scores of his fellow Porfirista, non-elected officials in the federal government. Meanwhile all existing disputes over land and property, including land claims by indigenous villages and campesinos, required resolution by Porfirian judges, and Madero declared his faith in the judicial system to address social grievances such as these.

These concessions angered many of the members of Madero's fragile coalition and sent Zapata's peasant agrarians into armed opposition. Such measures would have been unthinkable for later revolutionary vanguards like the Cuban Fidelistas or the Nicaraguan Sandinistas (let alone the much earlier Russian Bolsheviks). But we must remember that Madero was a nineteenth-century Liberal: he intended to tinker with the existing system, enacting political reforms that, in time, might provide a mechanism for addressing social issues. This tack, of course, was guaranteed to infuriate forces on both the Right and the Left. For Porfirian reactionaries, political reform went dangerously far, removing them from power while empowering the rabble. For most Mexicans, however, Madero's proposals did not begin to address pressing material needs and the structural inequalities that fed them. Madero may have been a benevolent hacendado, yet campesinos perceived him to be an hacendado all the same. His traditional brand of liberalism envisioned social change that would have to be gradual and modest lest it destabilize the nation's fragile economy. Such nineteenth-century Liberalism refused to entertain government intervention in the agrarian, labor, and educational spheres in the interests of the poorest citizens. Instead Madero insisted that his recipe allowed campesinos to press their grievances effectively by respecting democracy and due process at all levels.

The social message of the agrarians therefore did not reach Madero and his followers. Luis Cabrera, one of the leading reformers in Congress, a middle-class intellectual who appreciated the necessity of social reform, argued in the Chamber of Deputies, "The agrarian issue is the Achilles' heel of the revolution."[11] Without real, purifying change, Cabrera warned Madero, the people would return to violence and there would be no lasting social peace. But Cabrera's pleas fell on deaf ears. The portion of the budget dedicated to education was derisory—virtually the same level of funding as during the late Porfiriato; nor did Madero revisit the hated positivist curriculum of the científicos. To be sure, the urban working class felt a bit less intimidated under Madero, and workers established the anarchist Casa del Obrero Mundial in Mexico City. But the president did little to redress workers' material demands, and strikes proliferated. Similarly the president had little to offer land-hungry villagers; indeed he quickly refused Zapata's demands that lands be immediately returned to the villages (figure 3.2).

Irate, Zapata and his men issued the famous Plan of Ayala on November 25, 1911. The plan called for the overthrow of Madero for betraying the struggle of the pueblos and named Orozco (who had not yet asked for such an honor) the chief of the Liberating Revolution. The Zapatistas then outlined their own plan of agrarian reform. Significantly they envisioned a future that included *both* the great estate and the peasant village: one-third of the haciendas' lands would be expropriated in order to reconstitute the villages' landed patrimony.

Politically the return of democracy raised great hopes. In October 1910 de la Barra organized free elections in Mexico City and some parts of the republic—though by no means in all. These elections not only ushered Madero into power but also resulted in a politically diverse Congress. At the state and local levels, Maderistas had to share power with Porfirians and other elected politicians who had no affiliation with either the new or the old regime. In the federal Chamber of Deputies, open legislative debate flourished for the first time in generations, pitting old-line Porfirians against Cabrera's reformists and a few more radical representatives. In the nation's capital and other urban areas, Mexico flirted with democracy for the first time in its history. In Mexico City, as well as in much of the North, federal, state, and local authorities finally respected the freedom of the press after decades of repression.

But in other ways, Maderismo meant business as usual. The president followed the centuries-old precedents of nepotism and cronyism in re-

FIGURE 3.2 Madero and Zapata unsuccessfully negotiate the land question in Morelos, 1911. Fideicomiso Archivos Plutarco Elías Calles y Fernando Torreblanca, Mexico City.

warding his family members and friends with lucrative government positions, governorships, and seats in the federal legislature. This practice earned Madero some dangerous enemies, particularly Orozco, who was angry when he learned that the president (who considered Orozco a semi-literate bandit) would not recognize his service to the revolution in the form of an important political appointment. In addition, the pace of political change varied widely from region to region. In many regional peripheries the enduring political culture of patronage and clientelism operated with characteristic ruthlessness beneath a Maderista façade of democratization. In Yucatán, for example, Maderista rule was the Porfiriato redux, replete with imposed governors and municipal officials, rigged elections, and strong-armed district prefects who dispersed opposition rallies and smashed their presses. Finally, Madero's insistence (following his agreement with the Porfirians) that all rebels lay down their arms did not sit well with the self-proclaimed leaders of the revolutionary forces.

Not surprisingly, an increasing number of groups of different political persuasions pronounced against the new government. We have already mentioned Zapata's revolt, begun less than three weeks into Madero's term as president. Other revolts ensued, declared by General Reyes and Madero's erstwhile general, Pascual Orozco, among others. Finally, a rebellion led by Don Porfirio's nephew, Félix Díaz, set in motion events that led to the ouster of President Madero in February 1913.

Of these revolts, the Orozco rebellion deserves some discussion because of its large scope and its consequences for the future course of the revolution. Having been denied the governorship he felt he deserved, Orozco declared himself in rebellion on March 3, 1912. His former subordinate, Pancho Villa, remained loyal to Madero, and U.S. President William H. Taft authorized the export of weapons to the Mexican government; nevertheless the rebel general quickly demonstrated the value of having six thousand revolutionary fighters under his command. On March 23 Orozco dealt the federales a devastating defeat that resulted in the suicide of the federal commander. Two days later he proclaimed the Plan Orozquista, which assailed the Madero administration for corruption and fraud, subservience to the United States, and failure to carry out widespread social reform. Still, it is challenging to assign to the Orozquistas a definite political or social orientation. The group consisted of hacendados as well as middle-class leaders and rancheros, and Orozco's supporters included the state's most prosperous landowner, Luis Terrazas, whose holdings were larger than the U.S. state of Maryland. As the rebellion spread, Madero reluctantly charged the former Porfirian general Victoriano Huerta with the task of defeating Orozco, knowing full well that his reliance on the military of the old regime might come back to haunt him.

When the Orozco rebellion threatened neighboring Sonora, it brought onto the scene the last major protagonist of the armed revolution of the 1910s, the one who would imprint it with perhaps its most enduring impact: Alvaro Obregón Salido (1880–1928). Obregón was a rancher of Spanish descent from the environs of the town of Huatabampo in southern Sonora, where his father had once owned a prosperous farm on the banks of the Mayo River. But a catastrophic flood cost the family most of its possessions, and Obregón lost his father at a very young age. He came of age as an upwardly mobile, self-taught farmer best known for his invention of the garbanzo, or chickpea, harvester. Newly prosperous and a minor political officeholder during the last years of the Porfiriato, Obregón did not participate in Madero's revolution. But once the rebels had triumphed, he took advantage by winning election as mayor of Huatabampo, very much against the wishes of the town's old Porfirista cacique, who had desired the triumph of his own candidate. Obregón's debut in the fighting came in April 1912, when Governor Maytorena organized militias to defend Sonora from the Orozquistas. Obregón put together the most effective of these military groups, and his band chased the rebels back into Chihuahua, where he and General Victoriano Huerta of the federales congratulated each other on their successes.

Obregón's path to the revolution revealed the contradictions of the Madero era. Having sat out the Maderista rebellion, Obregón benefited from the political shakeup caused by the movement's triumph. Soon thereafter he joined the fighting to defend his native state and the social and political order that had made him a successful entrepreneur and local political leader. As he once allegedly confided, "Don Porfirio's only sin . . . was to grow old."[12] Like Obregón, many other upper- and middle-class Mexicans—for example, his eventual Sonoran associate Plutarco Elías Calles—initially desired nothing more than a reformed, politically stable version of the Porfiriato in which they could pursue their careers and ambitions. Yet as a series of rebellions progressively destabilized the Madero government, the idea of a *Porfiriato sin Porfirio* proved elusive, and the ever-spiraling violence served to convince these leaders of the need for social and economic change.

Ultimately Madero's obsolete brand of liberalism fell victim to a coup d'état engineered by Victoriano Huerta, the Porfirian general whom the president had summoned to vanquish his foes. Early in 1913 Bernardo Reyes and Félix Díaz, both serving prison terms for their respective revolts against Madero, conspired to launch another rebellion. On February 9 their co-conspirators freed them from their Mexico City jail. Reyes died during the escape, but in short order, Díaz led his troops across the city to ensconce themselves in the Ciudadela armory. Over the next few days, the Ciudadela area, not far from the city center, became the scene of a devastating artillery battle. Madero ordered Huerta to lay siege to the armory, and the general appeared to comply, as the federales shelled the Díaz forces. However, meanwhile, Huerta was engaging in secret negotiations with both Díaz and U.S. Ambassador Henry Lane Wilson, who used his offices to unite the two leaders in a common cause. In what became known as the Pact of the Embassy (the place where the final choreography of the coup was arranged), Wilson and the coup leaders decided that Huerta would support the rebellion in exchange for Díaz's assurance that the presidency would fall to Huerta. Thus the same North American business interests that had previously found Díaz expendable in 1910 now found Madero wanting on the same grounds of dollar diplomacy. The president had lost control of the political arena and was too weak to stem the kind of instability that jeopardized oil production and myriad other U.S. interests. On February 18, the end of what Mexicans remember as the *decena trágica*, or Ten Tragic Days, Huerta's men entered the National Palace and arrested Madero and Vice President José María Pino Suárez. A charade then commenced that saw the presidency held by three men in a span of twenty-four hours in order to legally validate Huerta's ascent to power. Three days later, Huerta's minions assassinated Madero and Pino Suárez at point-blank range—allegedly in the act of "trying to escape," a textbook rendition of the *ley fuga*.

Huerta's successful coup illustrated the bankruptcy of the nineteenth-century liberal political model in Mexico. Madero had not brought lasting peace. Socially motivated rebels like Zapata's agrarians took the field intent on toppling Maderismo, just as they had waged war against the old Díaz regime. The U.S. government reversed its course, helping to undermine a democratically elected administration; and the Porfirian military obligingly illustrated its resolve—and capacity—to foil the experiment in democracy. By early March 1913 it seemed as though Huerta might be able to restore the Porfirian model, absent the old dictator and his gerontocratic friends. Within two weeks of his coup, all but three state governors had recognized the new order of things in Mexico City, and the federales appeared firmly in control.

Yet Huerta's coup did not end the revolution. In particular, the assassination of Madero proved a monumental mistake, as the cowardly murder triggered cries of outrage throughout the republic. Much criticized in life, in death the former president entered his country's pantheon of martyred heroes, next to the Aztec emperor Cuauhtémoc and the fallen patriots who had fought for independence in the 1810s, Miguel Hidalgo and José María Morelos. Meanwhile Zapata and other agrarian rebels remained at war, content to fight Huerta just as they had battled Díaz and Madero. Even more ominously for Huerta, trouble was brewing in the North. The revolution was about to enter an even more violent phase.

With good reason, one leading historian of the Mexican Revolution sub-titled his benchmark work dealing with the 1910–13 years "Porfirians, Liberals, and Peasants."[13] The title aptly described the major groups — each of them diverse in composition — that vied for supremacy once the Díaz regime teetered on the brink of its demise. The Porfirians had proven re-silient, assuring not only their political survival in the Madero administration but also their renaissance in the Huerta coup, which simultaneously demonstrated their ability to marshal the support of U.S. diplomats and investors against a democratically elected government. Led by Madero, the Liberals (whether of the elite, hacendado, or middle-class variety) had assembled a broad-based coalition that quickly defeated the Old Regime, but just as quickly disintegrated when their focus on democracy clashed with both Porfirian recalcitrance and the broader, social goals of the nation's poor majority. Finally, the various poor agrarians often lumped together under the category "peasants" acted in myriad regional and local contexts to press their grievances. Some in the center and south of the country, like the Zapatistas, fought for the lands that had been stolen from them by hacendados and foreign corporations. Others, like the Villistas, experienced firsthand the adverse effects of liberal modernization on the northern frontier and took up arms to restore their liberty and to fight for economic and social advancement. As Huerta attempted to impose a neo-Porfirian dictatorship, he would soon find out that political and social re-form enjoyed the support of the vast majority of Mexicans. But what kind of reform, and for whom?

To them, *la revolución* was infinitely more than the Revolution of 1910. It was the long continuous movement of resistance, like a rolling wave, that had swelled against Cortés and his conquistadors, and the greedy Aztec warlords before them; that had engulfed the armies of Spain and . . . France as it now engulfed the hacendados. It was the struggle of these people for a birthright, to develop in their own way, in spite of strangers who came greedily to skim the cream, and, ignorantly, to make the people over. And so silent and vast and unceasing was the struggle that it seemed to me as though the sleeping earth itself had stirred to cast off the artificial things that lay heavy on it.

— ROSA KING, *TEMPEST OVER MEXICO*

THE VIOLENT CLIMAX OF THE REVOLUTION, 1913–1920 | 4

On March 13, 1913, officials from northeastern Sonora, the home of the famous copper mine of Cananea, issued a manifesto on behalf of what the signatories declared were five thousand armed men. The Nacozari Manifesto rallied Sonorans against the "absolutist" Huerta regime. As the insurrectionists declared with reference to Huerta's call to end the fighting, "None of us ignores the urgent necessity of reestablishing peace . . . , even at great sacrifice; but . . . the storms provoked by a popular rebellion are preferable to a peace sustained by the guns of a military dictatorship."

Indeed the revolution was far from over; in fact its most violent years lay ahead. Most immediately, the diverse remnants of Maderismo faced the substantial problem of how to defeat Victoriano Huerta's neo-Porfirian dictatorship. While the uprising against Díaz had focused on several pockets of resistance, the war against Huerta turned into a much more widespread affair, inaugurating the heyday of what the journalist Martín Luis Guzmán described as a "fiesta of bullets." In this bloody crucible, Mexicans tried once again to find an answer to the many political, economic, and social contradictions that had driven them to oppose the Díaz regime. As a result of this unprecedented degree of military mobilization, new actors came upon the stage of the revolution, people who became politically conscious during a destructive war. An upheaval that had featured a variety of insurgents from different social backgrounds became even more complex, and a resolution of their many grievances even more difficult.

THE WAR AGAINST HUERTA

Huerta soon found out that not all Mexicans would accept the charade by which he had reached the presidency. Indeed the dictator faced most of Díaz's enemies as well as a host of new ones. With their demands remaining unmet, Zapata's agrarian rebels remained in the field, as did a number of lesser-known campesino chiefs. Though most state governors quickly acknowledged the new state of things in Mexico City, Carranza, Maytorena, and Chihuahua's Abraham González did not. When Huerta, in true Porfirian fashion, had González assassinated, this action called Villa, an admirer of both Madero and González, back into the field. Among the new enemies of the government was the Sonoran group that had learned the art of war during the Orozco rebellion, people such as those who had signed the Nacozari Manifesto, as well as several defectors from the federal army. On March 26, 1913, Carranza proclaimed the Plan of Guadalupe. Subscribed to by Alvaro Obregón, Pancho Villa, and many others, the plan named Carranza "first chief" until the defeat of Huerta and the reestablishment of constitutional government. The rebels who supported this plan fought under the banner of "Constitutionalism," a clear reference to their allegiance to the 1857 Constitution that Huerta had trampled.

Like their Maderista predecessors, the Constitutionalists were a diverse lot. The insurgents harbored a variety of social and political motivations and were dispersed throughout a series of regionally based, caudillo-led "armies," actually congeries of local bands. These forces included Villa's powerful Division of the North, which originated in Chihuahua and Durango; the Division of the Northeast, based principally in Coahuila and Nuevo León and under the command of General Pablo González; and Obregón's Division of the Northwest, which operated in Sonora and Sinaloa. Zapata's Army of the South, based in Morelos and parts of neighboring states and united in its adherence to the agrarian Plan of Ayala, did not formally affiliate with the Constitutionalists but made common cause with them against Huerta.

The Constitutionalists hoped to receive assistance from outside. In particular, they stood to benefit from a change in U.S. leadership, as the

Democratic Party's Woodrow Wilson had replaced the Republican William Howard Taft in the White House. Wilson immediately reversed the course of U.S. foreign policy, which had played such an ominous role in Huerta's coup. Seeking to base his policy on moral principles, the prim and puritanical Wilson (no relation to Henry Lane Wilson) refused to recognize the Huerta government on the grounds that it had come to power through usurpation and assassination. Whether or not the Mexican people liked it, Wilson was determined to rid them of their dictator, whatever the cost to national sovereignty. Indeed the president pledged to save the Mexicans from themselves, if need be, as well as to refuse to do the bidding of Wall Street: "I have constantly to remind myself that I am not a servant of those who wish to enhance the value of their Mexican investments, [rather] I am the servant of the rank and file of the people of the United States."[2] While Wilson would recognize that he had "no right [to use the government of the United States] to express [his] own passions," these played some role in his policy toward Huerta. For now, Wilson pursued a policy of what he called "watchful waiting," content to withhold diplomatic recognition from Huerta. For their part, the rebels took matters into their own hands, seizing cattle from Huertista landowners and selling them for fifteen dollars a head in the United States in order to illicitly buy arms and smuggle them across the border.

Nonetheless the battle against Huerta proved far more difficult for the rebels than the war against Díaz. Much of the Mexican upper class united in the belief that a dictatorship appeared preferable to a continuation of the wars and rebellions that had plagued their country since Madero's Plan of San Luis Potosí. Huerta also received significant material assistance from France, Germany, and Great Britain — the great European powers jockeying for influence in Mexico on the eve of World War I. There is also no doubt that the Huerta regime made at least some attempts to co-opt the rebels. In the early 1970s, the historian Michael C. Meyer sought to rehabilitate Huerta from the condemnation that his colleagues had heaped upon the dictator in past decades. His analysis points out that, at least in social terms, the Huerta administration was no worse than Madero's, and that in some areas, such as educational spending, it may have been more proactive and forward-looking. While acknowledging Huerta's rash of political assassinations and his quashing of democratic institutions, Meyer sees the Huerta period as part of an emerging tradition of moderate revolutionary reform rather than a return to the Porfirian past.[3] Moreover Huerta's humble origin, as the son of poor Huichol Indians from the state of Jalisco, leads Meyer to suggest that he likely harbored some identification with the dispossessed.

Other scholars, however, have pointed out serious problems with this attempt to invoke Huerta's "revolutionary" legacy. For one thing, his hunting down of democratic legislators and journalists betrayed the worst aspects of Porfirian praetorianism, as Huerta opted too often to administer *palo* instead of *pan*. Witness, for example, the assassination of Senator Belisario Domínguez, an outspoken critic of the regime. And the regime's scant accomplishments in the areas of land, labor, and educational reform speak more to the comparative weakness of the social program of Madero than argue for Huerta's inclusion in an emerging tradition of revolutionary reform. Whatever the case, the dictator's personality increasingly alienated the population, whether rich or poor. An excessive drinker and marijuana user, Huerta shamelessly indulged his vices in full view of the public. Members of the elite who would have otherwise supported his regime would have concurred with the following assessment of a staunchly conservative German merchant in Mexico City: "The dictatorship of Huerta was the most baroque type of political rule we have seen in Mexico. The seventy-year-old was the prototype of the Mexican bandit: unscrupulous, impervious to pressure, asleep on a powder keg."[4]

Despite Huerta's shortcomings, the rebels initially made slow progress. After the assassination of Governor Abraham González of Chihuahua, the federal army chased Carranza out of Coahuila. Reduced to guerrilla warfare, Villa's and Zapata's troops blew up railroad tracks and bridges and burned and pillaged haciendas. In Robin Hood fashion, both factions seized land, jewelry, furniture, and money from the haciendas they occupied, swelling their ranks with campesinos who at long last glimpsed some hope for their future. Gradually both the Villistas and the Zapatistas sapped the strength of the Huertista governments in their states, and Villa in particular amassed a growing fighting force that would soon become the largest rebel army that Latin America had ever seen. But Huertista governors remained in the saddle.

Help came from Sonora, a state that had built a strong militia independent of federal authority. Even though Governor Maytorena took a leave of absence in Arizona rather than risk González's fate, both his replacement and the Sonoran legislature rallied to the Constitutionalist cause. They did so owing to pressure from below and only after one of the state's military commanders, Salvador Alvarado, barged into the legislature with some of his troops and threatened to dissolve the assembly if the politicians did not take a position against the dictator. Obregón was not so tentative; named commander of the Sonoran troops and enjoying the financial support of the state government, he took the initiative. Over the next six months, he and his allies took the state's garrisons one by one, and by September 1913 only Guaymas remained in the hands of the federales. Hounded by federales after the Huertista takeover of Coahuila, Carranza decided that Sonora offered him safety. In September 1913 the first chief arrived in the state capital of Hermosillo after a grueling march of more than two months. In short order he made Hermosillo the provisional capital of the Constitutionalist movement. Upon Carranza's arrival, Obregón reportedly remarked, "We have no *agraristas* here, thank God! All of us who are involved in this effort are doing it for patriotism and to avenge the death of Sr. Madero."[5]

Although reported secondhand, the comment highlights the fact that much of the Constitutionalist leadership still followed the precepts of Maderismo. Like Madero, Carranza and Obregón spoke in political rather than social terms. They represented the established order in the Mexican North, and Obregón in particular relied in large part on the militia that the Sonoran state government had commissioned during the prior year in response to the Orozco Rebellion. Embroiled in guerrilla-style conflicts, by contrast, Villa and especially Zapata experienced firsthand the frustrations of the humble people that made up their movements—movements organized from the ground up.

Therefore, even before the Constitutionalists had made any significant headway against Huerta, they were already betraying signs of dissension. In fact, once Obregón departed Sonora to attack federal garrisons farther south, tension mounted in Hermosillo, as the Sonorans divided into rival factions vying for supremacy. Often along lines of personal allegiance to cacique warlords, fissures such as these existed all over Mexico and slowed the progress of the rebellion.

This dissension became ever clearer as the three major northern armies slowly wended their way south. On the ground, these armies looked fairly similar (and clearly differed from Zapata's army, with its narrow regional base and focused social agenda). Each united people from all walks of life, including a majority of campesinos. The armies featured a loose hierarchy of self-anointed officers who based their claim to authority upon the number of troops loyal to them or their access to even more powerful officers. As these armies marched away from their regional bases, and as they recruited new troops from among the populations they encountered, they became more socially and regionally diverse. The vast distances covered during the campaigns made both officers and troops increasingly aware of Mexico's national problems, as opposed to the local conditions that had motivated their joining the revolution. At the top, however, differences emerged. Villa's División del Norte grew to be by far the largest of the three armies, and Carranza became jealous of its leader, a man he considered both his subordinate and a mere bandit. As a result, the first chief displayed increasing favoritism toward the other two northern generals, Pablo González and Obregón. As a civilian and noncombatant, Carranza knew little about the war that he formally directed, certainly far less than the powerful military chiefs.

In April 1914 President Wilson joined the fray and dealt the Huerta regime a fatal blow. He seized upon a rather minor incident to launch the first U.S. invasion of Mexican territory since the mid-nineteenth century. With relations deteriorating by the day and the U.S. fleet stationed in the Gulf of Mexico, U.S. sailors came ashore at Tampico to secure petrol. They were detained briefly by Huertista forces, which were bracing for an attack by rebels in the area. When Wilson learned of the imminent arrival in Veracruz of a German ship laden with arms for Huerta, he immediately ordered the naval occupation of Mexico's principal port. After massive artillery bombardment left parts of the city destroyed and hundreds dead or wounded, including many women and children, U.S. Marines took the port. Wilson's goal was to deprive Huerta of arms, supplies, and customs revenues, thereby sapping the strength of his army's campaign against the Constitutionalists. At first Huerta attempted to rally support for his beleaguered regime, calling for unity against another gringo invasion. In fact many of the nation's newspapers urged retaliation against the "Pigs of Yanquilandia." Demonstrations and anti-American riots swept the republic, leading U.S. citizens to flee and, in some cases, ride out days of violence on vessels offshore. But when it became apparent that the Marines would not move on Mexico City as they had done in 1847, the wave of xenophobia petered out. Huerta rushed forces to the Gulf, intent on making a show against the Americans, but thereby allowed the rebels to move with greater speed. Despite the unremitting opposition their occupation generated, the U.S. troops dedicated themselves to improving sanitation, eradicating disease in the port, and making the trams run on time. Local wags joked that following the gringos' arrival, the *zopilote* (vulture), the city's unofficial mascot, had abandoned them in search of more hospitable digs.

The gringos would receive no acknowledgment of their assistance from Carranza. The first chief steadfastly refused to sanction the U.S. invasion and occupation of Mexican territory. His nationalism is today commemorated by a huge statue in Veracruz Harbor, a powerful likeness of the bearded patriarch that points out to sea, as if to gesture for the Marines to return from whence they came. There is also no doubt that the U.S. occupation of Veracruz helped augment the role of nationalism in the ideological mix of the revolution. As Carranza decried the intervention as a blatant violation of Mexican sovereignty—the second such offense within eighteen months following Ambassador Wilson's role in the overthrow of Madero—his rhetoric introduced into the political debate the goal of limiting U.S. influence more generally. Because U.S. military intervention often followed the influx of dollars into Latin American countries, most Mexicans had come to appreciate that recovering national sovereignty entailed restricting the role of U.S. capitalists. Paradoxically, however, revolution-era xenophobia was directed more often against Chinese merchants and Spanish proprietors than against U.S. citizens.

Wilson's strategy of forcing the dictator to battle two enemies at once helped encourage the Constitutionalists to launch a major offensive. In June 1914 Pancho Villa took the central Mexican city of Zacatecas in the single greatest battle in the war against Huerta, and the Zapatistas gained control of Morelos, where they soon began to return lands to peasant villages. Obregón continued his march down the west coast, and González approached the oil-rich Gulf Coast region. As Huerta began to lose control of the regional peripheries, it became increasingly difficult to levy taxes and dragoon troops. Disillusioned regional elites resented the federales' impressment of their workers and peons and took up opposition to the regime, forcing Huerta to empty the jails for reinforcements. The rebels themselves had no compunction about raiding prisons for both recruits and matériel. Indeed the troops commandeered by Joaquín Amaro,

FIGURE 4.1 The triumphant entry of First Chief Venustiano Carranza and General Alvaro Obregón into Mexico City, August 1914. Fideicomiso Archivos Plutarco Elías Calles y Fernando Torreblanca, Mexico City.

a Constitutionalist leader from Zacatecas, were known as *los rayados*, or striped ones, in reference to the prison uniforms they wore on the battle-field.

In the face of insurmountable military, diplomatic, and economic obstacles, Huerta delivered his resignation on July 6, 1914. Mexicans watched closely to see which general would enjoy the honor of occupying Mexico City. Villa had appeared destined for that honor until Carranza ordered him to take his troops on a lengthy detour preceding the fall of Zacatecas. As a result, it was Obregón's army that entered the capital in August 1914. The inhabitants of Mexico City, who had been spared an encounter with Orozco's and Zapata's ragtag armies by the swift demise of the Díaz regime in 1911, now watched in horror as Yaqui soldiers rode into the capital on horseback. Among Obregón's first acts as conqueror of the capital was a visit to Madero's grave (figure 4.1).

More numerous and more militant than they had been in 1910, the nation's insurgents agreed only on the proposition that the revolutionary process needed to go beyond the channels of regular politics. Revolutionary chiefs unwilling to countenance at least some formula for the renovation of Mexico's factories and fields would lose out. Yet even as they stood momentarily united in triumph, their internal divisions were painfully obvious.

LA BOLA: THE WAR BETWEEN THE REVOLUTIONARY FACTIONS, 1914–1915

The most volatile cleavage pitted two powerful northern leaders against one another: Carranza, the former Porfirian senator and *hacendado* and the founding father of the Constitutionalist movement, and Villa, the onetime social bandit who had become the most famous revolutionary warrior (the "Centaur of the North") and commander of its most successful fighting force, the División del Norte. Carranza had already demonstrated his jealousy of Villa as a potential national rival when he delayed his advance on the capital, allowing Obregón to take Mexico City. For his part, Villa resented Carranza's patrician haughtiness and his failure to define himself on fundamental issues, such as the agrarian question and the shape of the new political order. Following Huerta's defeat, Villa attempted to obtain Carranza's approval of an agreement defining the revolution as "a struggle of the poor against the abuses of the powerful." He urged Carranza to commit the Constitutionalists "to implement a democratic regime to secure the well-being of the workers [and] to emancipate the peasants economically, making an equitable distribution of lands or whatever else is needed to solve the agrarian problem."[6] Not surprisingly, the first chief flatly declined.

As the potential for conflict escalated in late summer and early fall, Obregón proposed a diplomatic effort to defuse tensions and hammer out a unified program. The Constitutionalists painfully recalled that it had been the absence of consensus that had eroded the revolution's momentum and paved the way for Huertismo. All of the principal revolutionary forces therefore agreed to send delegates in October 1914 to the city of Aguascalientes in north-central Mexico. This was to be a military convention, and each faction received a set number of delegates (all military officers) based on its reported size. Hence the Villistas were by far the largest faction, followed by the Carrancistas, Obregonistas, and Zapatistas. Unfortunately the Revolutionary Convention of Aguascalientes only sharpened the animosity between Villistas and Carrancistas. It helped polarize the revolution into contending factions and trigger an apocalyptic War between the Factions that would ravage the country and cost hundreds of thousands of lives.

Supposedly Aguascalientes represented something of a neutral space, a territory under no faction's control; in actuality, it belonged to Villa. Not only were Villa's delegates in the majority, but the División del Norte lingered within striking distance of the city, a menacing presence for Carranza and others. In short order, the humble revolutionaries affiliated with Villa and Zapata made common cause against the Carrancistas, exasperated by the first chief's arrogance and more gradualist notions of reform. For them, Carranza's continued leadership augured an authoritarian style that reminded them of Don Porfirio. For Carranza and his supporters, the ascendancy of Villistas and Zapatistas represented anarchy and unlettered provincialism, the antithesis of Mexico's future as a progressive, modern state. Knowing that the Villistas enjoyed a majority due to the numerical weight of their faction, General Obregón attempted to mediate, making an impassioned speech that urged the delegates to work together. Despite these efforts, the Convention quickly degenerated into chaos, as armed revolutionaries occasionally rode their mounts into the chamber, shouted at one another, discharged their guns in the air to punctuate their points, and engaged in drunken brawls. As the armed delegates ran amok, their intellectual advisers stood aghast, powerless to influence the proceedings. All the while, Aguascalientes's *gente decente* barricaded themselves in their townhouses, fearful of the wrath of the losing faction.

Ultimately, when the Villista-Zapatista majority at the Convention decided to depose him as first chief, Carranza disputed the authority of the decision, then retreated with his depleted forces to Veracruz in November. He temporarily ceded the capital to the militarily powerful but tenuous "Conventionist" alliance that was Villismo and Zapatismo, but he never relinquished his claim to formal legitimacy. Establishing the headquarters of what remained of Constitutionalism in Veracruz was a bold stroke, affording him access to the Gulf's rich oil and customs revenues. Carranza counted on a talented staff of intellectuals and politicians, men like Luis Cabrera, who subordinated their personal distaste for Carranza's arrogance to a belief that Constitutionalism represented the best chance to avert another descent into chaos.

Even more fortuitous for the first chief, Obregón, whose forces represented the strongest counterweight to Villa's army, also continued to back the Constitutionalist rump, rebuffing entreaties from the Conventionists. The Obregonista leadership included men who had come to understand the social and political grievances of the poor majority amid the process of the military struggle. No longer would Obregón boast that there were no agraristas in his movement; instead he made himself into one of their champions. His supporters consisted of middle-class *rancheros*, small businessmen and merchants, artisans and mechanics, teachers such as Plutarco Elías Calles, and at least one pharmacist in Salvador Alvarado. (Both Calles and Alvarado would end up with a general's rank by the end of the war between the factions.)

The Obregonistas were prepared to enact reforms in the social sphere to modernize the economy. Their life on the border had introduced them to U.S. concepts of modernization. They wanted their nation to progress and ultimately to industrialize. To that end, they favored the breakup of large and inefficient haciendas manned by immobile debt peons, and the creation of dynamic, highly capitalized medium-size estates worked by true wage laborers. Here they drew invidious comparisons between oversized, unproductive, feudal-like Mexican haciendas and prosperous, efficient, midsize North American family farms, or even their own ventures in Sonora. At the same time, these middle-class reformers agreed to return to Indian and mestizo communities some of the lands they had lost, not because they were great agraristas but because it would bring social peace. They envisioned these campesinos as a potential modern wage-labor force that would provide work not only for the more efficient commercial estates they envisioned, but also for the nation's future industrialization. In other words, they appreciated that the peasant village's traditional land base would not alone suffice to support the rapidly growing population. These rural cultivators would then need to work as agricultural or industrial wage laborers to supplement their subsistence. This pragmatic, proactive approach to social reform—the willingness to implement a modest agrarian reform in order to accomplish longer-term development goals— distinguished the twentieth-century liberal ideology of the Obregón faction as well as the progressive wing of the Carrancistas.

Thus two parties—or better, two large, amorphous constellations of rival armies and bands, the Constitutionalists and the Conventionists— would contest Mexico's revolutionary future. At the level of the rank-

FIGURE 4.2 With the fate of Mexico hanging in the balance, Obregón and Villa meet with Governor Maytorena and U.S. military officers in Ciudad Juárez, 1914. From left to right: Colonel Francisco Serrano, General Alvaro Obregón, Major Julio Madero, General Francisco Villa, General John Sherman, and Lieutenant George Patton. Fideicomiso Archivos Plutarco Elías Calles y Fernando Torreblanca, Mexico City.

and-file troops, the rival factions resembled one another rather closely. Each constellation included a variety of former Maderistas, former federal soldiers, and opportunists who changed sides with each shift in the revolution's fortunes. The bulk of each faction's enlisted men consisted of humble campesinos, itinerant field hands and laborers, *vaqueros*, miners, drifters, and bandits. By contrast, the officers were frequently members of the middle sectors (e.g., rancheros, petty traders, artisans, teachers, successful social bandits).

The armies also included a growing number of women fighters, the *soldaderas*. Immortalized in the famous *corrido* "La Adelita," among other revolution-era songs, the soldaderas could be found in all factions (figures 4.3 and 4.4). Some went with the men in their lives; others found themselves the object of forced recruitment; and still others followed their own initiative. All signified both the additional opportunity that the revolution brought and the tragedy of a cycle of destruction. They expected much from the revolution but received few rewards; as one of them lamented years later, "[Women] helped make the revolution, . . . [yet] the government of our country, when the revolution was ended and they had taken advantage of our services, sent us home, saying that the place of a woman

FIGURE 4.3 These soldaderas fought for Plutarco Elías Calles and the Constitutionalists, and the photograph shows them accompanied by their children in Naco, Sonora, in 1915. Fideicomiso Archivos Plutarco Elías Calles y Fernando Torreblanca, Mexico City.

FIGURE 4.4 Women formed an integral part of the revolution. This photograph shows Valentina Ramírez, a soldadera from Sonora, in 1913. Fideicomiso Archivos Plutarco Elías Calles y Fernando Torreblanca, Mexico City.

is in her home."[7] The revolution's factional leaders varied in their opinion of the women fighters. At one end of the spectrum, Alvarado and, to a lesser extent, Zapata and González actively encouraged the participation of soldaderas. At the other end, Villa reportedly did not like the idea of women fighting; one historian reports that Villa once ordered the machine-gunning of eighty or ninety soldaderas and their children. In all likelihood, Obregón's opinion resembled Villa's more than Alvarado's; Villa and Obregón approximated the habitus of the traditional nineteenth-century macho caudillo more so than other leaders of the revolution. One historical account asserts that Obregón positioned women and children in front of his troops as human shields.[8]

At the top, significant differences in worldview distinguished the Constitutionalist leaders from their Conventionist counterparts. At the risk of overgeneralizing about a revolution as far-flung and chaotic as Mexico's, it seems fair to conclude that the Conventionists featured less of a social and cultural gap between chiefs and enlisted men than did the Constitutionalists. Zapata's men frequently commented that their chief was "one of them": "'Miliano, never Señor Zapata";[9] and chroniclers of Villismo made the same point about Pancho Villa. By contrast, a more ambitious and upwardly mobile middle-sector leadership characterized the Constitutionalist movement and set its tone; here the officers frequently built greater social and cultural distance into their relations with their troops, seeking to enforce a rank structure that would transform motley bands into a proper army. To be sure, intellectuals could be found in either camp, for instance, the famed journalist Martín Luis Guzmán (a former member of the Ateneo de la Juventud) among the Conventionists, and Luis Cabrera and others on the Constitutionalist side.

Constitutionalist leaders had a national program and vision and harnessed military discipline to it. Many of the movement's most talented military chiefs and top intellectual advisers epitomized the twentieth-century liberal ideological current; all were dedicated to bringing a modicum of social reform to Mexico. Their first chief was a more reluctant reformer, determined to dissolve the Porfirian bureaucracy and army while consolidating a strong central state, one that would *eventually* be capable of implementing social change. Still, he was pragmatic enough to accommodate more radical allies on social matters when national power hung in the balance. Carranza was undoubtedly the most nationalist leader in the

Constitutionalist alliance, stridently defending his country's right to self-determination even as he shrewdly collaborated with the U.S. and other foreign governments when it suited his purposes. Collectively the generals, ideologues, and local chiefs of Constitutionalism thought in national terms and carried out a deliberate strategy. Unlike the Villistas, who did a bit of plundering when the need or opportunity arose, or the Zapatistas, who fought to preserve what was theirs, Constitutionalist leaders sought the huge, socially acceptable fortunes that would fall to them as the legitimate future leaders of a new, modernized revolutionary state. Having defeated the Old Regime, they would purge its bureaucratic vestiges, then organize their own political system, predicated on the sound principles of bourgeois reform and nationalism. Craving legitimacy and the forms, routines, and rituals of the modern nation-state, these "official revolutionaries" could not tolerate the anarchic style and regional orientation of their Conventionist rivals. They were perfectly willing to subordinate individual rights to the collective good—not for nothing, then, were these twentieth-century Liberals characterized as illiberal by opponents to their right. Witness the following excerpt from a piece of Constitutionalist propaganda, published in 1915, which caricatures their opponents as savage beasts while affirming themselves as sober and trustworthy protectors of the nation:

> The history of Zapatismo is a long, terrifying criminal farce. . . .
>
> How can there be partisans of Zapatismo among people who boast of being civilized?
>
> How can the father of a family feel sympathy for a bestial mob capable of killing his own sons?
>
> If two and half miles outside Puebla a Zapatista band seizes women and outrages them, abandoning them full of shame and disgrace at the side of a road, how can you be sure, snooty Señora Zapatista . . . that tomorrow, for all your devotion, you and your daughter, coming from her first communion, pure in spirit and flesh, may not be the victims of the criminal concupiscence of those bandits? . . .
>
> The Zapatistas do not cost their chiefs much money. It is true, the Zapatista does not need clothes or comforts. He feeds on blood. . . .
>
> Those who follow [Francisco] Villa are mercenary soldiers, as mercenary and barbarous as those who besieged Carthage. For their complicity they demand payment in gold, in liberty to commit crimes, in

authority to rob, rape, and kill with impunity. This bestial, primitive, blind, and foolish mob is called an army because it consists of many men, but truthfully it is only a gang of bandits. For them the Republic is a stagecoach loaded with gold and women; what you do is hold it up....

Obregón's triumph over [Villa's] black hosts is the triumph of military expertise, calculation, calmness, and wisdom. Obregón takes no step that is not calculated, meditated, considered. His advance has been slow but sure, firm, definitive. ...

Mothers, you can sleep in peace. The rapists are fleeing. Bourgeoisie, don't worry so much now over your coffers. The robbers are dead. Hypocritical neutrals, your hope has gone out. Eternal reactionaries, the Revolution triumphs over all your selfishness. Privileges crumble, and the lights of Liberty go on![40]

By contrast, most of the Convention's top leaders, as well as their chief lieutenants, represented the agrarian currents of the revolution. With the exception of men like General Felipe Angeles, a former Porfirista who was one of the most important generals of the División del Norte, they espoused the goals of the common men in their ranks rather than aspiring to greater things. They abhorred official procedure and politicians, placing their faith in direct action to redress material and moral grievances. Nowhere is this sensibility more immediately illustrated than in Pancho Villa's encounter with Emiliano Zapata at Xochimilco on December 4, 1914. The Conventionist leaders were meeting at this little town south of Mexico City to seal their alliance against Carranza, the mere mention of whom triggered this intense and passionate exchange:

VILLA: As Carranza is a man so, so, so high and mighty, I realized that [he and his crowd] were going along getting control of the Republic, and me just waiting.

ZAPATA: All the fellows have already told you: I always said so, I always told them, that Carranza is a son of a bitch.

VILLA: [He and his crowd] are men who have slept on downy pillows. How are they going to be friends of people who have spent their whole lives in pure suffering?

ZAPATA: The other way around, they have been used to being the scourge of the people.... [The people] have lots of love for the land. They still don't believe it when you tell them, "This land is yours."

They think it's a dream. But as soon as they see others are getting crops from these lands, they'll say, "I'm going to ask for my land, and I'm going to plant." Above all, that's the love people have for the land. As a rule they never lose it.

VILLA: The [politicians] will soon see that it's the people who give the orders and that the people are going to see who are their friends.

ZAPATA: [People know] if somebody wants to take their lands away, they know all by themselves that they have to defend themselves. But they kill before they turn loose of the land.

VILLA: They no more than get the taste, and then we bring them the party [of politicians] to take it away. Our people have never had justice, not even liberty. The rich have all the prime fields, and the people, the raggedly little poor man, working from sunup to sundown. I think that in the future it's going to be another life, and if not, we won't turn loose of those Mausers we have now. . . .

ZAPATA: Those son-of-a-bitch politicians, as soon as they see a little chance to get in, then quick they want to make their way, and they take off to brown-nose the next big shot on the rise, like a son of a bitch. That's why I've busted all those sons of bitches. I can't stand them. In a jiffy they change and take off, now with Carranza, or now with another one farther on. They're all a bunch of bastards. I'd just like to run into them some other time.[11]

Although they held a military and political advantage after the Aguascalientes Convention, the Conventionists quickly squandered it. Ultimately the Constitutionalists' national orientation and shrewd political skills would triumph over their opponents' parochial perspective. Across a variety of fronts, the Conventionists' lack of national vision, and of a plan to gain and hold state power, cost them dearly. To begin with, the regionally based Villistas and Zapatistas communicated poorly with each other and found it difficult to coordinate movements of troops and supplies. At critical junctures, Villa denied ammunition to the beleaguered Zapatistas. Thus, for all practical purposes, the Conventionist alliance proved to be short-lived, allowing the Constitutionalists to take the offensive.

By contrast, the Constitutionalists managed a much more deliberate and coordinated campaign. Carranza's decision to locate his headquarters in the port city of Veracruz proved strategically wise, as the Constitution-

FIGURE 4.5   Villa and Zapata in the National Palace following the Conventionist occupation of Mexico City, 1914. Fideicomiso Archivos Plutarco Elías Calles y Fernando Torreblanca, Mexico City.

alists easily procured arms and ammunition through the port. From there, Carranza moved to extend his control over the southeastern states, whose ruling oligarchies had managed to keep the revolution at arm's length until then. In March 1915, for example, he dispatched Alvarado to conquer and govern the Yucatán peninsula, home of the immensely lucrative henequen economy. With the nation's principal port and its two most lucrative export commodities—petroleum and sisal fiber—under their control, the Constitutionalists gained a significant economic advantage over the Conventionists, who proved unable to restore the productive capacities of the war-torn regions under their control.

Ironically, although their movement's origins and concerns were genuinely closer to the peasants and workers, the failure of the Conventionist leaders to forge a clear national social program left the door open for Carranza's middle-class politicians, through skillful opportunistic appeals, to separate the Convention from its natural allies beyond its regional bases. In the January 1915 Veracruz Decrees, drafted by Cabrera and other progressive intellectuals, the Constitutionalists promised the return of traditional village lands and the right of workers to strike and organize freely.

Among the troops that Obregón used to launch an offensive against Villa several months later were six "red battalions" of urban workers who had allied themselves with the Constitutionalists in exchange for the promise to support the interests of urban workers.

The generalship of Obregón in pivotal battles in the Bajío in central Mexico in the spring of 1915 was also a determining factor in the Constitutionalist victory and similarly underscores the triumph of a broad, cosmopolitan outlook over a more narrow provincialism. A student of the military events then unfolding in war-ravaged Europe, Obregón employed barbed-wire entrenchments and withering machine-gun fire to rout the bold charges of wave after wave of Villa's crack gold-shirted cavalry. At the battle of Celaya in April, thousands of Villa's best troops were gunned down or impaled on wire, while Constitutionalist losses numbered in the low hundreds. In the months that followed, Villa's seemingly invincible División del Norte experienced new defeats as it straggled north—at León, Aguascalientes, and finally at the border town of Agua Prieta (Sonora). These crushing setbacks broke his army's offensive capabilities, driving him into a defensive posture in the Villista heartland in Chihuahua. Villa's demise isolated the Zapatistas in Morelos and sealed the fate of the Conventionist cause.

Not surprisingly, President Wilson also decided to throw his support behind Carranza's movement—despite a strenuous campaign to cultivate the North Americans by Villa, who even refrained from criticizing the occupation of Veracruz. In fact Carranza's tenacious nationalism did not prove much of a deterrent to the U.S. official recognition of his government in October 1915. Put simply, most North American businessmen and politicians regarded Villismo and Zapatismo as a greater problem than the Constitutionalists. These outsiders routinely cast Villa and Zapata and their followers as atavistic impediments to Mexico's development as a modern nation in partnership with U.S. capital. Recent research suggests that the U.S. naval forces that occupied and then abandoned Veracruz in 1914 left the approaching Carrancistas massive caches of arms and munitions that figured in the series of decisive battles waged in the Bajío the following year. The Constitutionalist commanders who successfully defended Agua Prieta from the Villistas in the last major battle of the revolution in November 1915 obtained weapons from the U.S. side of the border, and Arizona authorities even allowed Constitutionalist leader Plutarco

Elías Calles to move some of his troops across U.S. territory to shift reinforcements to the border city.

The "high politics" of the factional struggle, as critical as they were in establishing winners and losers and setting the terms for the institutional consolidation of "the Revolution," provide only a partial history of the twentieth century's first great social upheaval. Such high politics do not engage with the messy and often highly contingent local dimensions of the revolutionary process, what one historian has referred to as the internal "logic of the revolution."[12] As we have seen, Mexican popular culture has often characterized the factional struggle as *la bola*, which conjures up images of a gigantic boulder rolling erratically through the countryside. While this popular image privileges the arbitrary nature of revolution, it aptly suggests a revolutionary dynamic that was far from a phased and orderly affair fought between well-organized and disciplined units of combatants, who were in good communication with one another. In this regard the Mexican Revolution differed greatly from the more disciplined, socialist movements that shook Latin America later in the century (e.g., the successful struggles led by Cuban Fidelistas and Nicaraguan Sandinistas), though these too were not the neatly orchestrated affairs that their vanguards, once ensconced in power, proclaimed them to be. Rather Mexico's epic revolution remained notoriously disorganized as a whole and fell out differently from region to region, even from locality to locality.

Consider the issue of revolutionary violence and dislocation. Without question, the revolution was brutally violent. Approximately one million of Mexico's prerevolutionary population of approximately fifteen million died in the fighting or from social consequences of the violence. At the end of the decade, a devastating pandemic dubbed the Spanish flu would claim hundreds of thousands more, especially among those who remained famished and homeless after the war between the factions. The Mexican Revolution also led to the first large-scale wave of emigration north of the border.

Although the revolution constituted a major demographic event in modern Mexican history, the figures must be examined with some nuance. The one million Mexicans "missing" in the postrevolutionary census likely included potential births that were preempted by the upheaval's death and dislocation, as well as those who perished in the flu pandemic. Deaths directly attributed to combat have surely been overestimated. Aside from the pivotal mass encounters in the Bajío, revolutionary armies did not fight battles of attrition; indeed much of the fighting was done at long range and not very accurately. The chronic lack of artillery and machine guns certainly limited battlefield deaths outside of the Bajío campaign. Massacres and executions clearly contributed to the body count, but their frequency is debatable and some of their recounting in memoirs and oral histories appears to have crossed over from fact into myth.

Moreover violence and destruction varied widely across time and space. In 1915, at the height of the *lucha de facciones*, Mexico was indeed a bloody "fiesta of bullets" in most of the North, the Bajío in central Mexico, and Morelos. In these areas, intervals of peace were rare; indeed cease-fires became events for local balladeers to sing about. Yet as Obregonista killed Villista and worker fought peasant in the Bajío, the U.S. consul in Yucatán quipped, "Peace is raging down here, as usual."[13] By comparison, the entire Southeast (with the exception of waves of sporadic, low-level riot and revolt in the Yucatecan countryside during 1910–13) and much of the Gulf appeared relatively quiet during the worst moments of national factional strife. And following the apocalyptic "Ten Tragic Days" during the death throes of Maderismo, Mexico City also remained virtually free of violence.

Thus violence and social dislocation must be examined region by region — sound advice for analyzing any revolutionary situation. Between 1910 and 1917, for example, the Zapatista homeland of Morelos experienced a 45 percent decline in population (from 180,000 to 100,000) as government troops mounted a scorched-earth campaign against the agrarian rebels. Morelenses died in the fighting, faced deportation in large numbers to prison camps in the Yucatán peninsula, or became exhausted by the violence and left the state. In the process, the revolution gutted the extraordinarily lucrative sugar plantation economy of Morelos and destroyed or depopulated entire towns and villages. By contrast, during the same period, the Gulf Coast oil industry and Yucatecan henequen economy experienced a golden age in terms of export production and earnings.

This revolutionary-era bonanza in oil and henequen was not serendipitous. Mexico's war between the revolutionary factions coincided with the onset of World War I, and the United States made it clear to the Constitutionalists that disruptions in the production of these strategic commodities would not be tolerated. Oil fueled the Allied fleets and war-time economy, and henequen bound the midwestern wheat crop. Not only would a failure to guarantee shipments of oil and henequen bring an immediate end to U.S. arms shipments to Carranza's regime, but the United States did not rule out cruder forms of gunboat diplomacy. In 1915, for example, U.S. diplomats lectured the Constitutionalists that, if necessary, U.S. marines and seamen would come ashore, dump money for sisal fiber on the docks, and load the bales of hemp onto U.S. ships themselves. Such demands suggest perhaps why Carranza continued to maintain his seat of government in Veracruz, why it was so essential for him to dispatch powerful revolutionary proconsuls like Salvador Alvarado to Yucatán to control the situation economically as well as politically, and why Carranza took such pains to rein in local Gulf warlords like Manuel Peláez.

If the U.S. government intended to reap the benefits of political consolidation under the Constitutionalists after years of destruction, ironically it managed to reenergize factional division. Just a few months after the Constitutionalist triumph, Pancho Villa exacted a little revenge on the United States for its recognition of the regime of First Chief Carranza. On March 9, 1916, Villa crossed the border and went on a rampage in Columbus, New Mexico (figures 4.6 and 4.7). The attack, which, in effect, constituted the only Latin American invasion of the United States in history, prompted Wilson to send General John Pershing on a punitive expedition in hot but futile pursuit of Villa. (Earlier, "Black Jack" Pershing had chased the Apache chieftain Gerónimo over similar stretches of punishing northern Mexican desert.) "La Punitiva" burnished Villa's image as a national hero, as balladeers heralded larger-than-life exploits that enabled him to consistently elude and outwit hordes of Yankees trespassing on Mexican soil. Once again Villa became a force to reckon with, his ranks growing from a few hundred bedraggled fighters to tens of thousands of troops and supporters.

Villa's resurgence, and the presence of thousands of U.S. troops on Mexican territory, helped cement the ascendancy of Obregón, formerly the Constitutionalists' most powerful general and now minister of war under Carranza. To his chagrin, the first chief aimed to restore civilian rule and resented his reliance on the principal generals that commanded a hodgepodge of military forces. Thus began another round of divisiveness among revolutionaries. Merely allies of convenience, the Constitutional-

PROCLAMATION
$5,000⁰⁰ REWARD

FRANCISCO (PANCHO) VILLA

ALSO $1,000. REWARD FOR ARREST OF CANDELARIO CERVANTES, PABLO LOPEZ, FRANCISCO BELTRAN, MARTIN LOPEZ

ANY INFORMATION LEADING TO HIS APPREHENSION WILL BE REWARDED

CHIEF OF POLIC
Columbus
MARCH 9, 1916   New Mexico

FIGURE 4.6 Villa wanted poster displayed after the Columbus raid of March 9, 1916. Fideicomiso Archivos Plutarco Elías Calles y Fernando Torreblanca, Mexico City.

FIGURE 4.7 U.S. troops lining the border at Nogales, Arizona, following the accidental shooting of a U.S. citizen by a stray bullet that crossed the international boundary, 1917. National Archives, College Park, Maryland, RG 165, MID 8536–270C.

FIGURE 4.8 General Alvaro Obregón and U.S. Consul Ezra M. Lawton meet at
the border in Nogales, 1917. National Archives, College Park, Maryland, RG 165,
MID 8536–270d.

ists uneasily set about the task of restoring political order, a precondition
for the economic and social reorganization of the country (figure 4.8).

THE BEGINNINGS OF CONSOLIDATION, 1916–1920

After five years of fighting, the Constitutionalist victors faced an arduous
task. Despite its tremendous cost in human lives, the revolutionary upheaval had not yet fully run its course. While the Constitutionalist armies
had essentially reduced the Villistas and Zapatistas to guerrilla operations
in their respective regions, Félix Díaz remained at large in the Mexican
Southeast, and warlords such as Manuel Peláez and Saturnino Cedillo still
operated with substantial autonomy in their *cacicazgos*. Worse, the fiesta of
bullets had exacted a huge socioeconomic toll. The fighting had disrupted
many of the most significant export economies, including silver mining,
the production of cereals, and plantation agriculture. Only copper, oil, and
henequen production continued to prosper, fueled by the demand created
by the world war. Moreover the upheaval had wreaked havoc on millions
of families, with the men of the household dead, maimed, laid off from
work, or in the United States. Although women began to claim the political and social space left behind by these men, most of them were locked
in a daily struggle to save their families from destitution. Marauding gangs

continued to roam the land, without sufficient police or security personnel to control them. Commerce had collapsed in many regions, not only due to political instability and banditry but also because of the continuing emission of worthless paper money by the various factions. When trading resumed, Mexicans demanded payment in scarce silver and gold.

Foreign meddling also continued to plague the nation. The governments of Britain and France refused to confer diplomatic recognition, while German agents meddled in Mexican politics, hoping to exploit the nascent anti-American sentiments that accompanied Pershing's Punitive Expedition. Hence the ill-fated Zimmermann telegram, which invited Mexico to join Germany in an alliance if the United States entered the war on the side of the Allies. Although the Wilson administration had recognized the Carranza regime, it kept its troops in Chihuahua until February 1917, when its imminent entry into World War I occasioned a withdrawal. By then, however, Carranza—the revolutionary leader with the greatest nationalist credentials—had cleverly exploited growing Mexican outrage about the presence of U.S. troops on national soil to strengthen his own political position.

By late 1916, with the Constitutionalist presence established in the national capital and major urban centers, Carranza felt strong enough to begin the process of revolutionary consolidation. Although bitter memories of the Aguascalientes fiasco lingered, the first chief gathered a new convention to draft a revolutionary constitution that would legitimize his movement's triumph, reestablish the state's presence, and bring an enduring social peace. Learning from previous mistakes, Carranza and his advisers barred participation by the enemies of Constitutionalism; moreover they planned the gathering that assembled in the city of Querétaro in November as a less volatile and bellicose affair. Less than one-third of the delegates were revolutionary combatants. Over half were university-educated professionals, representatives of the young, new middle class that had languished under the Porfiriato. Left to his own devices, Carranza would have preferred a document that harnessed the tepid social doctrines of traditional, anticlerical Liberalism to a more powerful executive. Indeed the draft he circulated to delegates bore a strong resemblance to Juárez's Constitution of 1857. But ultimately the twentieth-century Liberals who constituted his most progressive advisers—the so-called "Jacobin" group, which included men such as Luis Cabrera, Pastor Rouaix, and Francisco

Múgica—carried the day, crafting a final document that privileged the kind of social reform that had animated the 1915 Veracruz Decrees.

This document drew upon the recent experiments of various Constitutionalist state governors, many of whom had received their first political experiences in Sonora. Although future president Lázaro Cárdenas would coin the phrase *laboratories of the revolution* to describe his own and other socially progressive state governments of the 1920s, the term is equally appropriate here. Sent to Yucatán by the first chief in 1915 to secure the state for the Constitutionalists, Salvador Alvarado unionized the state's urban workers and assailed its landowning oligarchy, particularly the owners of the vast henequen plantations in the northwestern quadrant of the region. His Agrarian Law of 1915 decreed that every Yucatecan adult had the right to his or her own parcel of land. Still, Alvarado knew that the henequen plantations constituted his state's main source of revenue, and he did not redistribute their lands. A self-styled proponent of women's rights, Alvarado also proclaimed all women free from positions of servitude and helped them organize in feminist leagues. Manuel M. Diéguez, the governor of Jalisco, joined Alvarado in mobilizing workers and spearheaded a radical attack on the Roman Catholic Church in one of Mexico's most devout states. Finally, Plutarco Elías Calles and Adolfo de la Huerta, who alternated as governors of Sonora for most of the 1915–20 period, imposed new taxes on foreign-owned copper companies, promulgated decrees aimed at temperance and the elimination of gambling, limited the power of the Roman Catholic Church, and set up a Workers' Chamber that adjudicated the demands of the copper miners and other blue-collar workers in the state. Out of this process, workers received retirement and health benefits as well as workers' compensation for injuries and illnesses related to egregious working conditions. It is not surprising, therefore, that the organized labor movements that these Constitutionalist governors helped to forge in these and other states (e.g., Puebla) became the key supporters of their rule. In those states where the governors were proconsuls imposed by Carranza, they were often the only reliable homegrown allies of Constitutionalist carpetbagger rule.

Despite their reformist bent where workers, women, and campesinos were concerned, Constitutionalist proconsular governors essentially sought to maintain the foundations of the economic status quo, viewing large corporations and agribusinesses as essential revenue generators.

Such a stance, however, made little headway in numerous states where the Porfirian oligarchy continued to rule. For example, heavily indigenous and impoverished Oaxaca, one of the cradles of nineteenth-century Liberalism and the birthplace of both Porfirio Díaz and Benito Juárez, whose son had served as governor under Madero, remained under the control of the old regime. In Oaxaca, Chiapas, and elsewhere, landowners rallied around counterrevolutionary figures such as Félix Díaz in an effort to stave off popular mobilization and reform. Thus the effort to craft a new constitution stemmed, in part, from the desire to assert federal supremacy over a variety of states whose governments ran the gamut from progressive to counterrevolutionary.

Although the assertion of central government control would ultimately depend on negotiation and compromise, the radical Jacobins forcefully pressed their agenda at the Querétaro Convention. Virtually all of the delegates were in favor of a strong position against the Church; radical anticlerical provisions abounded, reproducing and often exceeding the scathing rhetoric of the nineteenth-century Reform. Among the litany of new provisions limiting the powers of the Church: public worship and processions beyond church grounds would be prohibited; states could determine the maximum number of clergymen within their jurisdictions; and priests had to register with civil authorities and be native-born. Most important, primary education would henceforth be free, compulsory, and secular. These provisions inaugurated a conflict with the Catholic Church that would ultimately lead to religious violence in the Cristero War of the 1920s.

The Convention's debates about agrarian and labor reform resulted in resounding Jacobin victories and the inclusion of articles that heralded a new era of liberal social reform. In an effort to address the concerns of agraristas not just in Morelos and Chihuahua but throughout the republic, as well as remain true to their own nationalist and anticlerical sentiments, the Convention's radicals crafted Article 27 in a manner that looked backward and forward, transforming traditional liberal prescriptions with regard to the land. As in colonial times, the state would be the ultimate owner of all of Mexico's land, water, and mineral wealth. Henceforth private property—sacred and inviolable in traditional liberal conceptions— would be made conditional, something the state could concede to individuals provided their activities did not violate the general well-being of

Mexico's citizens. The state was therefore expressly permitted to intervene in private property in the name of "public utility."

With that end in mind, village lands despoiled during the Porfiriato would be restored to the pueblos; moreover provision would be made for those communities that could not prove legal title to receive lands anyway. Not infrequently landowners or unscrupulous caciques had seized a pueblo's title. Article 27 also empowered the new revolutionary state to expropriate the idle lands of large haciendas and to arbitrate the disposition of all mineral and subsoil rights. Thus, in a bold departure from the Porfiriato, "only Mexicans by birth or naturalization and Mexican companies" now had "the right to acquire ownership of lands [and] waters . . . or to obtain concessions for the exploitation of mines and of waters." The Mexican state might "grant the same right to foreigners, provided they agree[d] to consider themselves as nationals in respect to such property, and bind themselves not to invoke the protection of their governments . . . under penalty, in case of noncompliance . . . of forfeiture of the property acquired to the Nation." Finally, true to their Jacobin roots, the radicals incorporated a provision attacking the Catholic Church's right to own or administer real property. Henceforth "places of worship [were] the property of the nation . . . which shall determine which of them may continue to be devoted to their present purposes."[14]

Sensitive to the demands that animated the Plan of Ayala but inspired by the Jacobins' own hybrid notions of property, Article 27 paved the way for one of the most sweeping and contested agrarian reforms in Latin American and world history, one that remained on the books until the early 1990s. It also set the stage for Lázaro Cárdenas's landmark expropriation of foreign-owned oil properties in 1938.

The Jacobins similarly won the day in codifying Article 123 on the rights of labor. Here they drew from ideas appearing in the Magonistas' anticapitalist Plan of 1906, yet once again their article spoke more to their own pragmatic attempt to address subaltern demands within the limits of the capitalist system. In seeking to strike a prudent balance between the interests of labor and capital, the middle-class reformers enshrined the right of workers to organize, bargain collectively, and go on strike — demands for which so much blood had been shed during the late Porfiriato. They also included a series of provisions to improve working conditions: an eight-hour day, a six-day week, a minimum wage, overtime pay, equal pay for equal work regardless of nationality or gender, and safeguards against the use of labor by minors. These clauses made the Constitution of 1917 one of the world's most progressive labor codes at the time of its promulgation.

As we shall see in the chapters that follow, many provisions of the "Revolutionary Magna Carta" were honored sporadically, if at all, in the decades that followed. To what extent was the postrevolutionary Mexican state able to carry out its broad educational reforms, providing at least a free, secular primary education to all its citizens? Was the institutional revolution really willing or able to carry out its battery of escalated anticlerical provisions? How was the agrarian reform implemented: what kind of lands and accompanying services did campesinos receive, and under what terms? Did the agrarian reform meet the changing needs of a growing peasantry? Did the large estate disappear as the central agrarian unit in Mexico? Did Mexico truly regain control over its natural resources and subsoil rights? To what extent were the rights and conditions of labor meaningfully enforced? Did the postrevolutionary state tolerate an independent and assertive labor movement? These are only some of the larger questions with regard to the legacies of the 1917 Constitution—as well as those of the institutional revolution as a whole—and they figure critically in any account of Mexico's recent past.

Still, if only as a series of claims that campesinos and workers would invoke in the name of "the Revolution," the impact of the Constitutionalist document on the course of the twentieth century is beyond dispute. The 1917 charter provided a comprehensive blueprint for subsequent agrarian and social reform legislation during the institutionalizing phase of the revolution in the 1920s and 1930s and constituted a symbolic front for popular struggles after the Official Revolution moved irrevocably to the Right after 1940. Indeed it remains an intense symbolic battleground for neoliberal managers and grassroots social movements alike in the new millennium.

Although the formulation of the new constitution marked a decisive moment between the violence of the years 1910–15 and the beginning of institutionalization, this account would remain incomplete without reference to the bloody denouement of the personal animosities and political rivalries that had survived the war between the factions. A significant economic and demographic context framed this story. While Mexico appeared on the road to economic recovery in 1917 and 1918, the aftermath of

World War I again caused trouble. With the end of the war, Mexican raw materials such as oil, copper, and henequen no longer commanded the high prices that they had enjoyed as strategic wartime commodities. As a result, the balance sheets of mining and agricultural corporations suffered, and the managers passed the financial pain on to their workers. In addition, the tax revenues of state and federal governments declined. The aging Carranza did not handle this crisis well at all, blaming the United States and his political enemies for the trouble. As if these economic troubles were not bad enough, in 1918 the Spanish flu pandemic hit Mexico hard, accounting for hundreds of thousands of deaths.

While Carranza could ill afford to antagonize the U.S. government more than his government had already done in formulating the revolutionary constitution, he wrongly believed that his domestic rivals constituted easier targets. First, he moved against the Zapatistas. He ordered General González to wage a scorched-earth campaign against the rebels from Morelos, and in April 1919 the general decided to eliminate Zapata himself by means of a treacherous plot. One of his minions, an officer in the new federal army, approached Zapata with an offer to defect along with his men and asked the campesino leader to meet him in an abandoned hacienda building in order to hand over his assets. On April 12, 1919, Zapata entered the building, only to be gunned down by González's soldiers. This heinous deed alienated the already skeptical agraristas from the Carranza government and drove the remaining Zapatistas into an alliance with Obregón, who condemned the cowardly assassination of their leader and promised them that he would support their demand for the restitution of their village lands.

Carranza's second, and fatal, mistake was to stand in the way of Obregón's presidential aspirations. After Obregón declared his candidacy in June 1919, Carranza announced his opposition to military candidates. After months of silence, he threw his support behind a handpicked candidate, Ignacio Bonillas, a civilian without any political base of his own who was then serving as the ambassador to the United States. Obregón, who had never trusted Carranza, considered the president's move an act of betrayal. In April 1920 his Sonoran allies, Calles and Adolfo de la Huerta, launched the last successful revolt against a sitting president by means of the Plan of Agua Prieta, which accused Carranza of resorting to dictatorial political tactics. One month later, Carranza fled Mexico City by train en route to

Veracruz, a city that had always been good to him. But he never got there. In the state of Puebla, rebels destroyed the tracks and chased the president and his entourage into the hills. On the evening of May 20, 1920, Carranza's party arrived in the hamlet of Tlaxcalantongo. In the wee hours of the next day, assassins most likely in Obregón's pay entered the president's dwelling and shot him dead. With Carranza's death, leadership passed to the nation's last caudillo, Obregón, and the revolution entered a new phase.

Suffrage does not exist in Mexico. What does exist is the violent conflict
of groups contending for power, supported occasionally by public opinion.
That is the true Mexican constitution; the rest is a mere farce.

— MARTÍN LUIS GUZMÁN, *LA SOMBRA DEL CAUDILLO*

FORGING AND CONTESTING A NEW NATION, 1920–1932 | 5

General Abelardo L. Rodríguez had always wished to be a man of con-
sequence. A native of Sonora of lower-middle-class origins, he had
spent his youth on both sides of the border in search of his ticket to
a better life, dabbling in boxing, business, and singing. Born in 1891,
he was only nineteen when the outbreak of the revolution provided him
with new opportunities. He thus belonged to a new generation, a group
dubbed the *cachorros de la revolución*, or cubs of the revolution. His first
political post came in 1912 as police chief of the border town of Nogales,
and he joined the fighting in March 1913, less than two weeks after Huerta's
coup. When the Sonora state government disavowed the Huerta coup,
Rodríguez joined the state's military forces as a colonel. He did not have
any significant military victories to his name but made the crucial decision
early on to affiliate with Obregón, on whose coattails he rose to the rank of
general. Nonetheless, in May 1920, when Rodríguez received his general's
stripes, the payoff for his service in Obregón's army appeared minimal.

As it turned out, however, Rodríguez would be richly rewarded for
his loyalty. In July 1920 Interim President Adolfo de la Huerta put him
in charge of a military expedition to Baja California to dislodge a rebel
governor who refused to recognize his administration. Within weeks, the
rebel governor was in exile in Los Angeles, and Rodríguez was launched
on a ride to prosperity unparalleled among the other members of the

Sonoran coalition that had just assumed national power. Over the next decade, Rodríguez became the unchallenged cacique of Baja California, and he served as governor from 1923 to 1929, a period longer than that of any state governor since the beginning of the revolution. What had once been a sleepy backwater known only for Tijuana's and Mexicali's brothels and casinos, which catered to North Americans escaping Prohibition, became a bustling border state featuring booming fisheries, vineyards, and tourist resorts. Rodríguez himself got in on the act, joining U.S. investors by founding Agua Caliente, the finest casino in Tijuana. He also invested in wine making and agriculture. In 1930, Rodríguez received his first appointment to the federal cabinet and began to implement his strategy at the national level, acquiring spas, movie theaters, and soft drink factories. By the time he became president in September 1932, he was a millionaire.

Rodríguez's story is typical for its era, a time when a coalition of leaders from Sonora dominated the fledgling revolutionary state. The first three presidents of the 1920s—Adolfo de la Huerta, Obregón, and Plutarco Elías Calles—were Sonorans like Rodríguez. Bringing with them the fast and loose social conventions of the U.S.-Mexican borderlands, the Sonorans reshuffled the deck, giving campesino and worker organizations a chance to challenge entrepreneurs yet continuing to favor capitalist development. Behind it all lay a strategy of national reconstruction based on four pillars: (1) free market capitalism tempered by restrictions on foreign investment and social guarantees for the working poor; (2) support from agrarian and labor leaders in exchange for their political loyalty; (3) a cultural revolution that would promote secularism and inculcate all Mexicans with a set of core national values; and (4) repair and expansion of the country's tattered infrastructure. *Reconstruction* was also a code word for opportunities for individual enrichment. Rodríguez was only one of several revolutionaries to find wealth in the revolutionary era, joining such associates of the Sonorans as Juan Andreu Almazán, Manuel Pérez Treviño, Aarón Sáenz, and Maximino Avila Camacho.

The new elite's quest for wealth and power was only one important aspect of the Sonoran era. Another was the need to implement at least some of the social rights contained in the 1917 Constitution. Campesinos and workers found themselves included in the political debate to an unprecedented degree, as the new and initially weak revolutionary state needed their support. The middle classes not only found new opportunities for political and professional advancement; they also played a key role in one of the most important projects of the new state: the campaign to eradicate illiteracy and forge Mexican citizens out of the disparate regional and local identities that persisted across the nation. The new juncture itself fueled a sense of optimism and opportunity. One U.S. eyewitness, Anita Brenner, described "a lift, a stirring feeling... a sense of strength released: ... everything at the beginning."[1] But did the co-optation of *agraristas* and labor leaders engender substantial social and economic reforms that would benefit Mexico's poor majority? And would the government succeed in creating a new Mexican citizen who would foreswear regional and religious allegiances in order to serve the new national state?

THE MAKING OF THE SONORAN SYSTEM, 1920–1924

The Sonoran leaders shared a set of common values important for understanding the state project they engineered, as well as popular resistance to and participation in that project. As *norteños*, they favored individualism over collectivism, family farms over communal landholding, and a secular society over one in which the Catholic Church played a significant cultural and political role. They also broadly agreed on the need for a different type of modernization than that propagated by the Porfirians. In their view, modernization involved a set of economic, social, and educational reforms that put all Mexicans on an equal legal footing and eliminated the grossest of abuses that the wealthy had inflicted upon the poor. They also believed in the importance of organizing campesinos and workers, albeit in corporatist arrangements, in which such "popular" organizations would remain dependent on the state and its leader.

beliefs

Nonetheless, a sketch of the principal personalities involved in the Sonoran alliance — Obregón, Calles, and de la Huerta — reveals important differences in both policy and style. Obregón was the caudillo, the military leader who drew his strength from his charisma, the revolutionary army, and his ability to navigate among generals, politicians, entrepreneurs, and campesino and labor leaders. Calles was the administrator, drawing support from the up-and-coming urban middle class that demanded opportunities. And de la Huerta was the conciliator, who used his experience representing the Carranza regime as a consul in New York City to repair political divisions. Of the three, Obregón and Calles considered the ends of politics more important than the means and often used violence to achieve their objectives, while de la Huerta more closely approximated the Maderista tradition of political democracy. After Carranza's overthrow and murder in May 1920 — the last successful coup d'état in Mexican history — the three leaders formed what was known as the Sonoran Triangle, a group that henceforth set the rules of the political game.

As what one of his supporters called the "undefeated caudillo of the revolution,"[2] Obregón was the linchpin of the Sonoran Triangle and its undisputed leader. We have already traced his early career as one of the protagonists and the principal winner of the bloody factional conflicts of the 1910s. After a stint as Carranza's secretary of war, Obregón retired to his farm near Huatabampo. While he built up a thriving agribusiness, he kept an eye on the national capital, hoping to translate his military prowess into political success. He had the loyalty of many of Mexico's greatest military and political leaders, including agraristas such as Antonio Díaz Soto y Gama and labor organizers such as Luis N. Morones. Frustrated in his ambitions to win the presidency in the 1920 elections by Carranza's insistence on imposing a civilian, he had gotten a second chance after Carranza's defeat and death and intended to make the most of it.

Plutarco Elías Calles supplied the administrative brains of the Sonoran alliance. He was born in 1877 to a poor mother and a father of prominent origin whose life marked a slow descent into destitution. He lost his mother at an early age, and he grew up with his maternal uncle, as his father was an alcoholic who could not take care of his own children. Young Calles aspired to regain the social status lost by his father. He achieved a middle school education and then tried his luck as a teacher, hotel administrator, farmer, and mill operator. This circuitous career bred a strong-willed personality attuned to political opportunity but rigid in the face of challenges. By the time the revolution broke out, Calles had gained valuable political connections. In 1911 Governor Maytorena named him police chief of the border town of Agua Prieta. Calles formed part of the Constitutionalist leadership in Sonora after Huerta's coup. He proved himself a capable agent who helped smuggle cattle confiscated from his political enemies across the U.S. border; he also helped defeat Huerta and then the Conventionists, thanks to the infusion of food and supplies paid, in part, by the resulting revenues. In August 1915 Carranza rewarded him by naming him provisional governor. In that capacity, Calles oversaw one of the most progressive reform programs at the state level but also earned a reputation for ruthlessness. He was unforgiving toward his enemies, and one of his least popular measures included the prohibition of alcohol. In 1919 he joined the Carranza cabinet as secretary of industry, commerce, and labor and in April 1920 he became the first signatory of the Plan of Agua Prieta.

Adolfo de la Huerta was the diplomat of the group. Of the three leaders, he enjoyed the highest degree of education: a high school diploma from Mexico City. This achievement led him to seek a career as a professional, and he aspired to be a musician. Unlike the other two, de la Huerta never served in the military; his intellectual and civilian background attracted him early on to the Madero rebellion, in which he played an active part as a campaigner and organizer. He was elected to the Sonoran state legislature in 1911. Following the formation of the Constitutionalist alliance, de la Huerta became one of Carranza's aides and served in various diplomatic posts in the United States. In 1919 he was elected governor of Sonora. It was in this capacity that de la Huerta defied Carranza's authority in April 1920 and issued the call to overthrow him.

As the titular head of the Agua Prieta revolt, de la Huerta took the first turn in the presidency, albeit only in an interim capacity until the 1920 elections. He realized the dire situation of his government. Enemies besieged it from all sides, including vengeful Carranza supporters, the remains of Villa's army, the counterrevolutionary forces of Félix Díaz, and a large number of regional insurgencies seeking to forestall a strengthening of the central government. Agriculture and mining had not recovered from the ravages of war, and only petroleum production—protected by caciques in the pay of the oil companies—reached new heights. Finally, the Wilson administration did not recognize de la Huerta, contending that the regime emanating from the Plan of Agua Prieta had come to power through violent means.

Under these circumstances, de la Huerta's brief stint in power (May–November 1920) must be considered a considerable success. Unfettered by personal allegiances to military leaders outside the Sonoran group, de la Huerta negotiated with insurgents and got several of them to lay down their arms. The most important of these rebels was Pancho Villa, who offered to surrender to the federal government in exchange for personal guarantees. The interim president granted Villa and his personal guard the ranch of Canutillo in his home state of Durango, a ranch then in the possession of the federal government (figure 5.1). In exchange, Villa dis-

FIGURE 5.1   Pancho Villa on his ranch in Canutillo, Durango, 1921. Fideicomiso Archivos Plutarco Elías Calles y Fernando Torreblanca, Mexico City.

banded his army. In striking a deal with Villa, de la Huerta assumed a great personal risk, as both Obregón and Calles criticized the arrangement with their enemy. Obregón in particular lambasted de la Huerta for coming to an agreement with Villa. In his words, the majority of Villa's past actions had been "condemned by morality, justice, and civilization."[3] De la Huerta also allowed Félix Díaz to go into exile, and he overturned a court decision to execute General Pablo González, Obregón's erstwhile rival for the presidency, for plotting a coup against his government. There is no doubt that de la Huerta managed to achieve a significant degree of reconciliation with some of the most powerful enemies of the Sonoran alliance in the aftermath of its seizure of power.

Elected in July 1920 without significant opposition, Obregón took the next turn in the presidency, serving a full four-year term. From the outset, he faced a difficult situation. The new U.S. president, Republican Warren G. Harding, continued Wilson's policy of withholding recognition pending the resolution of claims made by his supporters in the oil industry and finance. He demanded the repeal of Article 27 of the new constitution, something Obregón could not accept. In the absence of U.S. and British recognition, the Obregón administration could not obtain loans from Mexico's principal creditor nations, and antigovernment rebels enjoyed free rein to organize in the United States. Not surprisingly, the reestablishment of diplomatic relations with the United States became a top priority.

Obregón also faced continued unrest in regions hostile to Sonoran rule, particularly the South and Southeast, where both indigenous campesinos and conservative landowners resented the authority of the revolutionary government. In some of these states—particularly Oaxaca and Chiapas, the two most heavily indigenous states in the nation—regional elites circled the wagons, resisting any attempt at implementation of economic and social reforms. In others, such as Veracruz, conservatives rallied around a powerful reactionary figure, in this case General Guadalupe Sánchez, who controlled a significant area of the state in defiance of the agrarista governor and staunch Obregón supporter Adalberto Tejeda.

The caudillo relied on Tejeda and other regional caciques to help him defeat both recalcitrant reactionaries and dissatisfied radicals. In the North, the Obregonista caciques were often pragmatists, such as his fellow Sonoran Abelardo L. Rodríguez. In the center of the country, the president enjoyed the firm allegiance of a powerful conservative agrarian cacique, Saturnino Cedillo. In the South, the Obregonista governors often professed radical and sometimes even socialist views. This group included the rabidly anticlerical governor of Tabasco, Tomás Garrido Canabal, and Felipe Carrillo Puerto, the governor of Yucatán. In these states, regional leaders and social movements experimented with economic, political, and social reforms that far exceeded Obregón's vision.

This far-flung network of alliances could not dampen the simmering discontent throughout the nation. Popular movements pressed for land and better working and living conditions. A prime example of this pressure from below was the 1922 rent strike in the city of Veracruz, touched off by prostitutes living in the poor neighborhood of La Huaca. In short order, the anarchist Herón Proal organized the Sindicato Revolucionario de Inquilinos (the Revolutionary Syndicate of Tenants). At its height, this movement counted on the support of over thirty thousand renters, all of whom refused to pay rent and demanded significant improvements in their rental contracts as well as in the condition of the tenements in which they lived. Tejeda, a strong supporter of the agrarians and the working poor in general, also favored the movement.

Obregón mitigated this popular discontent by striking deals with the leaders of the principal social movements spawned by the revolution. One significant ally was Luis Napoleón Morones, the secretary general of the Confederación Regional Obrera Mexicana (the Regional Mexican Workers' Federation, or CROM). The CROM had replaced the anarchosyndicalist Casa del Obrero Mundial, disbanded in 1916 on Carranza's orders. Obregón gave free rein to the CROM's political wing in Congress, the Partido Laborista Mexicano, or Mexican Labor Party, and he supported several PLM legislative initiatives. In exchange, the CROM supported the government. Another key Obregón supporter was the intellectual Antonio Díaz Soto y Gama, a former associate of Zapata, member of the Casa del Obrero Mundial, and one of the authors of the Plan of Ayala. At the Convention of Aguascalientes in 1914, Díaz Soto y Gama had made a name for himself by including Zapata on a list of history's greatest heroes that also featured the Buddha, Jesus Christ, and Karl Marx. He supported the Plan of Agua Prieta and returned to Mexico City as a federal congressman in 1920. Díaz Soto y Gama served as the leader of the Partido Nacional Agrarista (National Agrarista Party, or PNA) for the next eight years. The PNA adopted Zapata's program of land distribution but loyally supported Obregón and never once challenged the government over its failures to carry out wide-ranging land reform while Díaz Soto y Gama was alive. In 1922 Congress approved the Agrarian Reform Law, which targeted large "unproductive" estates for expropriation but protected profitable plantations and other agribusinesses producing for export. The law also prohibited the redistribution of land to individual peasants, instead creating the *ejido*, or agricultural cooperative, in which the government retained ownership of the land and parceled it out to residents. In the end, the Obregón administration expropriated and redistributed three million acres among more than 620 villages, particularly in areas such as the Zapatista heartland with strong agrarista influence. This redistribution amounted to seven times the total that had been achieved under Carranza, but still constituted a puny amount of Mexico's total acreage.

To further enhance government control, Obregón attempted to break the power of regional chieftains, particularly that of the powerful divisional generals. Carranza had named many of these generals to the post of *jefe de operaciones militares*, or zone commander of military operations. Drawing upon their formal control of army units, the jefes de operaciones had been able to consolidate regional power bases. Obregón diminished this power by playing a game of musical chairs: he moved them far away from their home bases and made sure they did not stay in any one zone long enough to build lasting clientelist allegiances. Even Rodríguez received his marching orders; having just begun to fashion a network of business alliances, he served four- to five-month stints in Nayarit, Sinaloa, Mexico City, and Oaxaca. Only after he had proved his value to Obregón during three additional short assignments throughout the republic did the caudillo permit Rodríguez's return to Baja California.

Obregón's fear of rebellions probably prompted one of the most cowardly acts in which he was ever involved as a political leader. On July 20, 1923, assassins gunned down Pancho Villa in the city of Parral, Chihuahua, on his way back to his hacienda. Although the killers claimed personal motives for their crime, it did not take long for ordinary citizens to blame Obregón and Secretary of Gobernación Calles. Both leaders had long been worried that the terms of de la Huerta's deal with Villa included an eventual alliance against them. This fear was especially timely in 1923, since Calles was now the odds-on favorite to succeed Obregón the next year, given his status as the caudillo's principal protégé. Thus one sarcastic joke had an imaginary Mexican on the street ask another, "Who killed General Villa?" To which the answer was "Cálles-e" (Shut up).[4] Recent research has convincingly argued that Calles and Obregón plotted the assassination; as president, Obregón likely bore the ultimate responsibility.

Shortly afterward, Obregón finally obtained the U.S. diplomatic recognition he had long coveted. In August 1923 U.S. and Mexican representatives met at Bucareli Street in Mexico City to negotiate a variety of pending matters. Obregón's men knew that U.S. bankers desired the reestablishment of diplomatic relations in order to collect their debts in Mexico and that the Teapot Dome scandal in the United States had discredited Senator Albert B. Fall and the oil lobby, which demanded a total repeal of Article 27 as a condition of diplomatic recognition. In the end, Obregón promised not to apply the article retroactively and vowed to repay his country's foreign debt. In exchange, the U.S. government recognized his regime.

Not surprisingly Obregón's growing control over the domestic political scene as well as his success in managing Mexico's international relations bred resentment among generals who did not belong to his inner circle.

Obregón had once quipped that no general could "withstand a cannon shot of fifty thousand pesos,"[5] but he found out that some military leaders were mobilized more by ambition than by greed. Those generals bided their time, waiting for the right moment to take advantage of political conflicts at the national level to support an organized challenge to the caudillo. That moment came in late 1923, when the Sonoran Triangle disintegrated.

Over the previous few years, relations between Obregón and de la Huerta—never as amicable as those of Calles with either one—had become increasingly strained. In 1922 de la Huerta, who served as Mexico's finance minister, had unsuccessfully attempted to obtain new loans from a group of U.S. bankers. Obregón believed that de la Huerta had offered wide-ranging concessions in exchange for the loans. He claimed that these concessions exceeded those authorized by him and charged that the treasury secretary had become too chummy with the bankers. This attack stung de la Huerta, especially as he watched Obregón make even greater concessions in the Bucareli agreements. Moreover he correctly suspected that Obregón and Calles were behind the assassination of Pancho Villa. Incensed when his Sonoran colleagues intervened in an electoral dispute over the gubernatorial elections in the state of San Luis Potosí on behalf of a politician who opposed one of his allies, de la Huerta finally resigned his cabinet post in September 1923. As the rift among the Sonorans became public, Obregón added insult to injury by appointing de la Huerta's archenemy, Alberto Pani, as his successor. The new finance minister alleged that his predecessor had embezzled funds from the national treasury. These fabricated charges forced de la Huerta to take a stand against the government in order to salvage his personal honor. On December 7, 1923, he proclaimed the Plan of Veracruz, calling Mexicans to arms against the imposition of Calles as Obregón's successor. Almost two-thirds of all military officers joined the revolt, including some of the country's most influential divisional generals, most notably Enrique Estrada of Jalisco and Guadalupe Sánchez of Veracruz.

As with many of the previous uprisings during the revolution, the trouble with this rebellion was that the participants agreed only on what they opposed. Thus the de la Huerta coalition included a wide array of participants: urban intellectuals, landowners opposed to Article 27, pro-clerical rebels eager to wipe out the secular provisions of the constitution, and a smattering of agraristas and representatives of urban labor.

Perhaps most strikingly, the Sonoran coalition witnessed a split along the lines of when its members had joined the revolution. De la Huerta had been a Maderista from the start. Among his supporters were former governors Manuel Diéguez and Salvador Alvarado, both also members of Madero's coalition from the outset. The cohort that had taken Obregón's belated path to the revolution, however, remained loyal to the caudillo, and included Calles, of course, as well as Rodríguez and Generals Arnulfo Gómez and Francisco R. Serrano. In the end, Obregón prevailed, just as he had at every twist and turn of the revolution. Well provisioned with fresh supplies from the United States, which had poured in after the awarding of diplomatic recognition, the government vanquished the disorganized de la Huerta rebellion after several months. Obregón could also once again count on urban labor, as several CROM battalions participated on the side of the government. On February 9, 1924, Obregón's federal troops won the last major battle of the Mexican Revolution at Ocotlán, Jalisco. When the smoke cleared, the revolution had devoured many more of its own. Among the dead were not only Alvarado and Diéguez but also one of Calles's more radical supporters, Governor Carrillo Puerto of Yucatán.

The triumph over the Delahuertista rebels gave Obregón an opportunity to purge the army of disloyal elements. It accelerated the process of professionalization of the military that he had begun. This process would greatly centralize political authority over the next two decades. Never again would disgruntled military officers succeed in overthrowing the national government. In many ways, the caudillo emerged strengthened from the internecine conflict, not least because Calles had come to depend on him more than ever for his own political survival.

REFORM AND REPRESSION UNDER CALLES, 1924–1928

Calles decided to counter this dependence by reviving a reform program that had been abandoned in the throes of the de la Huerta rebellion. He was aware that both labor leaders and agraristas were disappointed in the slow pace of reform under Obregón. He also knew that the existence of formal diplomatic ties with the United States gave him some leeway to use populist rhetoric to appeal to the poor majority. And he recognized the symbolism of the revolution and its martyred heroes. It was thus fitting that Calles formally inaugurated his presidential campaign at Zapata's gravesite in Cuautla, Morelos, on April 10, 1924, the fifth anniversary of the death of the agrarian rebel. In a gesture to the agraristas, he represented himself as the heir to Zapata's program. In other campaign speeches, he appealed to urban labor and the middle classes, lambasting the forces of reaction that, in his view, continued to impede the revolution. In July Calles won the national elections by a large margin over the Sinaloan general Angel Flores and soon thereafter embarked on a trip to the United States, France, and Germany. In Europe labor representatives hailed him as an exponent of the new Mexican social democracy. All of these efforts were designed to counter the political weight of the Obregonista cohort, a group that had emerged strengthened in Congress following the same elections that had brought Calles to office. Obregón had returned to his farm in southern Sonora, but no one believed that he had left the political spotlight forever. Indeed rumors circulated that Calles had promised the caudillo the opportunity to return to power after his own term ended, and some even believed that Calles and Obregón planned to alternate in the presidency for as long as they both lived.

Thus, still operating in the shadow of Obregón, Calles launched his presidency with an assertive agenda that registered his own imprint on politics, and his two first years in office constituted the high-water mark of the Sonoran Dynasty where its commitment to social reform was concerned. Calles's reforms demonstrated a greater adherence to the radical provisions of the 1917 Constitution than Obregón had displayed. Under Calles, indigenous villages received eight million acres of land — approximately five million acres more than under Obregón — and the Calles administration also established credit banks for campesinos (figure 5.2).

Even more important, the Calles era featured three enabling laws that brought national legislative congruence with several important provisions of the constitution. The Petroleum Law applied Article 27 to the oil companies, forcing them to apply for confirmatory concessions if they wanted to keep their holdings. The Alien Land Law limited foreign ownership of agricultural estates, while the Calles Law drastically restricted the activities of the Catholic Church. In all of these efforts, Calles drew on the support of leaders who had grown disaffected with the slow pace of reform under Obregón, most important being that of the CROM leader Morones, then secretary of commerce, industry, and labor. Unfortunately Morones became the caricature of the corrupt leader of an organization that purported to represent the interests of the working masses: fat, bejeweled

FIGURE 5.2 Agrarista peasants in Yaxkukul, Yucatán, receive their ejidal grant, 1930. Archivo Pedro A. Guerra, Mérida, Yucatán.

in diamonds, and clad in expensive clothes, he enjoyed lavish, decadent parties.

While Calles's reforms earned the president much-needed support among the official representatives of organized labor and the agrarian sector, the three major enabling laws also catalyzed an opposing coalition that threatened the progress that Calles sought to achieve. The Petroleum and Alien Land Laws provoked a U.S. Republican administration that was renowned for its defense of large corporations. In June 1925 U.S. Secretary of State Frank B. Kellogg proclaimed that Mexico was "on trial before the world."[6] At the end of 1926 Calles took the unprecedented step of lending military support to a rebellion in Nicaragua led by a group sympathetic to the Mexican Revolution. As the U.S. government considered Central America its exclusive sphere of interest, this effort to strengthen the Mexican position led to a further deterioration of U.S.-Mexican relations.

At the height of this crisis, Calles found himself improbably linked with the Soviet Union, with which his government enjoyed formal diplomatic relations. Several months before he had left office, Obregón had entered into negotiations with Soviet Russia. Russia had recently undergone a far more radical social revolution of its own, one that involved the elimination of the ruling elite as well as the wholesale nationalization of means of production. Soviet-style Bolshevism appealed to many intellectuals and workers dissatisfied with the slow pace of reform and opposed to U.S. influence in Mexico. Even though Obregón and Calles had no desire to turn their country into a Soviet republic, they appreciated the need to safeguard the national sovereignty—an endeavor that might benefit from ties with the world's largest nation. By the time Calles took office, a Soviet ambassador had served in Mexico City for three weeks. Alarmed by this token Soviet diplomatic presence and blind to the true nature of the Mexican government, U.S. Ambassador James R. Sheffield believed in the existence of a "Communist plan to acquire control in Mexico" and referred to both Calles and Morones as "Bolshevists."

Of course, no plan involving Bolshevism would ever come close to fruition. Indeed some of the most significant reforms of the Calles administration aimed to perfect capitalist development in Mexico. For example, the government successfully renegotiated its foreign debt. Calles and his associates also created the Banco de México as the nation's official bank of issue. Another set of reforms aimed to gain greater control over the military. Under the leadership of General Joaquín Amaro, the Defense Ministry reduced the size of the revolutionary army and introduced measures to further professionalize the officer corps, regularizing promotions in rank, which thus far had been based on fiat rather than demonstrable accomplishments.

The Catholic opposition was an even more formidable foe than the U.S. government. Catholic resistance to revolutionary anticlericalism began in the early to mid-1910s and reached its crescendo during the Calles presidency. As early as 1917, Mexico City Archbishop José Mora y del Río had declared that adherence to the anticlerical provisions of the new constitution amounted to "treason against [the Catholic] faith."[8] Although President Obregón pragmatically eschewed open conflict with the Catholic Church, knowing full well the deep roots of popular Catholicism, in 1923 he found himself embroiled in a conflict over the planned construction of a statue of Jesus Christ on Cubilete Mountain in Guanajuato, the geographical center of the republic. By far the most anticlerical of the Sonorans, Calles and his ally Morones took the conflict to a new level. In 1925 Morones assisted in the attempted creation of a schismatic Mexican church, which, like the Church of England centuries earlier, would have sworn fealty to the Mexican state rather than to the Pope. The following year, the Calles Law struck the nation's Catholics like an overt threat to their way of life. The law mandated the registration of priests; it allowed states to limit the number of clerics to one per ten thousand inhabitants; and it reiterated the constitutional ban on religious education and outdoor worship. All of these provisions, particularly the ban on outdoor worship, struck at the heart of religious practice. Throughout the republic, Mexicans expressed more than their faith in popular religious festivals on occasions such as Holy Week and the day of the local patron saint. These festivals not only celebrated local identity and, often, indigenous or African roots; they also served as a form of subaltern political expression. For example, a local Judas burning during Holy Week might feature the effigy of a hated landowner or public official as the Judas.

For his part, Calles argued that his law merely sought to apply the constitution and defend his government against threats from the Church. He pointed out that Archbishop Mora y del Río had recently declared that he still stood behind his declaration of 1917 to the effect that adherence to the constitution amounted to a transgression against the Catholic faith. Privately, Calles also worried about the existing ties between Catholic exiles in the United States, the U.S.-based Knights of Columbus, and former president de la Huerta, who lived in exile in Los Angeles. De la Huerta continued to be known among his supporters as the *jefe supremo*, or supreme chief, of the revolutionary movement of 1923–24, and Calles believed that his former ally harbored a U.S.-based plot to overthrow his government with the assistance of Catholics. Calles saw the Church as very much the same institution that had conspired to put Maximilian on the throne by force of French arms more than sixty years earlier, and he viewed himself as the heir of Benito Juárez, who had sought an absolute separation of church and state, the expropriation of church land, and a strengthening of lay education. Said the president:

> My enemies say that I am an enemy of the religions and cults, and that I do not respect religious beliefs. I . . . understand and approve all religious beliefs because I consider them beneficial for the moral program they encompass. I am an enemy of the caste of priests that sees in its position a privilege rather than an evangelical mission. I am the enemy of the political priest, the scheming priest, the priest as exploiter, the priest who intends to keep our people in ignorance, the priest who allies

with the hacendado to exploit the campesino, and the priest allied with the industrialist to exploit the worker.[9]

Fanned further by the Vatican and the Knights of Columbus, the religious conflict constituted a serious threat to the government. It alienated from the state a crucial group: the so-called social Catholics, who agreed with the government on the need for social reform but disagreed with the anticlerical provisions of the constitution. These social Catholics joined with the Church hierarchy and devout campesinos in responding to the state's challenge on two separate fronts. First, Archbishop Mora y del Río declared a religious strike, to go into effect on July 31, 1926. For the first time since the conquest, no masses or sacraments were performed in the nation's churches. Calles gravely underestimated the significance of this step when he told a French diplomat, "Each week without religious ceremonies will cost the Catholic religion 2 percent of its faithful."[10] He was badly mistaken: the church strike energized the faithful, who saw religious ceremonies as a space for contesting power. Indeed violence followed within six weeks of the onset of the strike. Throughout Jalisco, Guanajuato, Michoacán, and other neighboring states, peasants rallied in armed rebellion to the slogan of "Viva Cristo Rey!" (Long live Christ the King!). The phrase was designed to invoke popular religious devotion, a sense of Catholic community, and perhaps even the nationalist-Catholic tradition of the 1810 Hidalgo Revolt at the beginning of the Wars of Independence.[11]

Thus began La Cristiada, or the Cristero Rebellion, a three-year guerrilla war in central and western Mexico that claimed over seventy thousand lives. Under the leadership of a former Porfirian general, the Cristeros inflicted serious losses on the government through an unremitting campaign of guerrilla warfare. Although Calles dismissed the Cristeros as fanatical papists allied with large landowners, the rebellion drew on popular roots and merged religious concerns with political and social grievances. The Cristeros not only resented the state's persecution of the Catholic Church, but they also chafed at federal interference in local affairs. For example, Obregón's and Calles's heavy-handed tactics to centralize power had included intervention in state and local elections, and the federal mandate for lay public education in the countryside (of which more presently) antagonized the faithful. Staged largely in Mexico's breadbasket, the Cristero Rebellion led to a 40 percent decline in the grain harvest over three years. In June 1929 U.S. Ambassador Dwight Morrow helped broker an agreement between the government and Archbishop Mora y del Río that suspended several provisions of the Calles Law and allowed the Church to call off the religious strike. All the same, tensions between church and state would persist for another decade.

The destruction wrought by the Cristero Rebellion compounded an incipient economic crisis and helped inaugurate an eight-year period of recession and stagnation. The most significant reason for this crisis was a decline in the export sector, particularly in the value of mineral production. Between mid-1926 and mid-1927 the world market price of silver, copper, and other precious metals fell by 20 percent. To make matters worse, oil production fell as the foreign-owned petroleum industry disinvested for fear that their holdings might be expropriated. Companies such as Standard Oil, Royal Dutch Shell, and British Petroleum instead focused on Venezuela and other politically compliant oil-producing nations. As a result, oil production dropped almost 65 percent between 1924 and 1928. These developments propelled Mexico into crisis more than two years before Black Friday ushered in the Great Depression of 1929 — the worst economic cataclysm of the modern era. Between 1926 and 1932 per capita GDP dropped almost 31 percent. Not surprisingly federal tax revenues also declined by 10 percent in 1926–27 alone. This economic crisis transformed the dynamics of the revolution, robbing the state of resources needed to effectively prosecute the Cristero Rebellion as well as to make good on its promises of reform. Revolutionary programs such as education and public health campaigns cost money, and without funds from the federal treasury they were largely unsustainable. In response to this crisis, Calles decreed austerity measures and drastically cut back on federal spending.

The crisis also called Obregón back onto the scene. After Calles's election, the caudillo had returned to his farm and appeared to have retired from public life. Much like the ancient Roman dictator Cincinnatus, who had derived much of his political appeal from his insistence that he was just a humble farmer ready to serve his country when needed, Obregón proclaimed his happiness with his return to agriculture. However, no one in Mexico was really surprised when he announced his decision to enter the fray of the upcoming presidential elections. To be sure, presidents could serve only one term under the constitution. Yet this obstacle melted away when the large majority in Congress loyal to him passed an amendment that allowed nonconsecutive reelection. Of greater concern was the fact that two of Calles's and Obregón's Sonoran associates, Generals Arnulfo Gómez and Francisco R. Serrano, announced presidential candidacies of their own. As in the case of Pancho Villa, Calles and Obregón fashioned a violent response to this challenge, which, as they knew, enjoyed the support of the exiled Adolfo de la Huerta. On October 3, 1927, government forces apprehended and executed Serrano and dozens of his followers; a month later they killed Gómez, who had been hiding out in a cave in a remote corner of the state of Veracruz. As justification, the government claimed that Serrano and Gómez were conspiring against the Calles government. The killings ended any effective challenge to Obregón's return to power, and the caudillo won reelection in July 1928.

But Mexico's bloody revolutionary history had yet another cruel twist of fate in store. On July 17, 1928, two weeks after Obregón's triumph in the national election, the president-elect attended a luncheon in a restaurant in the village of San Angel, just outside of Mexico City. Passing himself off as an artist drawing sketches of the guests, a young man, José de León Toral, approached the caudillo seated at the head of the table and shot him dead from close range. Apprehended and interrogated, Toral confessed that he was a devout Catholic and a sympathizer of the Cristeros and that he had killed Obregón out of religious conviction. This made for a somewhat strange tale, as it had been Calles, not Obregón, who had pushed the anticlerical laws through Congress. Not surprisingly many Obregón supporters held Morones and Calles responsible for the assassination: Morones because he had harbored presidential aspirations of his own, and Calles because he was reputedly jealous of the caudillo's continuing political influence. Eighty years later historians have still not conclusively solved this mystery. However, no one ever came forward to challenge the confessions of Toral and his friends, and archival evidence does not indicate that high political players were involved in the assassination.

Toral's murder of Obregón removed the last protagonist of the fiesta of bullets of the 1910s. The assassination of the revolution's undefeated caudillo heralded the end of an era when military chieftains had determined the fate of the national government and most state administrations as well. President Calles summed things up in his final state of the nation address on September 1, 1928, observing that Mexico had moved, once and for all, from a "country ruled by one man" to a "nation of institutions and laws."[12] He enjoined his fellow citizens to embrace an institutional future in which parties and legislatures rather than caudillos and caciques would make and enforce the laws of the nation. His words foreshadowed a certain irony, as Calles himself would emerge as the *jefe máximo*, or supreme chief, of the Mexican Revolution, albeit without ever holding the presidency again.

Thus Obregón's death catalyzed the formation of an official party that ruled in the name of "the Revolution," the Partido Nacional Revolucionario (the National Revolutionary Party, or PNR). Formed in 1929, the PNR was originally designed as what one scholar has called a "confederation of caciques"—in essence, a political club that kept the ambitions of various local and regional military leaders at bay.[13] It included regional parties, many of which had served as platforms for individual caciques' political schemes, and it adopted a vague and wide-ranging program acceptable to these parties as well as to agrarian and labor organizations. No one knew at the time that Calles and his allies had created a future political behemoth. In the next nine years, the new official party would incorporate regional parties and organizations as well as all major social movements. In three different iterations, it would hold the presidency until the year 2000, a span of seventy-one years.

The formation of the PNR marked the beginning of the so-called Maximato (1928–34), the era in which Jefe Máximo Calles wielded power from behind the scenes. The idea of Calles as a strongman who held politics in his firm grip has often been exaggerated, to the point that he has been labeled a dictator who manipulated a string of puppet presidents. The reality is more complicated, as Calles's influence waxed and waned over time. Even before the inauguration of the PNR, Calles had handpicked former Tamaulipas governor Emilio Portes Gil to serve as interim president in order to fill the first two years of what would have been Obregón's second term. Portes Gil was an agrarista committed to land reform and, as a former governor, he enjoyed a strong regional base. But in March 1929, just as the PNR met to decide on its candidate for the presidential elections later that year, disgruntled Obregonistas under the leadership of General Gonzalo Escobar revolted against the Portes Gil government. Centered in Sonora, the Escobar revolt included a group of generals opposed to both Calles and the creation of the ruling party. To crush the rebellion, Portes Gil called Calles back into the cabinet as secretary of war. Soon thereafter, however, Calles spent six months in Paris recuperating from what had been a stressful nine years in the political spotlight.

While Portes Gil thus enjoyed considerable autonomy during the latter half of his presidency, his successor, Pascual Ortiz Rubio, found Calles's strong hand in his administration from the very beginning. Ortiz Rubio had not been Calles's initial choice to succeed Portes Gil; he was a last-minute replacement for Aarón Sáenz, a wealthy Protestant entrepreneur closely allied to both Obregón and Calles whom the delegates at the first PNR convention considered too conservative. As the nominee of the PNR, Ortiz Rubio was elected under allegations of fraud leveled by his opponent, the noted intellectual José Vasconcelos, who had served as Obregón's secretary of public education. On the day of his inauguration in 1930, Ortiz Rubio only narrowly eluded an assassination attempt, and he never gained any political footing thereafter. Over the next two years, the president squabbled with both the jefe máximo and Congress. So tenuous was the national government that Calles took part in political deliberations on an everyday basis. On two occasions the jefe máximo even met with the cabinet in the absence of the president. Finally, on September 4, 1932, he engineered Ortiz Rubio's resignation. Although the reasons for Calles's intervention have never been fully elucidated, Ortiz Rubio's political weakness and his membership in a political group from the state of Michoacán that had begun to challenge the Sonorans likely played a role. In retrospect, Ortiz Rubio would probably have failed with or without Calles's influence, given the intense political-economic stresses generated by the Great Depression.

Amid this crisis of leadership, a crisis accompanied by the worst days of the Great Depression, the revolution shifted away from its agrarian emphasis toward a more urban orientation. Seeking to address severe food shortages in the cities, Calles and his associates began to retrench publicly from their commitment to land reform and to focus on food production rather than social justice in the countryside. In 1930 the jefe máximo proclaimed that the era of land distributions had ended. At the same time, reform efforts continued in the labor sector even though the CROM remained under the now ineffective leadership of the discredited Morones, who could never shake the suspicion that he was responsible for Obregón's assassination. In 1931 Congress passed the Ley Federal del Trabajo, or Federal Work Law, a body of legislation that implemented the most significant protections for workers and their unions contained in the 1917 Constitution. Although much of this law remained unenforced for the time being, the national legislature had created a blueprint for a symbiotic relationship between the state and organized labor.

FORJANDO PATRIA

Building the new state involved a campaign to win the hearts and minds of ordinary Mexicans. Writing in 1916, the Mexican anthropologist Manuel Gamio labeled this effort *forjando patria,* or the forging of the fatherland.[14] This campaign involved a cultural nationalist movement that paid homage to both indigenous and mestizo traditions as the ingredients of a national culture in which all Mexicans participated. It also implied the expansion of education, secular and social reformist in nature, to transform a population that the Sonorans and their allies viewed as repressed, divided, and superstitious. As Calles proclaimed in Guadalajara, "The Revolution is not over. . . . It is necessary to enter into a new period, . . . the period of the psychological revolution. We have to enter and take possession of the conscience of children and youths, because they belong and should belong to the Revolution. . . . [The revolution must] uproot prejudices and form the new national soul."[15]

Although intended as a cultural revolution from above, this effort to turn campesinos into Mexicans proved to be far more complex and controversial than anticipated, and it had a number of unintended consequences. Reflecting on this cultural nationalism in the context of an era of extremes in which several other nations experimented with far more destructive forms of nationalism, one historian has called the Mexican version "a nationalism without a trace of xenophobia, . . . not anti-something, but above all, for Mexico."[16] Yet many Mexicans — whether they fought to maintain their identity or defend their faith from the state's anticlericalism — experienced cultural nationalism as an intrusion. Still others sought to shape or negotiate the nationalist discourse.

In an era prior to the advent of television, instilling a national culture across the far-flung regions was no small task. Few Mexicans owned a radio, a medium first used by the government during Calles's campaign for the presidency in 1924. More than half of all adults remained illiterate, which complicated efforts to convey messages by means of the printed word. Therefore the Sonorans' desire to turn campesinos into Mexicans by infusing them with a patriotic spirit required an education program designed to reduce illiteracy. That task first fell to José Vasconcelos, the head of Obregón's newly created Secretaría de Educación Pública (the Secretariat of Public Instruction, or SEP). The SEP first sent cultural missions into the countryside, and then, equipped with new textbooks that propagated the government's interpretation of the Mexican nation, founded a host of normal schools to train teachers. Their focus was on primary education, that is, to impart basic training in reading, writing, and math to adults and children. Secondary schooling, let alone university studies, would remain the privilege of the upper and middle classes, but the education program provided a significant boost to primary school enrollment across the nation.

Obregón supported the education program wholeheartedly but barely tolerated Vasconcelos, whom he considered a city slicker who could not relate to ordinary Mexicans. In particular he ridiculed the education secretary for his belief that the Mexicans needed to learn the Greek and Roman classics in order to understand the Mediterranean part of their heritage. A popular story tells of a time when Obregón and his party, which included Vasconcelos, traveled through the countryside. Having lost their way, the party approached a small hut inhabited by a poor indigenous couple. As the story goes, Obregón addressed the man of the house:

> "Compadre! . . . Can you tell us where we are?"
> The man shook his head.
> "But what place is this? What town are we near?"
> Again the man did not know.
> "Were you born here?" Obregón asked.
> "Yes."
> "And your wife also?"
> "Yes."
> "So you were born here, your wife was born here. You've both lived out your lives on this spot, and yet you don't know where you are?"
> "No," the Indian said indifferently.
> "José," Obregón said to Vasconcelos, "make a note of this man so you can send him a complete edition of the classics you've just edited."[17]

The story not only shows Obregón's contempt for Vasconcelos but also vividly illustrates the task before the SEP as it sought to teach locally rooted campesinos not only to read and write but also to embrace their place in the new nation.

The national education crusade met with mixed success. By 1940 the SEP controlled more than 12,500 rural primary schools enrolling over 720,000 students, and 70 percent of children between the ages of six and ten attended primary school. Yet the new teachers could not immediately reverse centuries of educational neglect, and illiteracy remained at levels over 50 percent. In addition, the government soon found out that what they had intended as acculturation from above was a two-way street, with those below proving active participants in (rather than passive recipients of) the cultural revolution. While teachers "nationalized" the countryside, they found themselves changed by their surroundings. Not only did they come to understand that a national culture could not be imposed on a re-calcitrant populace with strong local allegiances and traditions, but life in rural Mexico had also irrevocably altered their own political horizons. Many of them had grown up in comfortable middle-class families and had never confronted rural poverty firsthand. As revolutionary idealists, many of the teachers had sympathized with the agraristas' goals without understanding their everyday struggles. Their experience in the country-side also showed them the strength of religious convictions and the limi-tations of official slogans that tied social injustice to the oppressiveness of religious doctrines. As the teachers learned, many campesinos understood themselves as both agraristas and Roman Catholics, servants of both the national eagle and the Virgin of Guadalupe.

Artistic production, especially public art, constituted another impor-tant aspect of the state-sponsored cultural revolution. Works of art and monuments could reach those people who could not yet read. Particu-larly important were the three principal mural artists of the era: Diego Rivera, José Clemente Orozco, and David Alfaro Siqueiros. Between 1922 and 1928 Rivera emerged as the government's favorite muralist, thanks to his evocative and accessible style that included the liberal use of Aztec symbols and colors. During those years, he painted hundreds of murals on government buildings, especially the National Palace and the head-quarters of the SEP. Rivera's most accomplished and famous work was a giant triptych painted on the walls of the National Palace (figure 5.3). This mural depicted Mexico's past, present, and future from the Marxist per-spective of class struggle and predicted the eventual triumph of the work-

FIGURE 5.3 Diego Rivera's mural in the National Palace, Mexico City. Courtesy of
Ashleigh Blue.

ing masses in both the city and countryside. In this triumph, the country's
indigenous people redeemed the glory of the pre-conquest past, a glory
displayed in an idealized portrayal of Aztec civilization. Negative representations of foreigners, especially Spanish conquistadors and clergy as
well as North American bankers and politicians, dominated the central
part of the triptych, along with an image of Karl Marx pointing the way
into a better future. Rivera's murals not only educated Mexicans about
their history, but their radical message (one quite at variance with that of
the proto-corporatist Sonorans) also suggested that the new revolutionary
Mexico encouraged political pluralism and horizontal linkages between
workers and peasants. Although the government did not share the mural-
ists' ideology, it appreciated that it stood to benefit from their rousing
popular displays.

Monuments constituted another medium through which the government sought to disseminate its message. In particular, Obregón's death led
the rulers to propagate an alternative concept to Rivera's idea of the revolution as class and ethnic struggle: the myth of a "revolutionary family."
Centered on revolutionary leaders who had died violent deaths, this myth

united diverse social movements and their protagonists. In particular, the government propagated the martyrdom of five major leaders of the revolution—Francisco I. Madero (1913), Emiliano Zapata (1919), Venustiano Carranza (1920), Pancho Villa (1923), and Alvaro Obregón (1928)—all of whom had spent a good deal of time fighting one another. Zapata had gone to war against Madero, and the factions of Carranza and Obregón had fought those of Zapata and Villa. In uniting the cults of these men in a notional family, the government presented a monolithic and linear interpretation of "the Revolution" that erased the differences and even hostilities among them. The myth unified what history had divided: it presented the history of the revolution as progress brought on by personal sacrifice; it allowed the official revolutionary party to claim the legacy of Mexico's great upheaval as its own; and it made the jefe máximo the heir of Zapata, Villa, and Obregón. These slain heroes continued to have many admirers in Mexico; consider, for example, the proliferation of *corridos* (popular ballads) that paid homage to these three heroes. Their untimely, celebrated deaths stood in stark counterpoint to the daily reality of a revolution that had thus far failed to fulfill the expectations that so many Mexicans had placed in it. Not surprisingly the state would increasingly co-opt and disseminate these corridos in an effort to appropriate the popular political memory of the martyred revolutionaries.

Nowhere did this official idea of "the Revolution" find a better expression than in the Monumento a la Revolución in Mexico City. From 1933 to 1938 the government built this monument on the site of the Porfirian legislative palace. When the revolution came to Mexico City, only the iron structure had been completed, leaving unfinished that bombastic testament to modernization. Calles's architects ordered the rusting structure torn down but saved the cupola to make an open building that symbolized the triumph of "the Revolution." Later on, the monument came to house the remains of Carranza, Madero, and Villa, three of the slain icons (the fourth, Obregón, received a monument of his own at the site of his assassination). This monumental site of social memory propagated the myth of the revolutionary family by praising the accomplishments of all of the revolutionary leaders and eliding the divisions among them. Monuments such as this one coincided with the entrenchment of a great party that claimed for itself the exclusive mantle of *la Revolución*.

Finally, intellectuals played an important role in defining the nation. In the 1920s and 1930s Mexico City became a mecca for waves of progressive North American (and European) intellectuals and artists who were drawn by the transformative potential of the revolution defining itself next door. Nonconformist academics and writers like Anita Brenner, Frances Toor, Katherine Ann Porter, Frank Tannenbaum, and Carlton Beals, to name but a few, engaged in ongoing discussions with Mexican intellectuals, artists, and cultural workers commissioned by the new revolutionary state to define a new national culture, identity, and aesthetic. Many of these Mexican artists and cultural workers, like Diego Rivera, were similarly cosmopolitan and sought out kindred transnational spirits in polyglot circles that encompassed Mexico City, New York, and Paris.

One seminal intellectual contribution to an emerging national popular imaginary came from the education and cultural minister José Vasconcelos, who conceived of the nation as *la raza cósmica*, or "cosmic race."[18] Vasconcelos's work provided the intellectual underpinnings of the education campaign. It portrayed Mexicans as the amalgam of indigenous, African, and Spanish blood and culture, positing that this mixture represented the best of its ancestral traditions, with special emphasis on the indigenous and Spanish roots. On the surface, the notion of a cosmic race validated indigenous culture in a new way. However, more fundamentally, this vision implied that the nation urgently needed to assimilate its indigenous minority. Indeed Vasconcelos was a cultural elitist who did not truly believe in the value of indigenous culture, focusing instead — as many other Latin American philosophers did — on the difference between Mediterranean, Roman Catholic traditions and northern European, Anglo-Saxon modernity. Thus Vasconcelos made an invidious comparison between "high" art, which borrowed from European models, and "low" or popular art, which predominantly came from indigenous traditions. As one scholar has put it, for Vasconcelos, "all popular practices . . . were corruptions of high culture, and hence a mere 'parody of culture.'"[19] The philosopher Samuel Ramos rejected Vasconcelos's elitism. His *Perfil del hombre y la cultura en México* placed the *pelado*, the bum or popular everyman, at the center of analysis. According to Ramos, the pelado, usually a poor mestizo, was "the most elemental and clearly defined expression of national character." The pelado's precarious position in society, Ramos believed, made him into a macho — that stereotypical image of Mexican masculinity also embodied by Villa,

Obregón, and others. Thus Ramos also saw machismo, which he viewed as a product of the pelado's insecurity, as an essential part of *mexicanidad*.[20]

The issue of machismo invites a consideration of the role of women in Mexico in the 1920s and 1930s. Women had played important roles in the factional struggle, not just as *soldaderas* but also as increasingly important leadership figures at the local level, and some states had seen significant political mobilization of women's groups. Nonetheless Mexican women did not find their efforts during wartime rewarded — as German and U.S. women did just after World War I — with the right to vote. Verna Millán, a North American medical professional who moved to Mexico City with her husband, a physician, condemned in scathing terms the failure of the revolution to change the predominant patriarchal culture:

> Man is the Mexican woman's worst enemy. The very politicians, I soon found out, who drip with tears when they write about motherhood, have fought tenaciously, with every weapon in their power, the efforts of organized women to secure the vote and thereby obtain really effective laws to protect maternity, which the country does not possess at present; the very revolutionaries who praise with tremulous emotion the glorious lives of Rosa Luxemburg, Krupskaia and other heroines of the revolutionary movement refuse to let their own wives attend the meetings they address. "My husband is afraid I'll become infected with his ideas," one woman said to me dryly when I asked her why she had never heard her husband speak in public. "Mexican husbands are feudal Marxists," another explained, "Marxists outside and feudalists within their homes."[21]

Of course, it is not really surprising that a revolution that had produced a succession of macho generals in the presidential palace would fall short of the expectations that many women placed in it.

Despite the endurance of patriarchy, women began to play an ever-larger role. The rebuilding nation needed their services in new ways. While Porfirian Mexico had featured an overwhelmingly male corps of teachers in public schools, many of the teachers sent to the new rural schools were women. Thus women played a disproportionate role in education and also as members of the revolutionary state's expanding corps of social workers and nurses, which collectively served to modernize patriarchy and the domestic sphere. Several hundred women received university degrees in the 1920s. The emergent transnational intelligentsia in Mexico City and important provincial centers such as Cuernavaca and Mérida was composed of bohemian artists and intellectuals, many of whom were women. The most famous of these was Frida Kahlo, the wife of Diego Rivera and one of the greatest painters of twentieth-century Mexico. Kahlo's paintings graphically represent female suffering but evoke more complex and overlapping identities for women. Yet another front was labor organizing in the textile and tortilla industries, sectors that featured a high percentage of women workers. Prostitutes played a leading role in the tenants' strike in Veracruz. The women's movement would not coalesce until 1935, with the founding of the Sole Front of Women's Rights, but the 1920s and early 1930s witnessed the beginnings of that movement.

Women could be found not only on the feminist and intellectual Left, which, despite its misgivings about revolutionary machismo, supported "the Revolution" in general terms, but also on the Catholic Right. Construing themselves as the "guardians of tradition and 'eternal' values,"[22] they played an important role in the Catholic opposition, and their efforts to preserve their right to religious worship were arguably just as meaningful as the endeavors of the women's suffrage movement. Some women even returned to the battlefield as soldaderas in the Cristero army. Although conservative Catholicism attempted to push women to the side, the 1940s novel *Pensativa* by Jesús Goytortúa Sánchez portrays a fictional *generala* as a Mexican Joan of Arc who rescues the nation from godless infidels. Thus, like their pro-revolutionary counterparts, conservative women pushed the boundaries of female participation in the public sphere.

The period 1920–32 witnessed the beginnings of reconstruction in Mexico after a decade of warfare and revolution. Under the leadership of the Sonoran Dynasty, the government claimed the mantle of revolution for itself and laid out a modernizing vision. This modernizing strategy included the forging of a capitalist society with guarantees for Mexican ownership and a modicum of social reforms for campesinos and workers, the building of a nascent corporatist state in which the government began to mediate the interests of entrepreneurs and workers, and a cultural revolution designed to foster national cultural values and an official version of "the Revolution" across a far-flung nation. Both the revolution of the 1910s and the period of reconstruction had raised plenty of hopes for social reform, but only some of these had begun to be fulfilled.

As the Great Depression once again shook the country's economic and social foundations, many Mexicans asked themselves whether the violent and tumultuous struggle had in fact been worth it. The poor majority continued to live day to day, and promises of land reform and well-paying jobs had not materialized for most.

What impressed me most [about Cárdenas] was the strict paternal commitment with which he rejected any attempts to kneel to him or kiss his hand,
which . . . the village elders wanted to do in recognition of his authority. He
would take them by the hand with cordial energy and raise them up so that
they looked him in the eye.

— VICTORIANO ANGUIANO, *LÁZARO CÁRDENAS,
   SU FEUDO Y LA POLÍTICA MEXICANA*

RESURRECTING AND INCORPORATING THE REVOLUTION, 1932–1940 | 6

On March 28, 1936, hired gunmen affiliated with a local cacique assassinated the Maya activist Felipa Poot in Kinchil, Yucatán. The politically motivated murder was especially shocking because the victim
was a woman. In a patriarchal society, which boss would be so afraid
of a woman — even a politically active one — that he would order her killing? As so often occurs in Mexican history, Poot became a local martyr.
Over time, the story spread far beyond Kinchil and transformed into a tale
of heroic acts in the face of the forces of reaction. According to a local historian, "The landowners did not like that she was walking [active] in the
pueblo. Three hours before her death, three landowners came to her and
asked her how much money she wanted to stop her 'incitement' of the
peasants. She refused, saying that her parents were peasants and that she
would defend them. The hacendados then sent 12 horsemen to kill her."[1]

In fact the story of the death of Felipa Poot was more complicated.
She was not just a defender of the indigenous poor in Kinchil; she had
emerged as a significant power broker in local politics whose activities had
elicited envy among the male-dominated elite. The story embellished her
role as a defender of the community and at the same time downplayed her
political role. The fact that a cacique had ordered her death spoke to the
degree of Poot's political influence. Clearly she and other women like her

had claimed new political space for themselves and threatened the established order.

This story is emblematic of the process and legacy of the Lázaro Cárdenas period — without a doubt the most progressive phase of the Mexican
Revolution. More attuned to popular sentiment than Calles and his allies,
the Cardenistas responded to the growth of popular radicalism during the
Great Depression, articulating a political program that revived land reform and mobilized urban labor in new ways, while paying homage to economic nationalism and Keynesian doctrines. This chapter examines the
rise and retrenchment of Cardenismo in three stages: the transition from
the Maximato to the Cárdenas administration (1932–35); the Cardenista
reform program and the popular role in and response to it (1935–38); and
the waning of reform as the march toward World War II dictated cooperation with the United States (1938–40). *The 3 stages*

FROM THE MAXIMATO TO CARDENISMO, 1932–1935

As one of the *jefe máximo*'s principal protégés, Lázaro Cárdenas initially
appeared unlikely to break away from Calles and his policies. Like General Abelardo Rodríguez, whom he replaced in the presidency, he was a
member of the "cubs of the revolution," a generation that came of age in
the decade of factional struggle rather than during the late Porfiriato. Of
mixed descent, Cárdenas was born into a middle-class family in Jiquil-
pan, Michoacán, on May 21, 1895. At age sixteen he lost his father, a shop-
keeper, and became the primary breadwinner for a family of nine. After
only six years of primary education, young Lázaro left school to work at
a local print shop until June 1913, when anti-Huerta forces seized Jiquil-
pan. After a company of *rurales* reoccupied the town for Huerta and destroyed the print shop, Cárdenas joined the troops of a Zapatista leader. In
1915 he joined the Constitutionalists and thereafter stuck with Calles and
Obregón in all of their principal campaigns, first making his mark at the
Battle of Agua Prieta against Villa in November 1915. He aligned with the
two foremost Sonorans against Carranza in 1920, against de la Huerta in
1923, and against the Cristeros in 1926; then, in 1929, he supported the jefe
máximo and his government against the Escobar rebellion. Eighteen years
older, Calles was like a father to the young Michoacano, whom he pater-
nalistically called *chamaco* (kid). Cárdenas's loyalty earned him rapid promotions, and he attained a general's rank at the tender age of twenty-five.

Right picks = promotion

Cárdenas's political personality blended unique leadership gifts with a carefully concealed authoritarian streak. Early on, he displayed three crucial abilities: to side with the eventual winners of the revolution, to hide his true intentions, and to please those with whom he was interacting. In the words of one Callista cacique, he was a "fox."[2] Cárdenas was also known for his probity; unlike Rodríguez and many other members of the new revolutionary elite, he did not use his power to amass a great fortune. For example, in 1925, as military commander of the Huasteca region on the Gulf Coast, he insisted on applying the directives of the federal and state governments to the foreign-owned oil companies that dominated the economy. To the surprise of the operatives of those companies, Cárdenas refused the bribes that Manuel Peláez and other caciques before him had gladly accepted in return for their protection of the oil industry. However, Cárdenas's political wiles masked his determination to prevail in the chaotic atmosphere of revolutionary Mexico. Despite his willingness to listen to the concerns of ordinary people, he had no compunctions about enforcing his decisions. His political enemies knew him as authoritarian and unforgiving, and they also knew that he was more pragmatic and less idealistic than he appeared. _Perception v. reality_

Cárdenas's first major political post was as governor of Michoacán (1928–32), a state torn apart by the Cristero Rebellion. To reacquaint himself with his home state after years of absence, he announced his availability to all who wished to speak to him about their concerns and traveled around the state to learn more about the people he governed. As the epigraph to this chapter indicates, human interaction was Cárdenas's greatest strength, and he succeeded in healing some of the state's political divisions, although he pursued Calles's anticlerical policies. He distinguished himself by his zeal for reconstruction, especially in road building, school construction, and irrigation projects. Foreshadowing his later strategies at the national level, Cárdenas also organized his state's campesinos and workers into mass organizations. At a time when the pace of land distribution declined throughout the republic, the governor expropriated more than 350,000 acres of land and converted them into _ejidos,_ or communal cooperatives. This amount exceeded all the land parceled out by his predecessors in 1917–28. His success as governor won Cárdenas appointment to the national cabinet. By 1933 he had served as president of the National Revolutionary Party (PNR) and in various capacities in the governments

FIGURE 6.1   Jefe Máximo Calles and President Rodríguez present the PNR candidate, General Lázaro Cárdenas, August 1933. Fideicomiso Archivos Plutarco Elías Calles y Fernando Torreblanca, Mexico City.

of the Maximato, and he had emerged as a leading candidate for the presidential election of 1934. That endeavor required the approval of both the jefe máximo and his party (figure 6.1).

Fortunately for Cárdenas, the stars aligned for the nomination of a progressive candidate, as the jefe máximo had begun to retreat from his earlier dominating role under the Rodríguez presidency (September 1932 to November 1934). Stricken by the death of his second wife and an assortment of medical ailments, Calles no longer controlled the national government as he once had; with one of his closest associates in the National Palace, the Maximato appeared to be "on autopilot."[3] Although Calles remained the preeminent figure in the PNR, his involvement in the day-to-day operations of the government decreased significantly. He spent long periods far away from Mexico City, principally on vacation on the president's properties in Baja California. Moreover President Rodríguez desired to demonstrate that he would not be a puppet. The U.S. military attaché observed that he assumed an increasing number of the "responsibilities and decisions . . . formerly left to . . . Calles."[4]

While Calles sojourned far away, Rodríguez faced mounting popular discontent with the Maximato and the economic system over which it presided. To Mexicans laid off during the Great Depression, it became ever more apparent that the existing political system was a revolution in name only. Even as the government erected grand monuments to "the Revolution," the common people demanded real rather than symbolic benefits.

Despite his own pro-business views, Rodríguez felt compelled to provide some of those benefits. His government resumed the land reform program, and Congress passed the Código Agrario, which codified agrarian legislation and provided grievance procedures for dissatisfied campesinos. Rodríguez also established the nation's first minimum wage, indexed to the cost of living in each state. The government provided a state subvention for the founding of Petromex, the first Mexican oil company devoted to meeting domestic demand.

Finally—and not least in importance—Rodríguez defied the jefe máximo on a variety of political matters, including the ouster of one of Calles's key loyalists as finance minister. On one occasion, he explained to U.S. Ambassador Josephus Daniels that he was "no Ortiz Rubio."[5] Although Calles's supporters and members of the Rodríguez government sycophantically greeted the jefe máximo when he returned to the capital from his extended travels, Rodríguez assumed direction over the actual decision-making process. Calles meanwhile retained his powerful informal role in the PNR.

Aware that his understudy was not following his script as closely as he desired, the jefe máximo asserted his influence in the areas of education and church-state relations. Not only were these areas in the forefront of the state's everyday engagement with its people, but they also represented issues on which the former schoolteacher Calles continued to hold radical opinions. Anticlerical governors continued to stoke the church-state conflict, which lingered despite the 1929 accord that ended the Cristero War. For example, in Tabasco, Governor Tomás Garrido Canabal converted church buildings into schools. In Veracruz, Governor Tejeda had limited the number of priests to one for each 100,000 inhabitants. Meanwhile federal education policy continued to contravene the educational mission of the Church. Rodríguez favored lay education, the principle of secular instruction by public teachers, who, like their U.S. counterparts, could not legally promote one creed over another in the classroom. Just at the time when Rodríguez began to display his political independence, Calles asked one of his surrogates, Education Secretary Narciso Bassols, to up the ante by introducing "socialist education." The term was something of a misnomer, as Bassols never intended to impart Soviet-style indoctrination in socialist theory. Much like the positivism of the nineteenth century, socialist education stressed the teaching of rational and scientific rather than metaphysical explanations; it disavowed all religious dogma. An early version of the program also proposed sex education as a way to reduce the incidence of teenage pregnancies. Socialist education occasioned a new flare-up of the church-state conflict and set the stage for continuing tensions throughout the Cárdenas administration. In the fall of 1934 a second Cristero War broke out. Although the conflict was much less severe than the original Cristiada, it put Rodríguez on the defensive during the last months of his term. Catholics considered socialist education "the devil's work"; in the words of one witness, indigenous Mexicans believed that "the Devil [the state's maestros] turned men into animals or elements."[6]

In December 1933 the selection of Cárdenas as the presidential nominee at the second PNR convention in Querétaro took place against this backdrop of anxiety and dissatisfaction. The number of strikes registered by the federal government increased from 13 in 1932 to more than 100 in 1933 and up to 202 in 1934. Calles and Rodríguez could not ignore the mounting popular pressure on a party that labeled itself "revolutionary" and purported to represent the very best aspirations of the Mexican people in the great upheaval; still, they dragged their feet on meaningful social reform in the midst of the great economic crisis.

Cárdenas entered the PNR convention with Calles's calculated endorsement. The jefe máximo threw his support behind Cárdenas for several reasons. First, he shared a strong personal bond with a man he regarded as a political son and likely believed he could rein in Cárdenas's progressive tendencies (though he also appreciated that he could no longer subordinate the president of the republic). Second, Calles worried about political stability, and his selection of Cárdenas appeased many of his political opponents. Third, the jefe máximo had made a realistic assessment of the power shift within his ruling coalition, concluding that Cárdenas would enjoy the broadest support within the party. Thus Calles, a man often caricatured as the informal dictator of Mexico during this period, held less power than is commonly assumed, and he realized as much. Although the bond between Cárdenas and Calles was strong, it was not any more powerful than that between Calles and Cárdenas's principal rival for the nomination, General Manuel Pérez Treviño. Ultimately, Calles's choice, though it reflected the strong friendship he enjoyed with his protégé, was a pragmatic decision that was informed by his analysis of popular political currents and the leanings of significant power brokers, such as his own son Rodolfo and Tabasco's governor Garrido Canabal.

The other business conducted during this convention—the programmatic and organizational unification of the party—provided a blueprint for Cárdenas's eventual reforms as president. Calles and Rodríguez intended to unify the party by eliminating the constituent organizations and regional parties incorporated into the PNR after its founding. As the PNR still mediated the ambitions of powerful generals and political leaders, this proposal predictably elicited opposition. To secure its adoption required the party leadership to assiduously seek compromise with these regional organizations and their leaders. As a unifying measure, the PNR decided to commit itself more firmly to a set of political principles rooted in the revolutionary constitution. Upon Calles's recommendation, the party set about drafting a six-year plan to set the general policy direction of the Cárdenas regime. The delegates charged with formulating the plan came up with a draft that closely followed the letter of the 1917 Constitution and hence contained concrete commitments to additional land reform and improvements for labor.

Along with Rodríguez's relatively independent administration, the promulgation of socialist education, and the naming of Cárdenas as the presidential nominee, the PNR plan demonstrated the gradual transition from the Maximato to Cardenismo. Perhaps this transition can best be illustrated symbolically. Shortly after the convention, the jefe máximo invited Cárdenas and some of his friends to join him at his daughter Alicia's beach cottage in El Tambor in the northwestern state of Sinaloa. When Calles went to his favorite spot on the beach for a swim in the warm waters of the Gulf of California, Cárdenas and one of his friends demurred from the jefe máximo's invitation to join him, choosing to take a dip at another location several hundred yards away. The episode hinted that the new group would go its own way, carving out its place in history by including new groups in the revolutionary coalition.

Cárdenas's intentions to follow a new path became even clearer when he undertook an unprecedented campaign tour that included visits to every state and territory between December 1933 and July 1934. This tour constituted a remarkable effort given the fact that there was no way that the PNR candidate could lose the election. Its primary purpose lay in fashioning an independent political base. If Calles's presidential campaign ten years before had made history as the first to make use of the radio, Cárdenas registered his own imprint by connecting with voters at the grassroots level. In every part of the republic, the candidate took time to chat with ordinary people: men, women, and children, old and young, sick and healthy, rich and poor, urban and rural, indigenous and mestizo. In part this strategy reflected the global rise of mass politics evident in Franklin Roosevelt's New Deal in the United States and in populist regimes in South America.

Following his inauguration on December 1, 1934, the president asserted his authority while the jefe máximo was recuperating in the Mexican Northwest and in a clinic in Los Angeles. Aware that most members of the cabinet were allies of Calles, the new president first took symbolic and necessarily cautious steps. He announced plans to turn Chapultepec Castle, the residence of Mexican presidents since the days of Emperor Maximilian and Empress Carlota, into a national museum of history. He himself moved into a much more modest building at the base of the hill — ironically, the same building occupied by Calles when he was secretary of gobernación under Obregón. This move proved permanent: to this day, Los Pinos is the official residence of the country's president. Moreover Cárdenas did not wear a coat and tie to official functions. In another effort to promote modern and egalitarian communication, he allowed every Mexican to send one telegram each Sunday free of charge. Finally, Cárdenas displayed his desire to end what he viewed as immoral vices, ordering the closing of brothels and casinos — Calles's former practice as governor of Sonora. By necessity this initiative ultimately led him to confront former President Rodríguez, co-owner of the two fanciest casinos in Mexico: the Casino de la Selva in Cuernavaca and the Agua Caliente casino in Tijuana.

In short order, the president took more substantive steps to assert his own power at the expense of the jefe máximo. Unable initially to shake up his cabinet, Cárdenas targeted Callista dominance at the regional and local levels as well as among the military and popular organizations. Where the state governors were concerned (a position that had suffered from both a high turnover rate and incessant federal intervention), he promoted the election of younger leaders from his own inner circle to replace loyal Callistas. He applied the same strategy to the *jefes de operaciones*, replacing retiring generals with more junior officers loyal to him. At the same time, he used the increasing strike activity of workers to his advantage. The first half of 1935 witnessed more than 1,200 strikes, many of them wildcat strikes not registered with the authorities. In contrast to his predecessors, who had attempted to limit strikes, Cárdenas encouraged them as long as they remained nonviolent. He even stated that he sympathized with the workers, who had "always suffered injustices, disregard, and privations."[7] "The revolution was in the gutter," he told the journalist Anita Brenner. "It is necessary to raise it up."[8]

On strikes

This favorable disposition toward the strikers finally goaded Calles into a blunder that ended his political career, affording Cárdenas an opportunity to cast off the shadow of the jefe máximo. On June 12, 1935, the headline of the newspaper *El Universal* was "Sensational Declarations by General Plutarco Elías Calles." A now intemperate Calles criticized the "constant strikes that have rocked the nation for six months. In many cases, the labor organizations are showing . . . a lack of gratitude. The strikes . . . constantly obstruct the president's good intentions and tireless work."[9] Although these declarations did not criticize the president directly, they implied—in paternalist fashion—that Cárdenas could not handle the situation. They violated a cardinal rule in Mexican politics not to publicly question the president's abilities. Cárdenas seized the occasion to remind Mexicans that he, rather than the jefe máximo, directed the affairs of the nation. He immediately obtained the resignation of his entire cabinet and then appointed his own allies to the positions formerly held by Callistas. In Congress most Calles supporters switched to Cárdenas for fear that they too would lose their leadership positions. And at the state level, the president stripped power from fourteen Callista governors by having Congress declare the existence of a state of "internal disorder," a euphemism for blatant federal interference at the state level. In all fourteen states, Cárdenas loyalists succeeded Calles supporters. By early 1936 Cárdenas was firmly enough in the saddle that he commenced the expropriation of Calles's properties. On April 10, 1936, police arrested Calles, Morones, and two of their allies and flew them into exile in California.

As the jefe máximo settled in San Diego, where Cárdenas agents kept a close watch on his movements, a new era had begun. Cardenismo would significantly build on the Sonorans' achievements by expanding and fine-tuning the political machine that they had constructed. Strengthening a

Depression-era state that remained relatively weak at the time of Cárdenas's inauguration required significant cooperation from ordinary Mexicans. Thus the story of Cardenismo, like that of the other eras of the revolution, would involve the negotiation of power between those above and those below.

CARDENISTA REFORMS

For many Mexicans, Cárdenas remains larger than life even seven decades after his rule. Of all the revolutionary presidents, he enjoys the strongest hero cult, the only such cult that approaches the popularity of the slain popular heroes of the revolution, Emiliano Zapata and Pancho Villa. His enduring popularity rested on his radiant personality as well as a genuine commitment to social reform.

Just as he had shown in his governorship, President Cárdenas displayed an uncanny ability to relate to Mexicans from all walks of life. Cárdenas's personal appeal led ordinary Mexicans such as the Maya activist Felipa Poot to believe that they could transform their country and overcome centuries of exploitation and oppression. His popularity even won over foreign diplomats such as U.S. Ambassador Josephus Daniels, whose strong support gave the president greater leeway in implementing his reforms. Anita Brenner recounts an apocryphal anecdote that sums up the way many Mexicans thought of their new president:

> One morning while dispatching business in the capital, his secretary laid a list of urgent matters, and a telegram, before him. The list said "Bank reserves dangerously low." "Tell the treasurer," said Cárdenas. "Agricultural production failing." "Tell the Minister of Agriculture." "Railways bankrupt." "Tell the Minister of Communications." "Serious message from Washington." "Tell Foreign Affairs." Then he opened the telegram, which read: "My corn dried, my burro died, my sow was stolen, my baby is sick. Signed: Pedro Juan, village of Huitzlipituzco." "Order the presidential train at once," said Cárdenas. "I am leaving for Huitzlipituzco."[10]

Not surprisingly one member of the government observed that Cárdenas had "political instinct at the tips of his fingers."[11]

Cárdenas remains best known for a quartet of reforms affecting land, labor, the ruling party, and the oil industry. These popular measures formed the cornerstone of his presidency and integrated campesinos, workers, and intellectuals into the revolutionary state. A fifth measure—using the on-going campaign for public education as a means of mass mobilization—undergirded the four other major initiatives.

Cárdenas's first years as president focused primarily on agrarian reform. By the time he took office, previous administrations had handed over twenty-five million acres to campesinos in the span of seventeen years. Carranza had distributed approximately one million acres; Obregón, more than three million; Calles, eight million; Portes Gil, five million; Ortiz Rubio, three million; and Rodríguez, five million. These redistributions had provided some land to campesinos, but millions of them still did not own any land at all. Moreover the expropriations did not touch the hacienda as an institution. Most of the best land remained in private hands, and much of it was still under the control of foreign investors and members of the new political class. In addition, demographic pressures on the countryside had multiplied. The birth rate in campesino families remained high, and the Great Depression led to the repatriation of more than 400,000 Mexican immigrants, including some U.S. citizens of Mexican descent.

Thus Cárdenas first and foremost addressed the issue of the landless poor. In only six years, the president almost doubled his predecessors' combined efforts. He expropriated and redistributed a total of 49,580,203 acres. In the Laguna region on the Durango-Coahuila border, home to most of the nation's cotton production, Cárdenas parceled out eight million acres to more than thirty thousand families. Knowing that many small farms could not survive without help, and eager to maintain export-oriented agriculture, the president did not transfer most of the land to individual heads of household. Instead Cardenista land reform primarily benefited ejidos, the communal agricultural cooperatives first created in 1922 under Obregón. The president believed that the ejido offered the best solution to the problem of the landless poor, as large communal holdings parceled out to individual farmers often combined access to land with the advantage of farming on a large scale with shared resources. Thus the farmers of the Laguna engaged in the collective production of cotton, but they also produced enough food for their own consumption and even for sale to neighboring areas. To help campesinos obtain credit, Cárdenas created the Banco de Crédito Ejidal, which provided loans to more than three thousand ejidos in his six-year term. With this agrarian reform, Cárdenas had fulfilled one of the central promises of the Constitutionalists and also ensured for himself the admiration and unconditional support of most campesinos.

To be sure, the ejido system that replaced the large commercial hacienda was far from perfect. To begin with, it remained incomplete: in some regions, hacendados and Catholic priests prevented the full implementation of land reform; in others, landowners broke up their estates into small parcels, which they registered in the names of trusted associates or relatives, to avoid expropriation. In addition, the new bank could not provide sufficient credit, leading to a decline in agricultural production. The ejido system also made campesinos dependent on the state, not only for credit, but also for seeds, fertilizer, technology, and supplies. Moreover campesinos still did not own the land that they worked. Critics charged that the ejido system was no better than the Soviet *kolkhoz*, a system of huge collective farms established with the use of force under the dictatorship of Joseph Stalin. Perhaps most compellingly, the ejido did not offer a way out of poverty. More aware than ever of opportunities elsewhere, many rural Mexicans moved to the cities. The population of the three largest urban centers—Mexico City, Guadalajara, and Monterrey—grew an average of 35 percent during the 1930s.

Another significant reform concerned organized labor. Since 1928 the Regional Mexican Workers' Federation (CROM) had faded along with the political star of its leader, Luis N. Morones. The union had become Morones's corrupt sinecure and served as an ally of the Maximato governments. As a result, more radical labor organizations had emerged in opposition to both the CROM and the government. Cárdenas drew upon these new labor entities and helped them grow in membership, especially following the 1936 ruling of a labor arbitrations board that outlawed company unions. The president supported the efforts of an erstwhile Morones ally, Vicente Lombardo Toledano, to create a new national labor union, the Confederación de Trabajadores Mexicanos (Confederation of Mexican Workers, or CTM). With the help of a number of significant defectors from the CROM, the CTM brought together approximately three thousand different labor unions, many of them company or regional unions, and it came to comprise more than 600,000 members. Unlike Morones, Lombardo preached Marxist doctrine and saw the CTM as the vanguard of class struggle against the bourgeoisie. As he knew, it had often been the dissident wing of organized labor—not just high-profile railroad workers but also miners and stevedores, disaffected local and regional sectors of the CROM in northern and central states such as Coahuila, Zacatecas, and Guanajuato—that had maintained a stubborn autonomy from the official corporatism consolidating Mexico under the ruling party. In this sense, Lombardo appreciated that organized labor had done more than its share to keep the radical legacy of the revolution alive. Although Cárdenas was not a Marxist, he viewed the CTM as a useful ally in his quest to build a more inclusive and more just corporatist state in which the government mediated both class and political conflicts. For his part, Lombardo was substantially more pragmatic than his fiery speeches indicated; he was interested in obtaining influence for himself and the CTM in pursuing that more just society, which appeared hopelessly distant in the 1930s. Both men understood that the overt radicalism of the CTM provided an important incentive to striking workers, which allowed the state to enter conflicts between capital and labor as a mediating force that compelled solutions largely favorable to the workers. Lombardo and his CTM became one of the most useful pillars of Cardenismo.

Support for labor also came in symbolic form. Even after Calles's ouster, Cárdenas vehemently supported the right to strike, guaranteed under Article 123 of the revolutionary constitution but limited, in practice, to strikes that the government considered "legitimate." As we have seen, Cárdenas had angered the jefe máximo in part by allowing most strikes to proceed as long as they adhered to minimal regulation. After returning from a vacation in Mexico, the conservative British novelist Evelyn Waugh shared this undoubtedly embellished anecdote of a children's strike:

> On the first day of my visit traffic leading to the Cathedral square was paralyzed at midday. . . . We came upon the cause of the trouble: a huge procession of school children, of all ages . . . standing wistfully among their banners. . . . I asked, "Is it some football match?"
>
> "No, it is just a demonstration of the children. They are always having them."
>
> "What about?" . . .
>
> "They do not like one of their teachers. They have come to protest to the President."

"They seem very well organized."

"Yes, the children's committees do that. The Ministry of Education teaches them to organize like the c.t.m."

"What will happen?"

"The teacher will be dismissed. They are always changing their teachers in that way."[12]

Using sarcasm, this story illustrates the fact that Cardenista social reforms responded to the negotiation of power between ordinary Mexicans and the state. Hence Cardenismo was not just the result of top-down efforts, whether to improve the lot of the poor majority or to co-opt campesinos and workers. Because the state still remained weak, the reform effort remained messy and uneven. To be sure, owing to Cardenista initiatives, ordinary Mexicans acquired a real stake in the state's agrarian and labor reforms. Nevertheless the mass organizations often pursued their own agendas. For example, much to Cárdenas's chagrin, the CTM attempted to organize the *campesinado*, claiming that it represented all of the proletariat (of which more presently).

On the other end of the spectrum, resistance limited reform. Cárdenas and his associates could not overcome entrenched conservative alliances and local practices, and they often found themselves required to collaborate with leaders and movements antithetical to their stated political goals. In the end, many Cardenistas proved "time-servers and opportunists," lukewarm to ideology and political causes and primarily interested in individual betterment.[13] Even more important, the Cárdenas years witnessed the formation of an organized right-wing opposition with the foundation of the fascist Unión Nacional Sinarquista (National Synarchist Union), a group devoted, among other goals, to the restoration of the role of the Catholic Church.

Although women remained without the right to vote, and even though most men continued to believe in the notion of "separate spheres" that divided "male" public life from "female" private lives, women played a critical role in the Cardenista coalition. Cardenista women strove for inclusion in the nation as citizens and hence pushed suffrage and legal reforms to the forefront. The latter impulse targeted the civil and penal codes, both of which continued to discriminate against women. Even more important, they inserted themselves into the Cardenista political landscape as active participants. Women in the Comarca Lagunera region, the cotton-producing area that had witnessed the largest land reform of the Cárdenas period, mobilized and founded the Women's League for Social Struggle. This association allowed women, particularly poor women, to participate in local Cardenista struggles for bread-and-butter social and economic reforms without seriously challenging established gender norms. Yet women also participated in the right-wing opposition to Cárdenas, most notably in the Sinarquistas and other Catholic organizations.

Cardenista social reforms not only benefited those at the bottom but also improved the prospects of Mexican industrialists at a time when businesses worldwide continued to struggle with the impact of the Great Depression. Practicing Keynesian economics (at least prior to 1937–38), the Cárdenas administration increased the stake of the state in the economy in order to put capital into the hands of the consumer and foster industrial production. As the president announced during his inaugural address: "The state alone embodies the general interest, and for this reason the state has a vision of the whole. The state must continually broaden, increase, and deepen interventions."[14] Cárdenas confronted the Great Depression by fomenting industrialization that lessened the country's dependence on imports.

Indeed industrialists fared far better than the private landowners whose holdings the government had expropriated as part of the land reform, or the owners of the railways, which had also been nationalized. Nevertheless, for the most part, private ownership of industry remained untouched. Rising wages put spending money into the hands of consumers. Many Mexicans drank their first beer or soft drink, or purchased their first bar of soap or their first vial of pain medicine during the Cárdenas years. At the same time, many entrepreneurs (particularly the powerful Monterrey group) resented Cardenista labor policies and portrayed them as abuses of a repressive socialist regime. The Monterrey group had witnessed firsthand the Cuauhtémoc brewery become a target of CTM activism. However, despite their complaints, many industrial companies producing consumer goods, including the Cuauhtémoc owners, improved their balance sheets. Likewise merchants and other small entrepreneurs found ways to deal with Cardenista regulations. For example, the Casa Boker, a venerable German hardware store in downtown Mexico City, retained its company union despite an unfavorable verdict by the arbitration board.

The Cardenista economic recovery came to a screeching halt in the spring of 1937 with the sudden onset of an economic crisis. The U.S. economy, only then emerging from the Great Depression, experienced a deep recession, which drastically reduced demand for Mexican exports. In addition, falling food production, resulting from the implementation of the Cardenista land reform, caused the prices of basic commodities to skyrocket. Swelled by the influx of rural migrants, the larger cities experienced severe food shortages, and the cost of living leapt more than 20 percent in one year. Cárdenas attempted to intervene by eliminating the profits of gouging "middlemen" from the process that transported and distributed foodstuffs. These efforts, however, did not address the root cause of the problem: the scarcity of ejido-produced food coupled with steady population growth. In the end, the government resorted to the politically humiliating solution of importing food from the United States.

To show the nation that his reform agenda had not stalled, Cárdenas made an example of the most powerful foreign economic lobby: the oil industry. More than 90 percent of all oil production remained in the hands of foreign corporations headquartered in Great Britain and the United States. Since the promulgation of the revolutionary constitution, foreign control of the oil industry had served as one of the most contentious issues in foreign affairs. While the Mexican government attempted to levy sizable production taxes as part of a larger effort to regulate foreign oil, the companies insisted on the fulfillment of the Porfirian concessions that allowed them to extract millions of barrels at minimal taxation. The issue had greatly contributed to Obregón's difficulties in procuring diplomatic recognition in the early 1920s, as well as to the crisis in U.S.-Mexican relations in 1926–27. In 1936 the oil industry returned to the spotlight yet again, following a national oil workers' strike for better wages — and again the oil companies hoped that their governments would intervene on their behalf. This time, however, they were on their own. Although the oil workers received higher pay than most workers nationwide, Cárdenas sent the matter to a federal arbitration board, which ordered a raise of more than 30 percent. The oil companies appealed the board's decision to the Mexican Supreme Court, to no avail, and then decided to defy the court's decision. Meanwhile the oil workers got support from the CTM, and thousands of workers demonstrated in the streets of Mexico City against what they portrayed as the oil companies' greed.

On March 18, 1938, just as the eyes of the world were focused on Nazi Germany's recent annexation of Austria, Cárdenas decreed the nationalization of the oil companies on the grounds that their defiance of court orders violated Mexican sovereignty. This decision proved hugely popular. In the days following the expropriation decree, more than 100,000 people participated in boisterous celebratory rallies, and thousands of telegrams, written by ordinary citizens who offered to help pay for the expropriation, poured into the National Palace. Even the Catholic Church—normally a staunch defender of property rights—supported the expropriation.

Cárdenas succeeded in carrying out the expropriation despite retributions from the oil industry that included an embargo on the transport of Mexican oil, as well as pressure on the U.S. and British government to intervene on their behalf. The president fervently hoped that the U.S. government of Franklin Roosevelt would not join the fray. Five years prior, Roosevelt had pledged to pursue a new policy toward Latin America that would end the string of U.S. military interventions since the War of 1898. This new approach became known as the "Good Neighbor Policy." Concerned about the rise of fascism in Europe and Japan, and sympathetic to a reform effort that resembled the New Deal in some respects, Roosevelt and Ambassador Daniels protested against the oil expropriation but did not apply diplomatic pressure—let alone raise the specter of military intervention—in the manner of previous U.S. administrations. Meantime foreign investors protested against the expropriation through the means they knew best: divestment from Mexico. This capital outflow caused a 50 percent decline in the value of the peso, providing a powerful disincentive to further expropriation of foreign property.

To administer the newly nationalized oil wells and refineries, Cárdenas created a state-owned enterprise, Petróleos Mexicanos (PEMEX), which became the only company allowed to refine petroleum and sell gasoline to the general public. In a testament to the lingering popularity of the oil expropriation as an act of national pride, it remains today the only major state-owned enterprise that has escaped the neoliberal privatization drive of the 1980s and 1990s.

The popular excitement surrounding the oil expropriation restored Cárdenas's popularity and accompanied the final major Cardenista reform: the reorganization of the PNR. The Cardenistas desired to forge a more inclusive national party and especially wanted to include in its structure popular mass organizations such as the CTM and the Confederación Nacional Campesina (National Campesino Confederation, or CNC). They deemed such inclusion necessary for two reasons: to give workers and campesinos adequate corporate representation and to channel their ambitions and aspirations under the leadership of the president and his party. Thus Cárdenas proposed the creation of a corporatist party out of paternalistic concern for the lower classes and greatly increased the power of the presidency and the state party in the bargain. In 1938 a party congress deferred to the president's wishes and reorganized the official party as the Partido de la Revolución Mexicana (Party of the Mexican Revolution, or PRM). The PRM included four sectors: workers, agrarians, public employees, and the army. The party organized all of these sectors vertically, so that they directly negotiated with the president, and all popular organizations worked within the framework of the party. Of course, this reorganization could not eliminate *caciquismo*, and regional and local strongmen (or, as in the case of Felipa Poot, strongwomen) preserved their independent spheres of power. Nonetheless the transformation of the PNR into the PRM amounted to more than a name change. It marked the birth of a more mature corporatist state party in which the president mediated social conflict — the blueprint of the latter-day Institutional Revolutionary Party (PRI).

THE RETRENCHMENT OF CARDENISMO

The creation of the PRM coincided with the moderation of the Cardenista reform effort. Cárdenas had achieved his major policy objectives, and the 1937 economic crisis had demonstrated the cost of the reforms. Thus, little by little, Cardenista reformism waned. As early as 1936 Cárdenas had given up socialist education, a legacy of the Calles period, and as his six-year term wore on, the president became less tolerant of strike activities; by 1937 he began to crack down on strikes not authorized by his government. Finally, after the oil expropriation, land distribution slowed to a trickle.

The increasingly strained relations between the government and urban labor amounted to one important moderating influence in the last three years of Cárdenas's rule. The primary reason for this development was the CTM's desire to organize the campesinado. In Cárdenas's political universe, workers and campesinos inhabited two different planets. He conceived of workers as wage-earning employees, whether urban or rural, with the exception of middle-class professionals; campesinos were peasants tied to the land on which they worked. Cardenismo had improved the lot of the workers, and it had succeeded in giving land to hundreds of thousands of landless campesinos. In Cárdenas's opinion, the CTM leadership displayed a higher degree of political sophistication, and he feared that the union would drown out campesino concerns, particularly due to the workers' need for affordable food. Moreover, with the groups separate, the state loomed as the nation's supreme social arbiter. A second source of friction between the Cardenista government and urban labor lay in the refusal of organized labor to treat state-owned companies any differently from privately owned ones. Indeed many of the strikes suppressed by police forces in the late 1930s targeted formerly private companies that had been nationalized during the Cárdenas administration.

Cardenista moderation entailed compromise as well as cooperation with those who would otherwise have been inveterate enemies. The president's political machine included some unusual allies, such as two important Cardenista governors: General Maximino Avila Camacho of Puebla and Román Yocupicio of Sonora. Avila Camacho was a Cardenista in name only and a conservative in practice. He earned a reputation for corruption and cruelty, represented well in the 1985 novel by Angeles Mastretta, *Arráncame la vida* (Tear This Heart Out).[15] Yet above all, Avila Camacho shared Cárdenas's pragmatism, and the following judgment of his tenure as governor might just as well apply to the president: "He was able to step into a . . . tumultuous political scene and take advantage of existing conflicts, eliminating opponents and incorporating supporters into an expanding patronage network."[16] The son of a Mayo, Yocupicio had participated in the revolution as an Obregón loyalist and remained on the side of the government until 1929, when he joined the Escobar Rebellion. His involvement in that rebellion and his status as an indigenous Sonoran made him an anti-Callista and hence a potential ally for Cárdenas. Yocupicio was named substitute governor of Sonora in 1937 to finish out the term originally begun by Rodolfo Elías Calles, the eldest son of the former jefe máximo. Throughout his term, he opposed the federal agrarian reform effort and supported the state's large landowners and industrialists, even though he did support land reform in the fertile Mayo and Yaqui valleys, where his political clients resided. Yocupicio also attempted to keep the CTM from organizing in his state. His opposition to organized labor and his allegiance to the Catholic Church drove more orthodox Cardenistas to exasperation, to the point that CTM leaders labeled him a fascist. Yet the governor also found a great degree of support not only among the indigenous Sonorans who viewed him as one of their own but also among Catholics who had suffered under the anticlerical coalition that had dominated state politics since 1915. These examples demonstrate that Cárdenas increasingly realized the need to move toward the political center.

Yet this move did not placate those on Cárdenas's left or right. Within the Cardenista coalition, a radical faction pushed for a resumption and intensification of the reform effort. The CTM leader Lombardo as well as the artists Diego Rivera, Frida Kahlo, and David Alfaro Siqueiros identified themselves as Communists who yearned to take the class struggle against the bourgeoisie to new levels. During the 1930s Mexico's small Communist Party gained thousands of adherents. Meanwhile several factions emerged on the Right. The earliest was the *camisas doradas*, or Gold Shirts, of General Nicolás Rodríguez. This fascist paramilitary organization sought the overthrow of Cárdenas, who exiled Rodríguez in 1936. However, thousands of Gold Shirt supporters remained in Mexico, directed by their leader from the United States. In 1937 the founding of the Unión Nacional Sinarquista created an ultraconservative and pro-Catholic movement. Six years later the UNS claimed the support of half a million members, including many men and women who had supported the Cristero Rebellion. In 1938 Cárdenas nipped in the bud the rebellion of San Luis Potosí's venerable cacique Saturnino Cedillo, an opportunist par excellence who allied himself with right-wing elements in northeastern and central Mexico. Finally, in 1939 Catholic leaders and entrepreneurs founded a conservative opposition party, the Partido de Acción Nacional (National Action Party, or PAN). Given little credence initially, the PAN would gradually become the second largest party in Mexico (and stunningly defeat the official party in 2000). Just like their left-wing counterparts, right-wing movements influenced Cárdenas's policy at the national level, primarily by helping steer the government to the political center.

The polarization of the Mexican political scene reflected that of the world in general. Stalin's agents from the Soviet Union supported leftist movements in Mexico and elsewhere; although they could not put Communists in control, in 1940 they proved capable enough of murdering the prominent anti-Stalinist exile Leon Trotsky in Mexico City. On the Right, the late 1930s had witnessed the emergence of a dangerous alliance of the totalitarian regimes of Nazi Germany, fascist Italy, and Tojo Japan, formalized in September 1940 as the Axis Powers. Seeking world domination, this alliance opposed both the Communist Soviet Union and the Western powers (the United States, Great Britain, and France). Meanwhile Nazi operatives supported right-wing movements throughout Latin America.

In this struggle, Cárdenas opposed both extremes. He saw fascism, in particular, as a threat to Mexico and the world. The Cárdenas government was the only one to extend assistance to the Republican faction in the Spanish Civil War, an anarchist-socialist alliance pitted against a fascist coalition under Generalísimo Francisco Franco. When Franco won the brutally contested war, thousands of left-leaning Spaniards received asylum in Mexico, where they founded what is now called the Colegio de México, a superb graduate center in the humanities and social sciences. Cárdenas also allowed some Jewish refugees from Nazi Germany to reside in Mexico. On the other hand, the president also desired to keep his nation out of a global military conflict that appeared more inevitable each day. Trade with Germany remained important, as became clear by way of a 1938 agreement to barter Mexican oil for German-manufactured products at the height of the controversy regarding the oil expropriation. Occasioned by the oil companies' refusal to process and ship Mexican crude, this short-lived deal provided much-needed oil to the German Navy. Both the extreme Left and the Right demanded of Cárdenas the absolute neutrality displayed by Carranza in World War I, in case Axis aggression should lead to war, a position enhanced when the Hitler-Stalin Pact of July 1939 temporarily united Communists and Nazis in a common cause. Communists loyal to Stalin were unwilling to support Great Britain and France when the German invasion of Poland began World War II in Europe on September 1, 1939. Faced with a scenario in which the extremists cooperated with one another, Cárdenas inched toward the Western Allies. In 1940, the last year of his presidency, a significant obstacle to a pro-Allied position disappeared when the U.S. and British governments acquiesced in the oil expropriation.

That same year, the presidential election provided final evidence of the waning momentum for reform. This election season initially pitted the radical strain of Cardenismo against the growing Catholic and conservative opposition and eventually resulted in the victory of a compromise candidate. A former Michoacán governor, Francisco Múgica, a political mentor of Cárdenas's, represented the radical current. He called for continued expropriations of the remaining private land holdings and foreign-owned property and an aggressive campaign in favor of the working class. A prosperous general, Juan Andreu Almazán, opposed Múgica and his left-wing program. Almazán's rise to prominence had paralleled that of Abelardo Rodríguez and other revolutionary generals who had acquired substantial wealth. Enmeshed in the industrial sector, Almazán's power base resided in the state of Nuevo León, particularly in the city of Monterrey. His personal success story earned him the support of much of the middle class. Fearing that Almazán, backed by the support of the Sinarquistas and other right-wing groups, had a realistic chance of upsetting the PRM, Cárdenas supported General Manuel Avila Camacho as the PRM nominee, prompting Múgica to withdraw his candidacy. The younger brother of the Puebla governor, Avila Camacho was a bland and moderate conservative within the PRM. Unlike his brother, he had a reputation as a relatively honest politician, but, like most others among the Puebla elite, he rejected Cardenista mass politics and anticlericalism. The fact that the president backed someone on his political right over his own mentor once again demonstrated Cárdenas's pragmatism. As many Mexicans fully expected Almazán to rebel if he did not win, this election threatened to unravel the political stability that the Sonorans and Cárdenas had assiduously built over the preceding twenty years. With the support of both the PRM and the president, Avila Camacho handily won the election and became the final revolutionary general to sit in the presidential chair. Almazán charged fraud—a legitimate allegation given the lopsided official vote count—but ultimately backed away from launching a full-scale rebellion.

Cardenismo constituted the high tide of revolutionary reforms, finally delivering on many of the promises of the Constitution of 1917. Between 1934 and 1938 campesinos obtained land and urban labor acquired effective representation; the government expropriated the foreign-owned oil industry; and the ruling party reconstituted itself as an organization that embraced worker and campesino organizations as well as the army and the middle classes. Industrialization proceeded apace; women participated in politics to an unprecedented degree; and consumer culture reached the Mexican countryside. Only when yet another economic crisis and the long shadow of impending worldwide conflict began to engulf Mexico did the Cardenistas retrench from reform, pushed in equal parts by the emergence of conservative movements, foreign diplomats, and the opportunistic nature of their own diverse coalition.

The Cardenista heyday raises two important questions about the Mexican Revolution. First, to what extent did Cardenismo constitute a break from the trajectory laid out, successively, by Madero, the warring revolutionary factions, Carranza, and the Sonorans? This analysis has demonstrated that Cárdenas broke decisively from the Callista mold of attempting to tame social conflict by means of the CROM and agrarian organizations friendly to the regime. Yet Cárdenas greatly strengthened what was still a fledgling revolutionary state at the time of his inauguration, perfecting in many ways the strategy of state formation begun under Obregón and Calles. Cárdenas did not reinvent the revolution; his reforms finally implemented laws put on the books during the Constitutionalist and Sonoran periods. Second, to what extent did Cardenismo tap into popular roots? This chapter has suggested that Cardenista reforms enjoyed widespread popular support, even as an equally important counter-revolutionary and conservative movement began to emerge. In a global context, the 1930s were a time of political radicalism and mass mobilization, and Mexico was no exception. Both Cárdenas's labor policy and the oil expropriation responded to popular pressures rather than epitomizing top-down blueprints; similarly the retrenchment from reform occurred in large part because the regime confronted an emergent, organized Catholic and conservative opposition, which included mobilized peasants, during its last years in power.

Indeed, as Mexico entered the 1940s, its revolution encountered a new watershed. Yet another generation stood at its doorstep, a generation that had not participated in the "fiesta of bullets" of the 1910s. Could revolutionary reforms continue after Cárdenas, particularly during a time when World War II dictated closer cooperation with the United States?

It is an attempt to overthrow the government. They have already succeeded in making the union abandon the official party *en masse*; if this continues, how will you sustain yourselves, Mr. Undersecretary? Yes . . . that's the only way: to declare the strike non-existent, to send them to the army, to destroy them with the blows of clubs, and to jail their leaders.

— CARLOS FUENTES, *THE DEATH OF ARTEMIO CRUZ*

THE "PERFECT DICTATORSHIP," 1940–1968 | 7

On October 2, 1968, approximately five thousand student protesters assembled peaceably in the Plaza de las Tres Culturas (Square of the Three Cultures) in the Tlatelolco neighborhood of Mexico City. The square itself represents a conscious effort to remind Mexicans of their long and rich cultural heritage. The ruins of Aztec architecture dominate the center of the square, and a colonial convent lies on the eastern side. A high-rise that houses the Secretaría de Relaciones Exteriores (Foreign Relations Ministry) borders the southern side, and a modern public housing complex surrounds the square on the west and north. Carrying banners demanding democratic rights and the release of political prisoners, the students took advantage of the upcoming Olympic Games in Mexico's capital city to focus attention on their demands. They shouted "¿Díaz Ordaz, dónde estás?" (Díaz Ordaz, where are you?) and "No queremos olimpiadas, queremos revolución" (We don't want the Olympics, we want revolution). This personal appeal to the president, Gustavo Díaz Ordaz, a member of a long-ruling party that still referred to itself as "revolutionary," underscored the time-honored expectation that national leaders can redress popular grievances, just as Cárdenas had done in the 1930s. However, the government's response was not what the students had in mind. Around 6 p.m., tanks and armored cars appeared on the scene, and loudspeakers urged the protesters to disperse. When the students refused to leave, mayhem ensued. According to the most credible sources, a handful of special agents stationed on top of and inside the high-rises opened fire with automatic weapons, targeting both the protesters and the soldiers. In response, the soldiers machine-gunned the crowd, killing a large number of protesters. Popular *corridos* still mourn the death of "four hundred comrades," but the precise death toll is still unknown, since it appears the state may have removed and burned a number of the bodies.

In one bloody evening, state-sponsored violence had unmasked a system that the Peruvian novelist Mario Vargas Llosa in 1990 would dub the "perfect dictatorship": a political system that looked like a democracy but acted like a dictatorship. Since Cárdenas, elections have produced presidents serving nonrenewable six-year terms, and opposition parties have had candidates on the ballot. Yet until 1989 no opposition party was able to win a single state governorship, let alone the presidency. All winners belonged to the "official party": first the Callista National Revolutionary Party (PNR), then the Cardenista Party of the Mexican Revolution (PRM), and finally, after 1946, the Institutional Revolutionary Party (Partido Revolucionario Institucional, or PRI). Vargas Llosa's comments referred to this seemingly exceptional position among Latin American nations, especially the rule of one party with relatively little political opposition and a significant degree of consent among the governed. By contrast, most South American countries experienced a high degree of political instability and frequent military coups: between 1964 and 1976 Argentina, Brazil, and Chile all fell under the heavy hand of military rule. Although all three nations had returned to civilian rule by the time Vargas Llosa made his comments, their political systems appeared far more tenuous. One of the most important reasons for the political stability of the PRI system was the party's claim on the legacy of the Mexican Revolution—a claim tarnished indelibly with the blood of the students at Tlatelolco.

Thus as the sun rose on October 3, 1968, Mexico did not look so different from its authoritarian neighbors to the south. The regime's invocation of "the Revolution" as the justification for its existence sounded hollow indeed. The country appeared to have come full circle: from the authoritarian Porfiriato through the epic revolution to the authoritarian state of the PRI. As one historian rhetorically inquired in 1966, "Is the Mexican Revolution dead?"[1] Just four years before, another historian had written a book that implied an affirmative answer to this question, postulating that the period 1940–64 marked the transition "from revolution to evolution."[2] But the Tlatelolco massacre led scholars to use adjectives such as *demolished, abandoned,* and *betrayed* to describe the course of the revolution. Vargas Llosa's notion of the perfect dictatorship captures these tensions between popular expectations of continued reform and elite strategies to centralize political power by manipulating revolutionary discourse. Over time these tensions could not work themselves out, and ordinary Mexicans found room to articulate their own ideas of what an ever more distant revolution meant to them.

THE INSTITUTIONAL REVOLUTION

Mexico in the 1940s had changed greatly from Porfirian days. Cardenista reforms had shattered the hacienda system, nationalized the oil industry, and brought a political role to organized labor. While a powerful ruling party held sway in ways that Díaz and his allies never had, the political system also included opposition parties such as the conservative National Action Party (PAN). A sizable middle class bought both foreign-made and Mexican-made consumer goods. In the northwestern state of Baja California, vineyards and irrigated fields dotted a landscape that had been a vast expanse of desert only decades before. The country's communications and infrastructure had undergone significant improvements. In the age of the automobile, roads connected the cities and small towns. Mexico was becoming a significant tourist destination. Those who could afford movie tickets attended theaters that showed the latest productions from Hollywood and a burgeoning Mexican film industry, and radio brought news, political messages, and music to remote corners of the nation. Yet another mass medium, television, was in its infancy.

Still, in many ways, things had stayed the same. Despite a wave of urbanization brought on by industrialization and flight from the countryside during the decades of violence, Mexico remained a largely rural nation. The 1940 census estimated that almost 65 percent of the population resided in rural areas. The *ejido* system gave the state much of the power that the old hacendados had enjoyed. Real wages had increased, but a great majority of Mexicans remained in poverty, and illiteracy remained high despite the educational crusades of the 1920s and 1930s. Nor had the political revolution delivered liberty to all. As the dark and biting film satire *La Ley de Herodes* (Herod's Law) graphically illustrates, *jefes políticos* still lorded over villagers in rural areas, except they now wore the badge of an official party. As we have seen, controversy and allegations of fraud had followed Manuel Avila Camacho's triumph in the 1940 presidential vote. What the losers perceived as their inability to compete on equal ground left them embittered about a process they considered a farce. And the revolutionary regime continued to disenfranchise and marginalize women; promises to give them suffrage, full rights of land ownership, or even status as ejidal beneficiaries had not materialized.

However, if Avila Camacho started his tenure without a strong political mandate, he proved to possess the right political temperament for his time. Also known as the *presidente caballero*, or gentleman president, he desired to heal the remaining fissures among the people—most important, those separating secular from Catholic Mexico. He announced after his inauguration, "I am a believer. . . . I am a Catholic by origin, in moral feeling."[3] Stopping well short of announcing adherence to religious orthodoxy, these declarations indicated the mellowing of the revolution on the anticlerical front. The president postulated that one could be both a revolutionary and a Catholic, and that the church-state conflict would not continue during his administration.

Avila Camacho's *sexenio* (six-year tenure) enjoyed the good fortune of an improving economic and political climate. In particular, the new president took advantage of the stimulus provided by World War II to intensify the process of industrial development that had burgeoned since the late Cárdenas years. With the war, the prices of Mexican export products had skyrocketed, allowing the government to use revenue from these exports to stimulate industrialization. The U.S. entry into the war following the Japanese attack on Pearl Harbor on December 7, 1941, provided even greater opportunities. In addition, the U.S. wartime economy shifted away from producing exportable consumer products in order to manufacture items needed for the military campaigns in the Pacific and (later) Europe. Not surprisingly Avila Camacho committed his country to full participation in the war. Immediately after Pearl Harbor, he broke relations with the Axis Powers, and in March 1942 his government froze the assets of all Axis nationals. On May 23, 1942, Avila Camacho declared war on the Axis Powers after German U-boats torpedoed and sank two Mexican oil tankers in the Gulf of Mexico. Within a month, his government had seized all German, Italian, and Japanese businesses and jailed several hundred prominent Nazis. Avila Camacho also sent a squadron to fight in the Pacific theater, and tens of thousands of Mexican Americans fought in the U.S. armed forces.

World War II posed a set of unique challenges to a government that called itself revolutionary. Much of the revolutionary propaganda rested on the idea of economic nationalism, the notion that Mexicans needed to free their means of production from foreign control. In addition, Mexicans remembered the numerous instances in which the United States had intervened in their internal affairs. Just in the thirty short years of the revolution, U.S. troops had occupied their soil twice (Veracruz in 1914 and Chihuahua in 1916–17); U.S. Ambassador Henry L. Wilson had played a crucial role in the overthrow of Madero; and Mexico and the United States had stood on the brink of war during the Calles presidency. The wartime alliance required an effort to forget these recent conflicts, as well as to reach deeper into Mexican history to find a justification for collaborating with the northern colossus. One example was a deeply symbolic film made with the help of Hollywood filmmakers about Benito Juárez's struggle in 1864–67 to rescue his nation from the German-speaking emperor Maximilian. The 1943 film *Mexicanos al grito de Guerra!* (Mexicans to the Shout of War!) not only invoked the first five words of the national anthem; it also recalled a juncture when a heroic Mexican leader had worked with the Lincoln administration during a time of civil war in both the United States and Mexico. The war thus required a tweaking of the official discourse to the effect that "the Revolution" had made Mexico into a modern, democratic, and "Western" nation, eminently suitable as an ally of the United States, Great Britain, and France.

Even more important, the war contributed to Avila Camacho's efforts to promote national unity. In May 1941 he allowed former president Calles to return after five years of exile in San Diego. On September 15, 1942 — Independence Day — seven presidents posed on a platform erected on the Zócalo in a great display of national reconciliation. Fittingly, Cárdenas and Calles flanked Avila Camacho from the left and right, respectively, and Adolfo de la Huerta, Emilio Portes Gil, Pascual Ortiz Rubio, and Abelardo Rodríguez also attended. By all accounts, the event passed without an open display of animus. This photo opportunity displayed for all to see that the revolutionary family had finally come together (figure 7.1).

An excellent example of this rhetorical shift of the official revolutionary

FIGURE 7.1 During World War II, a moment of unity:
Abelardo L. Rodríguez, Plutarco Elías Calles, Manuel Avila
Camacho, and Lázaro Cárdenas. Fideicomiso Archivos Plutarco
Elías Calles y Fernando Torreblanca, Mexico City.

party toward a more politically centrist unity is the cult of General Alvaro
Obregón, celebrated each year on the anniversary of his assassination on
July 17. The ceremony takes place at the Obregón monument in San Angel,
Mexico City. As the last major revolutionary leader to die by assassina-
tion, Obregón offers an opportunity to highlight national unity and bridge
lingering resentments within the party. Not surprisingly it was President
Avila Camacho who turned the annual commemoration of Obregón's
assassination into a principal vehicle for official reflection on "the Revo-
lution" and the ruling party. Evidence of this refashioning appeared on
July 17, 1941, the first anniversary of the assassination celebrated under the
Avila Camacho administration. The association in charge of the Obregón

monument transformed Obregón's image as a slain caudillo into that of a national unifier and primary precursor of the ruling party. One of the event's speakers, formerly a close friend of Obregón, told the audience that Cárdenas had destroyed national unity by pitting the campesino against his landlord and the worker against his boss. He lamented that Mexico had "found many destroyers; great distributors of land; great expropriators of private wealth; great thieves of public wealth." "We have deviated," he declared, "from the authentic path of the Revolution."[4] Thus the speaker constructed the Mexican Revolution as a movement in the political center.

In 1946, Avila Camacho's last year in office, the Partido de la Revolución Mexicana underwent a reorganization and name change that reflected this shift toward the political middle. Unlike Cárdenas, who had brought new popular groups into his political alliance, Avila Camacho sought to put the revolutionary genie back in the bottle in order to focus on economic growth. Nonetheless the ruling elite knew that "the Revolution" as a concept remained critically important not only for political stability but also for the self-identification of the regime. Thus the party renamed itself the Partido Revolucionario Institucional (PRI), its name to this day. The structure of the reorganized party eliminated the military sector, a change that signaled the declining importance of military leaders within the party. The new party also concentrated more power in the hands of its National Executive Committee at the expense of the campesino, labor, and government employee sectors that remained vertically incorporated within the party. Four years later the party that did not lose elections even eliminated primaries — one of the ways that candidates at the regional and local levels could contest power. Henceforth running for office meant building a local power base and arriving at an understanding with a political patron at the next level above, rather than engaging in an electoral contest.

This new structure heralded the arrival of yet another generation at the helm of the revolutionary state: the *licenciados*, or college graduates, thus named to distinguish them from their predecessors, who had come out of the military, most of whom had no more than a middle school education. This new generation of leaders had no firsthand experience with the violent decade of the 1910s; indeed most of them had only heard their parents tell of it. The first of the licenciado presidents was Miguel Alemán Valdés, the son of a revolutionary leader and Obregón loyalist. In 1929 the elder Miguel Alemán had died fighting in the insurrection of José Gonzalo Escobar, who had taken up arms to fight the Calles-dominated government in the name of the slain caudillo. The younger Alemán had served as secretary of gobernación under Avila Camacho and had thus been responsible for internal security during World War II.

The Alemán administration marked a watershed moment in the entrenchment of the ruling party. It was under Alemán that the PRI state acquired its well-known characteristics: presidential absolutism, one-party monopoly on power, manipulation of mass organizations, the promotion of a nationalist unifying ideology in place of class and ideological differences, the elimination of the political Left from the official coalition, and state domination of the labor movement. Alemán's inauguration also signified the ascent of a conservative postrevolutionary oligarchy of financiers, businessmen, and industrialists. As one historian observed, "Alemán . . . profoundly changed the nation's course by allying the state with moneyed interests, wooing foreign capital, accelerating industrialization, and undoing or mitigating many of the reforms promulgated by Cárdenas."[5] In addition, Alemán brought a highly corrupt clique to power, as the movie *La Ley de Herodes* graphically illustrates by way of a junkyard operator who extorts thousands of pesos from an impoverished village simply by brandishing his authority as the local *jefe municipal*. During his rule, government officials illegally transferred funds from federal, state, and municipal accounts; politicians secured government contracts for themselves or members of their immediate family; and the famous *mordida*, or bribe—a standby in Mexico since precolonial times—became a common way of influencing decisions large and small. One prominent historian at the Colegio de México put it well when he stated, "The dishonesty of the revolutionary leaders, more than anything else . . . has split the very heart of the Mexican Revolution."[6]

No organization reflected this shift toward institutionalization more than the Confederation of Mexican Workers (CTM). The new leader of the labor federation, Fidel Velázquez Sánchez, was a former milkman and Zapatista. Heading an affiliate union of Luis Morones's Regional Mexican Workers' Federation (CROM), Velázquez broke with the Federation in 1929 and joined Vicente Lombardo Toledano in establishing the Cardenista CTM in 1936. In 1941 he succeeded Lombardo as CTM's leader, forced Communists and Lombardistas out of the union leadership, and moved the organization to the political center. Velázquez remained the

CTM's principal figure until 1997. During his tenure, *charrismo* (boss rule) increasingly characterized the labor federation, as he repressed democratic tendencies inside the CTM and in independent unions throughout the country as a whole. Under Velázquez, the CTM became a reliable and often uncritical appendage of the official party and, by extension, the president. Like Alemán, Velázquez parroted the party line about pursuing "the Revolution's" aims of national development and social justice; also like the president, the labor czar cared far more about the former than the latter.

Nonetheless the PRI was far from a monolithic party bound to the mere whim of the president. The three sectors within the PRI — labor, peasants, and "popular," a catch phrase that combined middle-class party members as well as women, youth, street vendors, and many others — remained in constant competition, as did the state governors and mayors who lobbied for the attention of the central government. At least every six years, the jockeying among several *presidenciables* (plausible presidential aspirants) to receive the president's *dedazo*, or nomination as the official party's candidate, brought these groups into play. Although the president's authority informally extended to wielding decisive influence in the selection of state governors and even *diputados* and *senadores* in the federal congress (a legislature that never once seriously challenged an executive initiative in the period covered in this chapter), the nation's top PRIista often did so in ways that accommodated local power structures. Finally, Mexicans expressed their opinions through biting political humor that collectively influenced the policymaking process in ways that historians have only begun to understand.

Indeed lest one desire to promote a top-down, Mexico City–centered focus on the PRI's ability to maintain power, one must analyze as well the "informal" local and regional power dynamics involved in the PRI's "perfect dictatorship." As recent scholarship has demonstrated, the presence of the PRI throughout Mexico has always been uneven. Even more important, the rule of the state has always been shaped in many ways at the regional and local level. As with the 1920s and 1930s, the post-1940 state did not simply impose itself upon the countryside; rather it contended with, and worked through, the regional and municipal structures of power and the historical relations of control that it found throughout the nation. While we should pay attention to the *formal* corporatist structure of PRI rule, it should not completely dominate our understanding of how the

PRI negotiated its power across Mexico. The state and its ruling party constantly needed to respond to various forms of resistance and accommodation at the grassroots level, in ways that are specific to local and regional populations and circumstances. Occurring outside of the formal political arena, these subnational contingencies represent significant historical, political, cultural, and economic factors, variables such as traditional indigenous authority in highland Chiapas and cults of the Virgin in devoutly Catholic Michoacán.

All of these local and regional variables became crucial sites of conflict and negotiation for the ongoing rule of the PRI. They not only served to complicate or hinder the party's national, centralist program, but they also shaped local people's daily lives and understandings of themselves and, in turn, of the state and their place within or outside it. Mirroring the early history of the PNR, when the ruling party was a conglomerate of regional parties and their bosses, local and regional cultural factors influenced and created political forms after 1946. The way the PRI responded and adapted to these forms determined the successful transition from a postrevolutionary government with few centralized institutional mechanisms to one with an array of corporatist and regional mechanisms of control. The PRI was born of, and existed with, powerful regional bosses and caciques who carefully measured their relations with the party, shrewdly using both accommodation and resistance to ensure their own control over local economic and political worlds. In Chiapas and Michoacán, in Yucatán and Chihuahua—indeed across the breadth of the country—local history, identity, and politics informed the ways the PRI and the people negotiated rule beyond the bounds of Mexico City. In the process, grassroots dynamics and social movements challenged the form and function of centralized rule and helped shape the ways the PRI modified its policies and positions.

Thus, rather than a large Leviathan spreading its fearsome girth across the Mexican landscape, the PRI has been shaped and structured by the very subjects it attempts to dominate and discipline. The PRI is a more subtle creature that has based its longevity on *infiltrating* local realities, co-opting whenever possible—offering local power brokers positions within the PRI hierarchy—and modifying its methods of rule according to the cultural requirements of local populations. Occasionally the PRI has imposed its will rather clumsily, as in the case of the Tlatelolco massacre. But more often than not, there was a dialectic at work in which the center and the regions and localities shaped one another, in constant motion. The result was a modus vivendi that should dispel any reflexive notion of a brutish Leviathan unwilling to negotiate its rule. The "perfect dictatorship" was what one Mexican historian has dubbed a *dictablanda*, or soft authoritarian state very much aware of its weakness, rather than a *dictadura* that unflinchingly imposed its decisions.[7] Another historian has pointed out, "Precisely because the postrevolutionary process of state formation in Mexico engaged local communities so intensely, the very construction of state principles and ideals depended upon how they were understood, reshaped, and discarded at the local level."[8]

THE REVOLUTION IS CAPITALIST AND ANTI-COMMUNIST

We can find one example of such a dialectic in the state's projection of Mexican nationalism in the Cold War era and the ways this projection reflected on a revolution that appeared to fade in the rearview mirror. The creation of the PRI coincided with the coming of the Cold War, a global (and Latin American) confrontation that circumscribed and redefined both the official and the popular discourse about the revolution. During World War II, fascism had been the enemy, and Mexican Communists enjoyed a modicum of toleration. The victory over the Axis Powers, however, had left the Western European Allies exhausted, leaving the United States and the Soviet Union as the world's preeminent powers. The two rookie superpowers soon squabbled over control of Europe and East Asia. Soviet-supported governments imposed Communist rule in the Eastern European countries occupied by the Red Army at the end of World War II. In 1949 the triumph of Mao Zedong's Communist movement in China — a triumph achieved with only limited Soviet assistance — demonstrated the ongoing appeal of radical ideas of social transformation. Alarmed at what appeared to be a victorious march of Communist governments, the U.S. government formulated the Doctrine of Containment, which called upon the "free world" (that is, capitalist nations) to fight the worldwide spread of Communism. As part of its campaign to ensure cordial relations with the United States, the Alemán government eagerly seized upon containment discourse to portray itself and the revolution that it claimed to represent as part of the free world. Anti-Communism became official policy, as Alemán proclaimed Communism incompatible with *mexicanidad*. In tandem with this anti-Communist rhetoric, U.S. representations of the Mexican Revolution came to stress its positive nature, as well as its alleged fundamental affinity with North American values. North Americans perceived that their differences with the mildly social democratic PRI were small compared to fundamental conflicts with the Communist Soviet Union and China.

A good example of this emerging view of the Mexican Revolution as an anti-Communist and capitalist movement is the renowned Hollywood film *Viva Zapata!*, released in 1952 with Marlon Brando in the lead role. The director Elia Kazan and the screenwriter John Steinbeck were liberal Cold Warriors who cast Zapata as a defender of the time-honored values of life and liberty. Brando's Zapata was a handsome, charismatic, and honest campesino leader fighting not only for land but also for the right to local self-determination. Although it recognized the struggle for land as the central pillar of Zapatismo, the film emphasized the hero's tragic fight against scheming military dictators and their civilian stooges. *Viva Zapata!* thus played to a U.S. audience that wanted to see the popular hero as a Mexican Tom Paine fighting for liberty. As depicted in the film, Zapata defined his movement with limited input from below, and the audience caught few glimpses of the grinding poverty that had prompted campesinos to take up arms against the repressive Díaz regime. Indeed the land issue was cast as a struggle between valiant peasants and greedy landowners over property stolen by the latter, not as a conflict in which the notion of unqualified landownership was very much at stake.

The official cult of Obregón offers another illuminating window onto this changing discourse. Since 1943 the Obregón monument has displayed the caudillo's famous arm, lost in battle against the Villistas and preserved by Obregón's private physician in formaldehyde. This public display made the monument into a tourist attraction as the only place in the country where a body part of a political leader was on view. In the words of one cultural commentator, the arm "infused charisma into a bureaucracy that insistently called itself revolutionary."[9] The sacralization of the limb was part of a larger aim: Obregón's apotheosis as a revolutionary hero to assist the PRI's claim to a revolutionary heritage that the party had in fact abandoned. In 1950 Luis L. León, a stalwart of the ruling party since its founding and a close personal friend of both Obregón and Calles, announced, "The Revolution is a sacred movement. . . . To defame the great revolutionaries is to insult and betray the Revolution." He called upon revolutionaries "of all the 'isms' to express solidarity with [this] great movement and always know how to defend it," and he asked his audience to defend "not only Obregón, but also the triumphs, the greatness, and the accomplishment of all the dead leaders of the Revolution."[10] Not surprisingly, not everyone was happy with this interpretation. For example, one of the caudillo's sons, Humberto Obregón, opposed León's appropriation of his father's symbolism. In a letter he portrayed his father as "a caudillo of a revolution of extreme leftist tendencies." Demonstrating the continuing battle over the legacy of the revolution, he labeled the PRI a "group of plutocrats" that resembled the inner circle of the Old Regime of Porfirio Díaz.[11]

At the same time, the PRI realized the need to celebrate the other dead heroes of the revolution as well. It found that opportunity in the Monumento a la Revolución. Unlike the Obregón monument, the regime had thus far not utilized the structure for official celebrations, in all likelihood because popular memory associated it too closely with Calles's Maximato. As if to show that Alemán had no such compunctions, he organized an annual November 20 commemoration. Over time that monument, like the one to Obregón, became the repository of revolutionary relics. In 1942 Congress ordered the transfer of Carranza's ashes to the monument, and over the next decades the remains of Madero (1960), Calles (1969), Cárdenas (1970), and Villa (1976) joined those of Carranza. Thus, beginning in the late 1940s, the Monumento a la Revolución eclipsed the Obregón monument as the primary locus of the memory of "the Revolution," moving the emphasis of the commemorations toward a more inclusive celebration of the recent past.

Ordinary Mexicans, on the other hand, embraced popular culture to create their own rituals that reflected the legacy of the revolution. In particular the advent and rapid spread of television communicated cultural symbols relating to what it meant to be Mexican in ways that no other medium had been able to do. Mexican cinema was also experiencing a golden age, in which the national industry created unforgettable stars. For example, in 1957 the funeral of the popular singer and actor Pedro Infante, following a tragic plane crash, attracted 150,000 people, far more than those of the major revolutionary heroes combined. Another popular actor who represented mexicanidad was José María Moreno, better known as Cantinflas. In his many roles, Cantinflas represented the *naco* or *pelado*, the "uncultured" and impoverished urban lumpen despised by the upper classes for his rough manners and poor taste. As one historian put it, Cantinflas "symbolized the underdog who triumphed through trickery over more powerful opponents."[12] Finally, there was the famous wrestler El Santo, the masked, premier practitioner of the uniquely Mexican sport of *lucha libre*. Also known as the "Silver-Masked Man," El Santo made his debut performance in 1942 by defeating seven opponents in an eight-man battle royal, a form of wrestling in which multiple opponents fight each other in the same contest until only one of them is left standing. His wrestling career lasted almost five decades, and he remains one of the sport's greatest heroes. El Santo appeared in movies and comic books and came to represent the ordinary Mexican's everyday struggle for justice.

The disconnect between PRI propaganda and the desires and expectations of ordinary people was not lost on Alemán and the PRI, especially as the nation underwent a serious economic crisis after the Allied victory in World War II. Between 1946 and 1950 Mexico experienced low rates of growth occasioned by a drop in postwar commodity prices, high inflation due to a steep decline in the value of the peso, and high unemployment caused in part by the return of tens of thousands of Mexican *braceros* who were no longer needed in the U.S. economy. As real wages dropped precipitously, Alemán waited in vain for the kind of U.S. economic assistance that was rebuilding Western Europe and Japan. Even though Mexico and several other Latin American nations had made material contributions to the war, the U.S. government did not reward them for their loyalty, believing the western hemisphere to be relatively safe from Communist infiltration. Soon Mexicans from all walks of life grew restless about the deteriorating conditions in their country. In 1951 five thousand miners from the northern town of Nueva Rosita, accompanied by ten thousand family members, marched all the way to Mexico City in a "caravan of hunger" designed to demonstrate their plight to President Alemán. Their immediate grievance was the PRI's takeover of the miners' union, but a stunning decline in real wages served as the backdrop for this desperate action; it took the miners fifty days and nights to reach the nation's capital. It was a testament to the PRI's grip on news coverage that the media hardly covered this arduous trek.

Another protest movement had coalesced around the aging Zapatista Rubén Jaramillo. Born in 1900, Jaramillo had joined Zapata's army at the tender age of fourteen and continued the fight after his leader's murder in 1919. Encouraged by the Cardenista land reform but believing that Zapata's legacy remained incomplete until all land was in the hands of campesinos, he organized a cane cutters' union that rose up in arms in 1943. Two years later, following an amnesty from the state, Jaramillo founded an agrarian party in Morelos that was soon repressed by the local branch of the PRI. In the course of his struggles within and outside the system, Jaramillo inspired a new generation to continue to fight for Zapata's ideals of "land and liberty," thereby validating the continued vitality of revolutionary icons and ideas at the popular level. For the Jaramillistas, Zapata's legacy was more palpable and politically nourishing than Obregón's, and they pushed for a continued commitment to land reform rather than vacuous homage to dead leaders at the Obregón monument, the Monumento a la Revolución, and Zapata's gravesite. In Morelos and elsewhere, popular revolutionary legacies held greater relevance than state-sponsored propaganda designed to cloak a less than revolutionary reality.

Alemán felt the need for a strong economic stimulus to address simultaneously the economic downturn and the criticism of his administration. He committed his government to state-sponsored economic development to guide the nation out of its postwar doldrums. The president was familiar with the argument of the Argentine economist Raúl Prebisch that Latin America's structural dependence on U.S. and European manufactured products lay at the heart of its economic malaise. Prebisch counseled Latin American leaders to act assertively to prevent further erosion of the region's terms of trade, and specifically to provide government funding for import-substitution industrialization, even at the cost of running a high budget deficit. Alemán's government spent millions of pesos to build up industry, a sector that had already grown considerably during the 1920s and 1930s. It imposed punitive tariffs on more efficiently produced foreign imports that competed with Mexican products. The government also invested in the nation's infrastructure to attract tourism to resorts such as Acapulco, as well as to picturesque colonial cities and towns in the states of Guanajuato, Michoacán, Morelos, and Puebla. These moves came at a fortuitous time, as the Korean War (1950–53) motivated a remobilization of the U.S. military complex, which once again accelerated U.S. demand for Mexican raw materials.

As a result, Mexico experienced high economic growth during an era many observers dubbed the "Mexican Miracle." Measured at the macro-economic level, the Mexican Miracle appeared to yield impressive results. Annual growth rates averaged 6.4 percent between 1940 and 1970, and per capita gross domestic product doubled between 1950 and 1973, adjusted for inflation. These boom years witnessed stunning productivity increases in both industry and agriculture. Dozens of multinational corporations built partial assembly plants in Mexico, and a "green revolution" occurred as new planting and irrigation techniques expanded both arable acreage and yields nationwide. The emergence of Acapulco as a world-class resort heralded the golden age of Mexican tourism, when millions of North Americans and Europeans annually visited the country's beaches and cultural attractions. By 1968 workers had finally recovered, in real terms, the purchasing power they had enjoyed at the end of the Cárdenas years. Economic growth in the United States attracted a new wave of immigrant labor, and Mexicans in the United States sent back sizable remittances to their families.

Significant advances in education and health care accompanied economic growth. Illiteracy fell from about 70 percent in 1940 to approximately 20 percent in 1960. Following advances made under the Sonorans and Cárdenas, improved sanitation contributed to the eradication of yellow fever and the most virulent forms of amoebic dysentery. With the help of widespread vaccination and antimosquito campaigns, the government also made significant progress against malaria and other infectious diseases. As a result, the annual death rate declined from twenty-three per thousand in 1940 to ten per thousand in 1970. Infant mortality dropped dramatically.

Of course, there was a downside to such progress. The Mexican Miracle accentuated rather than attenuated social inequality. At 0.56, Mexico's Gini coefficient during the 1950s and 1960s (a measure of the degree of social inequality) was the second highest in Latin America, behind only Brazil's. Mexican families remained large, and few Mexicans used contraception due to its cost and prevailing opposition from the Catholic Church. The fertility rate remained stable even as infant mortality declined, and the population grew at increasing annual rates: 2.7 percent in the 1940s, 3.1 percent in the 1950s, and 3.4 percent in the 1960s. Thus the population increased by 150 percent between 1940 and 1970, when almost fifty million lived in Mexico, half of whom were under the age of twenty. No economic model could accommodate such explosive population growth.

In addition, the so-called Miracle belied the uneven nature of development. Economic growth primarily benefited manufacturing, export agriculture, tourism, and the border region. In the heavily indigenous rural South, however, subsistence agriculture continued to struggle as the population exploded and the government kept the ejidos undercapitalized and undersupplied. In addition, industrialization attracted millions of rural migrants to the cities, and not all of them could find work for decent pay. By the 1960s a ring of *ciudades perdidas* ("lost cities," or shantytowns) surrounded the nation's major urban centers. Runaway urbanization of this kind induced the government to pay even less attention to the languishing countryside. In addition, high inflation initially accompanied industrialization, and in 1954 alone the peso lost half of its value against the U.S. dollar. In response, the government intervened to stabilize wages, prices, and currency exchange rates, a strategy known as *desarrollo estabilizador*, or stabilizing development. While this strategy limited inflation for the next twenty years, it also circumscribed salary and wage increases for both workers and professionals. State-assisted development also imposed a heavy burden on the federal treasury and created a new kind of dependence on capital goods such as industrial machinery. As early as 1958 Franz Böker, a German merchant and longtime resident of Mexico City since Porfirian days, wrote, "As a European who does not believe in miracles, I can only express my greatest concern about the future. . . . The expensive machinery and technological innovations [necessary for industrialization] threaten Mexico's foreign currency holdings no less than the previous imports of manufactured goods."[13]

The overriding emphasis on modernity and economic progress further moved the PRI away from its revolutionary roots. The growth of a new bourgeoisie under the aegis of what Böker called "firmly entrenched ex-revolutionaries" contributed, in the judgment of one historian, to the maturing of a commercially constructed mexicanidad, an "attempt on the part of the state to create a mass media–based cultural nationalism."[14] As long as the macroeconomic figures looked impressive to the government, and as long as both campesino and labor groups remained loyal, the official party felt little incentive to change. Thus until the 1960s the PRI did little more than tinker with Alemán's system; in 1953, for example, Congress finally implemented women's suffrage, decades after the measure had first been debated. Otherwise the developmentalist wing of the PRI remained firmly in charge. In the 1952 presidential elections, Alemán's hand-picked successor, Adolfo Ruiz Cortines, easily thwarted a challenge from General Miguel Henríquez Guzmán, whose supporters included many former Zapatistas and other agrarians and workers dissatisfied with the pro-business orientation of the Alemanistas.

REVOLUTIONS "GOOD" AND "BAD"

Significantly the PRI showed the ability to engage in self-correction when popular pressure and political circumstances so dictated. In 1958, as women prepared to vote in their first presidential elections, the PRI leadership was well aware of the fact that its prior three presidential administrations had successively steered the party and the country to the Right. Presidents Avila Camacho, Alemán, and Ruiz Cortines (1952–58) had presided over governments that privileged economic development over social justice. At a time when Brazil and other Latin American nations experimented with left-wing populism, the PRI sought to correct its course. Encouraged by former president Cárdenas, Ruiz Cortines nominated as his successor the secretary of labor, Adolfo López Mateos, a leader with progressive credentials who had distinguished himself by successfully mediating a series of labor conflicts.

Immediately after his inauguration, the railroad workers, a radical segment within the Mexican working class since the beginning of the revolution, decided to test López Mateos's political persuasion. Their strike targeted a government-owned sector rather than greedy foreign investors. President López Mateos wasted no time demonstrating that he would not tolerate labor unrest in state-owned businesses. He forcibly broke up the strike and arrested the leader of the railroad workers, Demetrio Vallejo, on charges that he promoted "social dissolution." The president also ordered the jailing of the Marxist muralist David Alfaro Siqueiros, who had declared his solidarity with the strikers.

However, López Mateos subsequently moved several degrees to the left. He signaled his intention to address one of the workers' major grievances, invoking a constitutional article that mandated profit sharing. In a speech in Guaymas, Sonora, on July 1, 1959, the Mexican president declared that he stood at "the extreme left within the limits set by the Constitution."[15] A few months later he nationalized the country's electrical industry; and beginning in 1962 the government required most Mexican businesses to distribute a portion of their profits among their employees. López Mateos also offered the agrarian rebel Rubén Jaramillo full protection in exchange for laying down his arms (again), and he appointed him a special delegate of the Confederación Nacional Campesina (CNC) in Morelos. And much as Cárdenas had forged his brand of populism by visiting every corner of the republic, López Mateos visited sixteen different nations in the Americas, Asia, and Europe in an effort to become a major player in the "nonaligned" movement, which sought to assert a middle ground between the U.S.-led North American Treaty Organization and the Soviet-led Warsaw Pact. The Mexican president also received visits from such dignitaries as India's Jawaharlal Nehru and Yugoslavia's Josip Broz Tito. His extensive travels earned him the moniker "López Paseos" (a loose translation would be "the Peripatetic López"). This joke aside, Mexicans from all walks of life held López Mateos in high regard. Whereas Cárdenas would have alarmed foreign and domestic investors alike if he had declared himself on the "extreme left" within the Constitution, conservative entrepreneurs and journalists reacted to López Mateos's speech in Guaymas with indifference, knowing full well that the PRI machine would keep the nation on its sure path of state-sponsored capitalist development.

The Cuban Revolution provided an external stimulus to this more progressive and nationalist posture, and hence another example of the dialectic that shaped the PRI amid pressures from without and from below. On New Year's Day 1959, Fidel Castro's bearded rebels rode triumphantly into Havana, ending a three-year guerrilla campaign against the U.S.-backed dictator Fulgencio Batista. This guerrilla campaign had originated on Mexican soil, as Castro and his group (which included the young Argentine revolutionary Che Guevara) had trained in Veracruz and departed for Cuba from the port city. As the first social revolution in Latin America since the Mexican Revolution to triumph by the force of arms, the Cuban Revolution invited comparisons with the Mexican case. From the outset, that comparison showed the Cuban Revolution to be far more ideologically focused and their leaders to be far more radical in their methods. After his victory, Castro referred to the Mexican Revolution as a guide during the struggle against the Batista regime. What he failed to mention was that the Mexican experience had helped convince him to conduct his revolution rather differently. He desired to avoid the fate of Madero, Carranza, and Obregón, all murdered by their opponents, by quickly and decisively consolidating his power.

Soon, the "romantic image of Castro's Revolution began to catch the public imagination" in Mexico.[16] In February 1959 twelve rebels from Castro's days in the Sierra Maestra visited Mexico, and the group found an enthusiastic reception. As the year unfolded, Cuba's early revolutionary program struck a chord with many Mexicans as well. As the Mexican ambassador in Havana, Gilberto Bosques, pointed out, Castro's policies, which included agrarian reform and the nationalization of foreign property, resembled Cardenista initiatives. Bosques even went so far as to lament the lack of an international propaganda office for the Cuban Revolution. "This revolution," he noted, "deserves good spokespeople."[17] Of course, he would not have to wait long, as the Cuban Revolution produced one of the most enduring icons of the twentieth century in Che Guevara. Guevara became a symbol for social revolution in Latin America, immortalized by the famous *guerrillero heróico* image created by the Cuban photographer Alberto Korda in 1960. Even today Korda's image endures on T-shirts and bumper stickers, commodified and often divorced from its political message. In Mexico Guevara continues to serve as a reminder of a more radical revolution than the Mexican one—devoted, at least in theory, to the redemption of the poor. At a time when many veterans of the Mexican Revolution remained active in public life, the events in Cuba resuscitated debates about the nature of Mexico's own revolutionary upheaval.

A good example was the emergence of former president Cárdenas as the principal Mexican advocate for the Cuban Revolution. Since his departure from the presidency, Cárdenas had remained involved in politics as the unofficial leader of the left wing within the official party. A revered figure within Mexico and much of Latin America, the ex-president had paid close attention to progressive movements in other Latin American nations, particularly the democratic governments of Juan José Arévalo and Jacobo Arbenz in Guatemala (1944–54). Known as the "Ten Years of Spring," these two administrations had sought to weaken the power of the giant banana companies and return land to Guatemala's impoverished indigenous campesinos. Cárdenas had praised Arévalo as an "example for oppressed peoples."[18] In 1949, as U.S. foreign policy increasingly targeted social reformist governments like Guatemala's as enemies of the free world, Cárdenas had pledged his support to Arévalo against "the armed aggression of the great interests opposed to progress."[19] Five years later, when the U.S. government labeled the Arbenz administration a Communist threat, Cárdenas came to its defense, professing his "personal friendship and sympathy" with Guatemala's experiment in social reform.[20] When a CIA-assisted coup overthrew Arbenz in June 1954 and ushered in a repressive military regime that would remain in power for almost forty years — an event witnessed by Guevara, among others — Cárdenas's principled position appeared prescient. Five years later, when another Latin American revolution promised a better life to the poor, many Mexicans looked to the ex-president for support. On July 26, 1959, the anniversary of Castro's attack on the Moncada barracks, Cárdenas traveled to Havana to show his personal support for Castro's triumph. In an effort to draw parallels between the Mexican and Cuban experiences, he declared, "The agrarian reform in Mexico received [its] most virulent attacks from the enemies of an anti-feudal struggle. . . . We Mexicans know well that revolutions are not exported and imported. We respect the integrity of emancipation movements in other countries, as we have asked for respect for the Mexican Revolution."[21]

Prodded by Cárdenas, López Mateos recognized the symbolic power of the Cuban Revolution. He knew that Castro's triumph could remind Mexicans that the momentum of their own revolution had long expired. Siqueiros, for one, noted in a newspaper interview that Castro's movement had left the Mexican Revolution far behind. Therefore the president defended Castro both against the United States and against conservatives within his own country, who sponsored anti-Communist demonstrations. In June 1960, on the occasion of the visit of President Osvaldo Dorticós of Cuba, López Mateos declared, "We, who have gone through similar historical stages, understand and value the Cuban effort at change. . . . We trust that the Cuban Revolution will be — just as ours has been — one more step toward the greatness of America."[22]

This verbal support of the Cuban Revolution, however, soon became more difficult to sustain. Even during Dorticós's visit, the conservative newspaper *Excélsior* had dissented from López Mateos, stating that the Cuban government was a satellite of Moscow. Afterward many Mexicans, particularly the Alemán faction, liked even less what they heard about Cuba. As tensions grew between Castro and the United States, the new Cuban government ordered the execution of hundreds of prominent Batista supporters, landlords, and leaders of the army and it increasingly turned toward socialism. In April 1961 a CIA-sponsored invasion near the Bay of Pigs sought to put an end to the Cuban Revolution. After quashing this invasion, Castro and Guevara moved their revolution even further to the Left, expropriating almost all private property and forging an alliance with the Soviet Union.

The Bay of Pigs invasion demonstrated the ambivalence of the López Mateos administration toward revolution in the present rather than the past tense. The president faced the problem of placating two opposing groups. On the one hand, the leftists and nationalists around Cárdenas demanded that López Mateos support and defend Castro, whom they considered the new standard-bearer for social revolution. The former president led a demonstration against U.S. intervention on the Zócalo in Mexico City and even announced that he might go to Cuba at the head of thousands of volunteers, organized into "Pancho Villa Brigades," to help Castro fight U.S. invaders, should that become necessary. Cárdenas's actions — unprecedented because they amounted to a critique of the current government — created an image problem for the government. The left wing within the PRI argued that Castro, and not López Mateos, represented revolutionary change. And on April 18, 1961, just days after the invasion, angry protesters sacked the Instituto Cultural México-Norteamericano in Morelia, Michoacán, an institution that was a visible symbol of U.S.-Mexican cooperation. This leftist response might be summed up by the cries of "Cuba sí, Yanquis no!" that emanated from large-scale demonstrations in the capital and several other Mexican cities.[23] On the other hand, former presidents Alemán and Rodríguez led a conservative faction within the PRI that urged the Mexican government to condemn the Castro regime. This faction considered Communism anathema and "un-Mexican." Also on the Right, pro-clerical elements shouted, "Cristianismo sí, comunismo no!" Only in their rejection of U.S. military intervention in Latin America did these ideologically opposed groups find common ground.

Seeking to maintain a balancing act between the two camps, López Mateos launched an abstract defense of Cuba's right to national self-determination. Without commenting on the merits of either the Castro regime or its opponents, his ambassador to the Organization of American States (OAS) made an impassioned plea to his colleagues to prevent further assistance to rebels trying to overthrow a sovereign government. López Mateos's support of time-honored diplomatic principles cloaked the fact that he avoided Cuban officials after the Bay of Pigs invasion. The Mexican president also stopped emphasizing the similarities between the historical experiences of Mexico and Cuba. From the standpoint of the Mexican elite, Castro was a Marxist dictator who embraced an economic doctrine alien to Latin America instead of pursuing the rightful path of fighting for land and liberty represented by the idealized "Revolution" represented by the PRI. That "Revolution," the origins of which now lay half a century in the past, remained an anti-Communist revolution firmly allied with the capitalist West — a "good" revolution counterposed to the "bad" Cuban example. In this context, rebels such as Jaramillo were no longer as useful as they had been only a few years before. On May 26, 1962, the judicial police and the army arrested Jaramillo, together with his wife and three children, and assassinated them.

However, since the polarity between a good and a bad revolution was useful to the Mexican government, it continued to defend Cuban sovereignty even as it cracked down on rebels and protesters at home. Thus López Mateos's representative voted against a motion in the OAS to expel Cuba in early 1962. At the end of that year, unlike most other Latin American nations, Mexico did not break diplomatic relations with the Castro government after the stationing of Soviet missiles on Cuban soil led to the infamous Cuban Missile Crisis in October 1962. In 1964 López Mateos refused to heed an OAS resolution that mandated the suspension of air service and other commercial travel to Cuba. Thus Mexico City became the only possible layover point in the western hemisphere for travel between Havana and any other city in the Americas.

One reason the Mexican government increasingly distanced itself from the Cuban Revolution was the increasing political polarization within Mexico itself. In August 1961 Cárdenas helped found the left-wing Movimiento de Liberación Nacional (National Liberation Movement, or MLN), a group committed to national control over resources, social justice, and peace. In response, right-wing elements coalesced under the Frente Cívico Mexicano de Afirmación Revolucionaria (Mexican Civic

Front of Revolutionary Affirmation), a faction organized with the help of former presidents Alemán and Rodríguez and several notable ex-Callistas. In December 1961, concerned about a possible split in the official party, López Mateos invited all seven living former presidents to join his cabinet. Fortunately for him, all of them accepted his invitation and restored a semblance of unity to the national government. Cárdenas thus turned his back on the MLN and showed that loyalty to the party ultimately trumped all other considerations. Throughout the remainder of his life, he remained circumspect about supporting other radical protest movements with agrarian or pro-labor aims, such as the rural insurgency led by the teachers Arturo Gámiz and Pablo Gómez in Chihuahua.

These mounting tensions between the grassroots and an increasingly authoritarian state that labeled itself revolutionary ultimately culminated in the student movement of 1968. This movement mirrored other radical student-led protests around the world, particularly in France, Germany, and the United States. With its epicenter in the nation's capital, and principally among scions of the middle class, it was by far the most prominent and visible protest movement against the PRI, and one in which women shared center stage. The students took advantage of the spotlight cast on their city by the 1968 Summer Olympics, the first such event to be held in the developing world. Their demands were primarily of a political nature: release of all political prisoners, implementation of a democratic structure of governance at the national university, dismissal of a police chief known for his brutality, and dissolution of the paramilitary riot police known as *granaderos*. If students believed they would be able to express their grievances as freely as their counterparts in the United States and Europe, however, their government soon dashed these hopes. On August 27 approximately half a million protesters gathered in the Zócalo, only to be dispersed when tanks moved into the area after nightfall. In mid-September the army occupied the campus of the national university and made hundreds of arrests (figure 7.2).

The bloody massacre of October 2, 1968, was therefore both the climax of a long confrontation and the beginning of a new era. The conflict had deep roots in the public's disaffection with the PRI, a ruling party that appeared to have forgotten its revolutionary origins. The massacre had wide-ranging effects besides destroying the time-worn myths of the PRI. It confronted protesters with the choice between giving up the struggle

FIGURE 7.2 Police hold students at gunpoint inside an apartment building in Tlatelolco, Mexico City, after the massacre of October 2, 1968. Associated Press.

for reform and continuing the struggle underground, thereby sowing the seeds of the armed rebellions of the 1970s. The carnage also recalled Cananea and Río Blanco, the most notable Porfirian-era protests broken up by state-sponsored violence. [Many Mexicans — including noted historians — believed that their country had come full circle in the past sixty to seventy years.]

On October 19, 1971, two somber men took the stage during a ceremony at the Monumento a la Revolución. With President Luis Echeverría Alvarez in attendance, a man who had played a significant role in the Tlatelolco massacre as the secretary of gobernación, Plutarco Elías Calles Chacón and Cuauhtémoc Cárdenas read prepared speeches to reflect on an ironic twist of history. One year before, Lázaro Cárdenas had passed away, precisely twenty-five years after Plutarco Elías Calles's death on October 19, 1945. Now the monument housed the remains of the two men who had contributed more than any other to the creation of the architecture of the postrevolutionary Mexican state. On the occasion of this joint anniversary, their sons read eulogies that reflected not only on historic coincidence but also on their fathers as the twin pillars of the ruling party. It was time, Cuauhtémoc Cárdenas declared, for the "authentic revolutionaries to close ranks." Aco Elías Calles concurred: "Men are ephemeral . . . and what persists . . . is the ideals of our Revolution, aspiring toward a better humanity, always to be perfected. These ideals need to unify us rather than divide us."[24]

These statements revealed not only the PRI's official version of history—one that emphasized the existence of a revolutionary family capable of working out its many squabbles—but also the crisis of the party's brand after Tlatelolco. In particular, Cuauhtémoc Cárdenas's comments expressed the need for unity because the massacre had shattered the party's cherished myths. Not surprisingly the massacre defined the era that followed, one in which the embers of revolution would continue to burn even while "the Revolution" sponsored by the official party had lost all momentum. *Critical of PRI*

My real commander is the people.

— SUBCOMANDANTE MARCOS

THE EMBERS OF REVOLUTION, 1968–2000 | 8

uring a dinner in July 1995, Alejandra García Quintanilla reflected
on her recent experiences with the Zapatista movement in Chiapas.
A Monterrey native who had relocated to Mérida, Yucatán, and a
scholar of Mexican history with a doctorate from the University of
North Carolina at Chapel Hill, Alejandra wore a traditional Maya *huipil*
dress. Her face was radiant as she described her involvement in running
food and medicine into the highlands near the provincial center of San
Cristóbal de las Casas, appropriately named after the Franciscan friar who
had first brought the plight of indigenous campesinos to the world's attention in the sixteenth century. Before graduate school, Alejandra had spent
time underground as a member of various clandestine opposition movements. Now she formed part of a vast network in civil society that assisted
the Ejército Zapatista de Liberación Nacional (Zapatista National Liberation Army, or EZLN). The year before, the EZLN had seized San Cristóbal
and several nearby towns and villages, but the federal army had encircled
the movement, which drew its name from Emiliano Zapata and called
for a wide array of improvements for the country's indigenous and rural
population. Nearing starvation, the rebels could only count on allies like
Alejandra for their survival. "The EZLN," said Alejandra, "is all that is left
of the revolution!"[1]

In fact the efforts of Alejandra and others like her represented the embers of the Mexican Revolution at the close of the twentieth century. Veering from a neopopulism that vainly sought to recapture the magic of Lázaro Cárdenas to a neoliberalism that embraced global capitalism in order to make Mexico a First World nation, the PRI and the state it directed had struggled to regain traction after the Tlatelolco massacre. Amid this struggle, Mexicans such as Alejandra found new political meaning outside the self-proclaimed Institutional Revolutionary Party. Thus even as the PRI continued to decline, the symbols of revolution remained relevant to many Mexicans.

THE NEOPOPULIST REVIVAL (AND COLLAPSE)

In 1970, the year Mexico hosted its first soccer World Cup, the PRI was still reeling from the Tlatelolco massacre less than two years before. In 1970 Díaz Ordaz gave the *dedazo* to former secretary of gobernación Luis Echeverría Alvarez, who inevitably became the party's standard-bearer in that year's presidential election. An attorney from Mexico City and from a politically prominent family, a PRIista who had never stood for a single political office, Echeverría had represented the government in its negotiations with student leaders just prior to the massacre. At first glance, Díaz Ordaz appeared to have made another mistake. But Echeverría played his cards well at this difficult juncture, ably shifting the official party's direction according to the needs of the moment. Associated with the unpopular and draconian Díaz Ordaz regime, the candidate rehabilitated his image by embarking on a national tour that evoked memories of the great campaigns of Madero in 1910 and Cárdenas in 1934. Echeverría's political pilgrimage covered thirty-five thousand miles and featured visits to approximately nine hundred municipalities in all twenty-nine Mexican states and the then-territories of Baja California Sur and Quintana Roo. Clad in the traditional tropical shirt, the *guayabera*, the PRI candidate reinvented himself as a populist, making frequent references to Lázaro Cárdenas as his mentor. At one rural campaign stop, Echeverría declared, "If the vote of the people favors me and I am elected President of the Republic, I will not be able to sleep at night during the six-year term unless I have the certainty of having done that day something for the agricultural progress and the welfare of the peasants." In September 1970 the federal government declared that Echeverría had won the election with 86 percent of the vote. Although some of this margin was the work of PRI machine politics and even outright ballot box stuffing, the candidate's victory was impressive under the circumstances. As the journalist Elena Poniatowska recounted, Echeverría also reached out to the young in an effort to wash the stain of blood from the hands of the regime: "[His] government carried the stigma of Tlatelolco, which it tried to remove at all costs. . . . The president set out to conquer the students with a vehemence that would have been unthinkable without Tlatelolco. . . . The government recognized that the student movement, with all its faults and virtues, was . . . a vital force in the country."[3]

From the outset, the new president faced difficult times. In particular his government confronted the violent aftershocks of Tlatelolco. The killings had radicalized the student movement, and many of its adherents had turned toward Marxism, some of them going underground. Some joined urban guerrillas, and others participated in rural rebellions such as the ones commanded by Lucio Cabañas and Genaro Vázquez in the mountainous state of Guerrero—since the 1810s, a hotbed of insurrection. The northern part of this state had been one of the mainstays of Zapatismo during the revolution, and Cárdenas's home state of Michoacán bordered Guerrero from the west. Both Cabañas and Vázquez were Marxist schoolteachers inspired by the Cuban Revolution as well as Cardenismo and the iconic figure of Zapata. They were leaders of popular organizations that had confronted state-sponsored violence against militant campesinos during the 1960s, before themselves opting for clandestine action and armed struggle. In 1973 an urban guerrilla group, the September 23 Communist League, killed a wealthy industrialist, Eugenio Garza Sada, patriarch of the Monterrey Group and one of the wealthiest men in the nation. Cabañas's forces kidnapped a federal senator, and in 1974 yet another revolutionary group held for ransom Echeverría's father-in-law, the former Jalisco governor Guadalupe Zuno Hernández.

Borrowing a page from the South American dictatorships that coincided with his rule, President Echeverría unleashed a veritable *guerra sucia*, or dirty war, against them. He sent over ten thousand federal troops (roughly 15 percent of the army) into Guerrero to carry out a scorched-earth campaign that killed hundreds of innocent civilians along with Cabañas and twenty-seven of his closest collaborators. As one campesino, whose neighbor had been brutally tortured and killed by the army in hot pursuit of Vázquez, lamented in a letter to the secretary of defense, "We have returned to Porfirian times!" A month later, soldiers ambushed the campesino, forced him to dig his own grave, and buried him alive after knocking him unconscious.[4] *Damn*

The government also encouraged private efforts to crack down on the organized Left. For example, on June 10, 1971, a right-wing paramilitary group known as Los Halcones attacked peaceful protesters in Mexico City while police and security forces stood by. Later on, it was revealed that the Halcones were on the payroll of the government. Echeverría also ordered agents from the Dirección Federal de Seguridad (DFS) to infiltrate university student, staff, and faculty organizations to get advance warning of any planned protest activities. Founded in 1947 as part of the Secretaría de Gobernación during the Alemán presidency, the DFS aimed to defend the political order against subversion and terrorist threats, congruent with the prevailing Cold War doctrine of internal security.

While Echeverría thus brutally repressed left-leaning groups *within* Mexico, he sought to appease the Left by offering verbal support for left-wing and nationalist movements *outside* the nation. For a country that had experienced half a dozen foreign invasions since independence, no aspect of government policy was fraught with more symbolism than foreign affairs. Moreover the international panorama offered a unique opportunity for Echeverría to burnish his preferred image as a champion of the Left. In the early 1970s the United States was bogged down in Vietnam, with no apparent way out. In Latin America, Mexico increasingly appeared to represent a middle road between two opposing tendencies: the rise of military regimes in Brazil, Paraguay, and Uruguay, and of socialist ones in Cuba and Salvador Allende's Chile. Echeverría watched both of these tendencies closely: the military dictatorships, because Mexico was emerging as a destination for political exiles, and socialist regimes, because the Cuban and Chilean revolutionary processes represented far more radical experiments in social justice than Mexico's own fraying revolutionary tradition.

Increasingly Echeverría cast himself as a friend of social revolution in Latin America, particularly of Allende, who had come to power in a democratic election in 1970. Even more important, he offered his country as a safe haven for victims of the South American dirty wars. In September 1973, after General Augusto Pinochet's right-wing coup overthrew Allende's Popular Unity government—a bloody takeover that claimed the life of the president—Echeverría granted asylum to thousands of refugees,

including Allende's widow. After another coup ousted President Isabel
Perón of Argentina three years later, Echeverría again opened Mexico's
doors. Between 1973 and 1982 thousands of left-leaning Argentine and
Chilean professionals entered the country. These refugees proved useful
to the government for three reasons: many of them were highly educated
and possessed skills in demand in Mexico; they proved as loyal to their
host as the Spanish Republicans had been in the 1930s; and the president's
welcoming stance toward left-leaning South American refugees diverted
attention from his own scaled-down dirty war against the Left. Secure in
his position, Echeverría confronted his critics on the Right, who charged
that he was following Allende's path to socialism, by stating, "There will
never be a Pinochet in Mexico."[5]

• In the process, the president also emerged as a critic of the Cold War.
Following in López Mateos's footsteps, Echeverría became one of the
leaders of the "nonaligned movement" within the United Nations, and he
maintained a dialogue with Cuba's Fidel Castro. He even posed for photo
ops with the Palestinian leader Yasser Arafat, a symbol of anti-Zionist and
anti-imperialist sentiment in the Middle East.

• Simultaneously Echeverría participated in the front ranks of a campaign to negotiate a new economic world order. He became one of the
world's primary exponents of an aggressive *Tercermundismo*, or "Third
Worldism." Pointing to the unfavorable terms of trade of most developing
nations, he called for global economic justice with vaguely defined references to a new commodity price structure. The president's trade policy
was unabashedly protectionist, and he continued his predecessors' practice of levying punitive tariffs on imported goods. During his administration, many of these tariffs exceeded 100 percent, and the government impeded the entry of some manufactured products, particularly industrial
goods that competed with domestically manufactured items. At the other
end of the trade spectrum, Echeverría aggressively promoted the export of
strategic minerals. When oil prices skyrocketed following the Yom Kippur
War of 1973, he publicly rejoiced at what he viewed to be redress for years
of depressed prices for raw materials. In the meantime he nationalized the
tobacco and telephone industries, pointing to these sectors as examples of
foreign exploitation.

Echeverría also made a number of substantive social reforms. His government revived the long-dormant land distribution program, parceling

out more land to peasants than his four predecessors combined. In particular he targeted northern Sinaloa and Sonora, areas where large landowners had hitherto largely avoided expropriation. Under Echeverría's tenure, Congress lowered the voting age to eighteen; it inaugurated an ambitious profit-sharing scheme designed to increase the gross pay of workers; and it expanded the purview of the social security program to cover an additional ten million Mexicans. The administration established housing subsidies for workers, with the costs shared between employers and the federal government, and it set maximum prices for basic foodstuffs. In an effort to make amends with the student movement, Echeverría released most of the political prisoners captured during the Díaz Ordaz regime. Perhaps most important for scholars of the Mexican Revolution, the Echeverría administration opened up a number of previously classified government archives to researchers, supported the establishment of more professionally organized regional archives, and gave generous assistance to research projects in history and the social sciences. With the collaboration of El Colegio de México, his government sponsored the twenty-three-volume, state-of-the-art *Historia de la Revolución Mexicana*. These policies encountered widespread support among the intelligentsia and earned Echeverría kudos from many eminent social scientists — scholars who otherwise might have found themselves in the opposition.

In 1973, however, a worldwide economic crisis hit Mexico hard enough to negate these efforts to reclaim for the PRI some of its past luster. Rather than helping all petroleum-producing nations, as Echeverría had hoped, the surge in oil prices in the aftermath of the Yom Kippur War triggered a global economic slowdown that drastically reduced demand for Mexican export products. To make matters worse, the massive infusion of billions of dollars into the economy to fund Echeverría's social programs created runaway inflation. In 1974 credit became tight, raising the cost of the government's foreign loans that helped pay for the new social programs. Showing that he did not understand the roots of this crisis, Echeverría shifted his populism into a higher gear by raising taxes on the wealthiest and calling for mandatory wage hikes of up to 18 percent. The rich did not take such redistributionist measures lying down, moving billions of dollars out of the country and refusing to pay taxes at the higher rates. Facing a veritable mutiny by the business community, the government frantically attempted to prop up the peso in order to prevent its devaluation and

a concomitant increase in consumer prices. Nevertheless this most serious economic downturn since 1948 ended with the peso losing half of its *Whoa!*
value. By 1976 a dollar bought twenty-five pesos, up from a 2:1 ratio in the
1920s and a 5:1 ratio as recently as the late 1940s. Rapid population growth
made this crisis feel even worse at the grassroots level. In the 1970s the fertility rate of the average Mexican woman was 5.4 children, and the population grew at more than 3.5 percent annually. In other words, the economy
needed to grow 3.5 percent each year just to accommodate the population
growth, and as Echeverría found out during the last years of his rule, the
heady days of 6 to 8 percent growth lay in the past. Rather than gallop-
ing down the stretch of his *sexenio* as the Second Coming of Cárdenas, he
faded badly, finishing his tenure in ignominy. *Weak finish*

Echeverría's successor, his boyhood friend and former law partner José
López Portillo y Pacheco, nevertheless vowed to continue Echeverría's
populist policies, hoping they might yet revive some of the promises—
and legitimacy—of the PRI's "Institutional Revolution." A former law pro-
fessor at the national university, López Portillo was the first scholar at the
helm of the official party. The new president was extremely fortunate in
that the recent discovery of vast oil deposits in Chiapas, Tabasco, Cam-
peche, and the Gulf of Mexico afforded his government an opportunity to *New oil*
spend its way out of the economic doldrums. Once exploited, the newly *reserves found*
discovered oil fields made Mexico the fourth largest oil producer in the
world. Moreover petroleum prices had hit unprecedented highs following
the 1973 crisis in the Middle East, and López Portillo intended to take advantage of this windfall. To supplement this revenue, the president hiked
taxes, initiating a new value-added tax that added 15 percent to the price of
each good or service sold in the country, except basic foodstuffs. Even the
wealthy, always seeking ways to reduce their tax burden, did not know a
way around the VAT. López Portillo then set about systematically spending
these newfound financial resources. He greatly increased the size of the
federal bureaucracy by establishing new agencies, among them six cabinet-
level secretariats. In response to the decline in real wages, his government
increased housing and food subsidies. It also launched a family planning
program that helped reduce the fertility rate from 5.4 in 1976 to 4.6 in 1982.
Equally important, López Portillo's initiative contributed to a shift in social values by attacking two deeply rooted notions: that it was *muy macho*
to father many children and that women fulfilled themselves by giving

birth to many children. This shift in values supported a further decrease in the fertility rate to 2.9 in 1993, thereby slicing the rate of population growth in half. While this drop in fertility occurred worldwide, Mexico went from exceeding the global average in 1976 to trailing it in 1993.

Like Echeverría, López Portillo pursued an activist foreign policy that displayed his country's independence from and criticism of the United States. In particular his government was a staunch ally of the Nicaraguan Sandinistas, a left-leaning movement that overthrew forty-two years of Somoza family dictatorship in July 1979. Significantly, after Anastasio Somoza Debayle's resignation, the Sandinista leadership arrived in the capital of Managua on a Mexican jet, singing Mexican revolutionary *corridos* and extemporizing a few ballads about their own victorious insurrection. Two years later López Portillo joined President François Mitterrand of France in granting "belligerent" status to the Marxist FMLN guerrilla in El Salvador, a diplomatic step that awarded the group recognition as a legitimate political force in their struggle against a repressive right-wing regime. López Portillo also continued Echeverría's practice of giving asylum to refugees from Latin America's military dictatorships; hundreds of thousands of Guatemalans took up residence in Mexico, chased out of their native country by the scorched-earth policy of a U.S.-backed military government. Unlike Echeverría, however, López Portillo ultimately found a determined adversary for his policies in the strongly anti-Communist U.S. President Ronald Reagan. After his inauguration in January 1981, Reagan assailed both the Sandinistas and the Salvadoran rebels as mere proxies of Cuba and the Soviet Union. Bypassing congressional approval, the Reagan administration gave military assistance to the repressive Salvadoran military as well as a Nicaraguan opposition group, the Contras, and the U.S. president made it clear that he would not tolerate Mexican interference in an area the United States had long considered its own backyard.

The economy proved a much greater disappointment. As López Portillo prepared to leave office in 1982, Mexicans learned that his government was mortgaged to the hilt. Mexico owed tens of billions of dollars to foreign banks at interest rates exceeding 10 percent, a product of the efforts of the U.S. Federal Reserve to root out the double-digit inflation that had plagued the world economy for several years. In 1982 Mexico defaulted on these loans. López Portillo expressed anger at what he portrayed as a foreign plot to destroy the nation's economy, insisting that he would "de-

TABLE 8.1 *Estimated Real Wages during the López Portillo Administration, in US$*

INDEX 1976 = 100

Year	1977	1978	1979	1980	1981	1982
Legal minimum wage	110.0	125.5	146.6	172.5	230.4	309.2
Real wages	85.6	88.0	83.4	77.7	81.0	66.0

Source: Francisco Salazar Sotelo, "Balance global de la política económica en el sexenio 1976–1982," in *Estudios cuantitativos sobre la historia de México*, ed. Samuel Schmidt, James W. Wilkie, and Manuel Esparza (Mexico City: UNAM, 1988), 48.

fend the peso like a dog."[6] However, the very next day he announced a catastrophic devaluation of the currency. In the course of the year, the peso lost 85 percent of its value against the U.S. dollar, and billions of dollars fled the country in search of safer investment opportunities. In December 1982, posturing as a latter-day Cárdenas, López Portillo nationalized Mexico's major banks and made all capital transactions with foreign countries subject to government approval. To celebrate this achievement, his government even renamed one of the squares in downtown Mexico City the Plaza de la Banca Nacionalizada. These measures, however, only deepened the crisis. Nor did the U.S. government help out: offended by Mexico's support for progressive movements in Central America, President Reagan stood by as the Mexican economy sank into its deepest quagmire since the Great Depression.

The quagmire commenced what many Mexicans still refer to as the *década perdida*, or "lost decade." During the remainder of the 1980s, millions lost their jobs, and hyperinflation and capital flight aggravated the decline in real wages that had continued throughout López Portillo's presidency despite the oil boom (see table 8.1). The crisis led to biting popular humor that further undermined the official myth of "the Revolution" propagated by the ruling party. For example, in reference to López Portillo's earlier pledges to defend the country's currency, cynics dubbed the Los Pinos presidential residence the Casa del Perro, or doghouse.

•As if this serious economic downturn were not bad enough, mounting reports of mismanagement and corruption sullied López Portillo's outgoing administration. To be sure, decades of sordid experience had inured Mexicans to news reports about corruption. Ordinary Mexicans knew when to pay a *mordida*, or bribe, to an official or police officer; most of them regarded all government officials as a *bola de rateros* (gang of thieves). Since World War II, massive government-sponsored industrial and public works projects had afforded increasing opportunities for large-scale graft. By all accounts, however, López Portillo and his allies set new standards for illegal self-enrichment. As a British journalist estimated, during the oil boom "almost every purchase by Petróleos Mexicanos involved a kickback of 10 or 15 percent."[7] Most notorious was the head of the Mexico City police, Arturo Durazo Moreno, a.k.a. El Negro, or the black one, a term that referred both to his origins in a heavily indigenous part of Sonora and to his prodigious ill-gotten wealth during public service. At the time of his appointment, this childhood friend of the president had already earned a grand jury indictment in the United States for narcotics trafficking. As police chief, he built the biggest racketeering operation in the capital's history. With these proceeds, he constructed two enormous residences in southern Mexico City, and Mexicans dubbed a third residence near the Pacific port of Zihuatanejo "the Parthenon," a reference to its likeness to the famous temple in Athens. Durazo's greed was rivaled only by his vanity. Even though he had not served any time in the military, he insisted that his charges call him "General de División," the highest military rank. Other prominent Mexicans who took full economic advantage of their political roles included Carlos Hank González, the mayor of Mexico City, and the president himself. López Portillo lived in inexplicable luxury and appointed his son, his wife, his mistress, and four other family members to important positions in his government. By any measure, the corruption of the López Portillo years made all previous rulers — even Miguel Alemán's self-enriching clique — appear relatively honest by comparison. In 1982 the president left office in infamy.

"REFORMING THE REVOLUTION"

The collapse of 1982 administered the coup de grâce to the PRI-led "Revolution" as an economic and social program fourteen years after the Tlatelolco massacre had mortally wounded it as a political model. The crisis severely weakened the state as a player in the economy. In exchange for facilitating new credit, the International Monetary Fund demanded an austerity package to bring down government spending. To meet IMF targets, the administration of Miguel de la Madrid Hurtado (1982–88) under-

took deep cuts in social programs. For example, de la Madrid slashed government subsidies for low-rent housing as well as basic foodstuffs such as
rice, beans, and tortillas. Added to the decline in real wages, the cuts devastated both workers and the middle class. Worse still, the austerity package
did not stanch the bleeding. Inflation ran well over 100 percent annually
for several years, and the peso fell from a rate of 150 to the dollar to 2,200
in a span of five years. The rate of unemployment, as reported by the government, reached 25 percent in the middle of the decade; most likely it was
much higher than these official figures. Not surprisingly people voted with
their feet, and millions of migrants added to the large population of Mexican descent in the United States and Canada. U.S. census data suggest a
doubling of that population during the 1980s. The 1990 census counted 13.5
million people of Mexican descent, and by the year 2000 that number had
ascended to 20.6 million. These official figures included several million undocumented workers but likely underreported the true number, as many
indocumentados refused to answer census surveys.

[handwritten margin note: slashing public services, severe inflation, unemployed rise in immigration]

From today's vantage point, the 1982 debt crisis appears the most significant watershed in postrevolutionary history, the moment when the PRI
gave up on its own rhetoric and accepted the fact that "the Revolution"
was over. In this regard, de la Madrid's comments regarding corruption
were revealing. Like his predecessors, the incoming president portrayed
himself as a tough opponent of corruption and announced plans for the
"moral renovation" of society. However, this Harvard-trained technocrat
with a master's degree in public administration—the first Mexican president with a graduate degree awarded in the United States—went one step
further, predicting the demise of the PRI regime if the party could not
put its affairs in order. He announced that his government would not "accept corruption as the cost of our system's stability or efficiency in the
management of the affairs of the state."[8] He also denounced López Portillo's "financial populism," that is, his irresponsible management of public
finances.[9]

A devastating natural disaster brought the human cost of corruption
home to Mexicans at the midpoint of the de la Madrid sexenio. On the
morning of September 19, 1985, an earthquake measuring 8.1 on the Richter
scale shook Mexico City. Another quake struck the next evening. According to some estimates, the tremors left approximately 10,000 people dead,
50,000 injured, and 250,000 homeless. The city center was devastated, with

roads impassable due to cracked pavements, scattered building debris, and broken water lines, and the hardest-hit areas resembled war zones. The aftermath of the earthquakes revealed fresh evidence of corruption. For example, the collapse of two state-owned apartment buildings in Tlatelolco near the site of the 1968 massacre laid bare massive violations of the building code in force at the time of construction in the early to mid-1960s. While the government-approved plans for the apartment buildings had strictly adhered to these standards, contractors had colluded with building inspectors in skimping on construction costs, splitting the difference with these officials for personal benefit. Corruption within the PRI had thus directly contributed to the loss of human life. Continuing this theme, rumors circulated that the de la Madrid administration was siphoning off some of the international relief assistance for its own use.

Moreover an inadequate emergency response to the disaster contributed to a general sense that the government was part of the problem rather than the solution. After each of the quakes, victims waited for hours for rescue workers to appear. The police response was similarly insufficient, leaving looters to descend upon the disaster zone after nightfall. This lack of response was particularly offensive to the residents of the capital because the government was assiduously preparing to host the 1986 World Cup. Rather than attending to earthquake victims, the de la Madrid administration preened before the world, hosting the World Cup in expensive soccer stadiums such as the one in Ciudad Nezahualcóyotl, the nation's largest slum with almost four million inhabitants.

Governmental ineptitude in the wake of the earthquakes ultimately empowered victims to take matters into their own hands, especially in the Tlatelolco neighborhood. Residents formed impromptu cleanup crews and dug through the debris in search of family members and neighbors. Doctors and nurses living in the area established makeshift clinics. Neighbors unafraid of violence banded together to provide defense against looters. Others collected food and blankets provided by neighbors who had escaped unscathed. In all, grassroots action rather than government-sponsored relief provided the most tangible assistance to the 100,000 residents of the Tlatelolco neighborhood. The 1985 earthquakes contributed to a new type of middle-class political mobilization in defense of urban neighborhoods. Outrage about government incompetence permeated this movement. In a letter to the head of the National Housing Fund, one group of citizens expressed "strong feelings of pain, rage, impotence, and uncertainty": "Pain for our dead brothers; rage because this strategy could be avoided . . . ; impotence for not being able to rescue more survivors in the rubble; and uncertainty for the present and the future of our housing complex."[10]

Along with the economic crisis, the earthquakes contributed to the administration's abandonment of even a theoretical commitment to the goals of "the Revolution" as enshrined in the 1917 Constitution. In his last three years in office, as capital continued to flee and the peso declined further, de la Madrid openly embraced neoliberal strategies designed to tear down the social compact that lay at the center of the PRI's political message. As formulated by the University of Chicago economist Milton Friedman, neoliberalism effectively challenged several key tenets of the PRI state: spending on social services, protectionist tariffs and import regulations, currency and price controls, and state ownership of significant sectors that controlled natural resources and infrastructure. De la Madrid moved to implement many of the foremost components of the neoliberal agenda. As a former employee of Petróleos Mexicanos (PEMEX), the president knew that the sale of state-owned companies would attack corruption and mismanagement at their roots. He also appreciated that the privatization of state-owned businesses could provide cash to a strapped national treasury. Therefore the government sold 40 percent of the approximately one thousand state-owned businesses to private investors, but not PEMEX, which remained an icon of economic nationalism for many Mexicans. Indeed at the same time that de la Madrid completed the sale of billions of dollars worth of the public stake in businesses, his government issued a 5,000-peso coin to commemorate the fiftieth anniversary of Cárdenas's 1938 oil expropriation.

Not surprisingly the disgraced ex-president López Portillo later portrayed himself as the "last president of the Mexican Revolution" and argued that his selection of de la Madrid as his successor was a "mistake."[11] To be sure, López Portillo had helped create the economic mess that made neoliberalism possible. But he accurately pinpointed the de la Madrid sexenio as the end point of "the Revolution" as a political program. Not only had the PRI lost its hegemony in the political landscape, but opposition movements from both the Right and the Left found spaces to operate after the 1982 debt crisis. Ever so gradually, the PRI leadership, and particularly de la Madrid, realized that the days of their party's dominance were drawing to a close.

Most significantly, the PRI's turn toward neoliberalism led to a split in the official party and the emergence of a new Cardenista alternative on the eve of the 1988 presidential election. None other than Cuauhtémoc Cárdenas, son of the former president, broke with his party and formed an opposition organization, the Frente Democrático Nacional (National Democratic Front, or FDN). Cárdenas announced his candidacy for the presidency in opposition to that of Carlos Salinas de Gortari, another Harvard-trained PRI technocrat. The conservative National Action Party (PAN), advocates of liberal capitalism and vocal critics of neopopulism à la Echeverría and López Portillo, also fielded a competitive candidate, the northern businessman Manuel Clouthier. But all eyes were on the younger Cárdenas, a highly visible politician whose departure from the PRI further highlighted the crisis of the ruling party. Although Cárdenas lacked his father's charisma, he symbolized the revolutionary past. His name conjured two icons: the courageous last Aztec emperor and the most popular president of the twentieth century. His supporters expected him to fix all that was wrong with Mexico. As one of his admirers wrote in a personal letter, "Long live Cárdenas[,] who will support the poor and . . . the humble[;] who protects the humble mexican[;] who will stand up for justice and truth because he is mexican like us[.] Death to foreign toadies[;] we will transform Mexico and defend it."[12]

Therefore the summer of 1988 witnessed the most closely contested presidential elections since 1940. Exit polls indicated that Cárdenas had done very well, and early returns suggested that he and Clouthier might both finish ahead of the PRI candidate Salinas. However, a few hours after the closing of the polls, the computer system that tallied nationwide election results crashed under mysterious circumstances. When the system resumed operation approximately a week later, Salinas had won over 50 percent of the vote in the narrowest victory for a PRI candidate to date. The PRI also triumphed in the national legislature, but taken together, the FDN and PAN had won enough seats to impede the customary PRI steamroller in Congress. Naturally the FDN alleged fraud, but in the absence of a fair and impartial national elections board, these allegations went nowhere.

In the end, the split of the official party between the neoliberal Salinas and the Cardenista alternative only accelerated the demise of what remained of "the Revolution." Although he came from a politically radical family, and even counted Zapata's biographer John Womack among his close friends while at Harvard, Salinas stepped up his predecessor's neoliberal agenda. Jetting about the nation in his private plane, the *Emiliano Zapata*, the new president announced his intention to "reform the Revolution" in order to make Mexico a First World nation. This effort signified tearing down the social compact embodied in the economic nationalism and redistributive reform of the 1917 Constitution, while preserving the paternalistic state that the PRI had created. Salinas made common cause with the Catholic and antirevolutionary PAN in relegating the revolutionary provisions of the constitution to the garbage heap. Under his aegis, Congress modified Article 27 to delete the strictures on foreign investment in agriculture and the subsoil. It also dealt a fatal blow to the old Cardenista land reform by making provision for the conversion of all *ejidos* to private land holdings. Henceforth campesinos could buy and sell plots of land, and in time much of this land seemed destined to end up as the property of large domestic producers or landowning multinational corporations like Nestlé or Del Monte. Salinas sold off most of the remainder of the public sector, including Teléfonos Mexicanos (Telmex), a telecommunications firm that enjoyed a monopoly over the national market. The president also came to an agreement with Pope John Paul II that restored diplomatic relations with the Vatican for the first time since the revolution. In particular Salinas reversed the Calles-era laws and allowed churches to own buildings that had been nationalized during the revolution.

In the short term, Salinas's reforms met with considerable success. The administration lowered annual inflation from 159 percent in 1987 to 7 percent in 1993. The fire sale of the state sector of the economy not only stimulated private investment but was also a one-time infusion of much-needed cash to help the government address its spending priorities and international obligations. Delighted with these neoliberal reforms, the business sector reinvested billions of dollars in the Mexican economy, capital that for years had been parked abroad in multinational corporations, Swiss bank accounts, and real estate. After eighteen years of extreme volatility, annual rates of growth reached an average of 3.5 percent —a more modest expansion than that associated with the Mexican Miracle but one occurring in the context of slower population growth. International investors happily bought up Mexican stocks, grateful for opportunities in what they considered a prime "emerging market." Finally, privatization afforded Salinas's cronies new opportunities for enrichment. For example, Salinas placed a close personal friend, Carlos Slim Helú, at the helm of Telmex. Slim acquired a commanding share in Telmex for a fraction of its value, and the company flourished quickly thanks to an infusion of foreign investment and the spread of mobile telephony. Unlike other governments, which coupled the privatization of the telecom sector with legislation encouraging competition, the Salinas administration kept the Telmex monopoly in place, allowing Slim to rack up stunning profits. From this base, he invested in other companies abroad, soon building the largest business empire ever assembled in Latin America. As of this writing, Slim is the world's richest individual. *Narcotraficantes*, or drug lords, also greatly expanded their influence in collusion with PRI bureaucrats.

The idea of reforming "the Revolution" was not only profitable but also matched the spirit of an age in which other ideological certainties surrendered to globalization oriented by the capitalist model. Salinas's term coincided with the disintegration of the Soviet Union and its bloc in Eastern Europe. Just a year into his administration, the world looked on in amazement at the razing of the Berlin Wall, long considered an immutable barrier between East and West. The Soviet state, like the postrevolutionary Mexican state, had emerged from a violent social revolution, and both Soviet and Mexican revolutionaries had founded ruling parties that claimed to represent the true heritage of their nation's upheavals. The similarities ended there, but in the late 1980s, PRIistas watched keenly as Soviet Premier Mikhail Gorbachev dismantled his party's hold over the Soviet Union and its satellites through the policies of *glasnost* (openness) and *perestroika* (restructuring). At the very least, the collapse of the Soviet Union raised two significant questions for Mexicans: After seven long decades, was "the Revolution" worthy of upholding as a set of values? Did the crisis of Communism presage the inevitable decline of social compacts such as Mexico's predicated on a large state role in the economy? Without a doubt, the disappearance of the Soviet Union emboldened leaders like Salinas who saw themselves as capitalist reformers of a cumbersome and outdated system. Similar thoughts of reform occupied the rulers of the People's Republic of China, which transitioned into capitalist practice without seeing its authoritarian form of government disintegrate. With

Soviet falls

the collapse of Communism, the only alternative to Western capitalism had disappeared.

Another significant element in the reform of "the Revolution" was the attempt to rewrite the Mexican history textbooks used in the nation's elementary schools. Since the early 1960s, the government had commissioned and distributed free textbooks to all students. The Libros de Texto Gratuitos program mandated the use of these texts in both public and private schools, and it allowed students to keep the books after using them in class. For decades the official history textbooks used in the fourth, fifth, and sixth grades had depicted the revolution as the culmination of the struggle of the Mexican people for democracy and social justice. For many poor families, whose children abandoned school after sixth grade in order to work, these books were the only available source of historical instruction. In Manichaean fashion, the texts contrasted official national heroes such as the last Aztec emperor Cuauhtémoc, Hidalgo, Juárez, Madero, Obregón, Zapata, Villa, and Cárdenas with an assortment of villains that included the Spanish conquistador Hernán Cortés, the nineteenth-century caudillo Antonio López de Santa Anna, various U.S. diplomats and foreign investors, and, of course, the dictator Porfirio Díaz. During an August 1992 public ceremony, Salinas and Education Secretary Ernesto Zedillo unveiled the latest edition of the textbooks. Written by Héctor Aguilar Camín and Enrique Florescano, two prominent historians close to the administration, this edition featured an interpretation that downplayed the negative aspects of the Díaz dictatorship. Instead the authors highlighted Porfirian modernization as a necessary precursor to Salinas's efforts to bring Mexico into the era of globalization. Likewise they drew a more ambiguous portrait of revolutionary leaders than their predecessors had, suggesting the leaders' authoritarian and militaristic tendencies along with their desire for reform. This effort to de-emphasize "the Revolution" as the heroic centerpiece of Mexican history displayed the degree to which Salinas and his allies (in particular his friend Aguilar Camín) had dissociated themselves from the PRI's core program.

But before the new textbooks could enter the classroom, a public outcry over the newly emerging interpretation forced the Salinas administration to withdraw them. This widespread reaction to the new texts revealed the fact that "the Revolution" as an idealized process and a blueprint still mattered deeply to many Mexicans. Even though a large number of Aguilar Camín and Florescano's revisions matched the findings of contemporary scholarship, the public resented these efforts to rewrite official history in order to complement the administration's neoliberal policies. Those more familiar with historical scholarship marveled at the manner with which Aguilar Camín, formerly a revisionist historian with Marxist leanings, had reconciled himself with the neoliberal economic and political elite. Moreover detractors attacked the new textbooks for the positive spin they put on the role of foreign investment in the modernization of Mexico — an obvious validation of Salinas's globalizing objectives.

These objectives and the concomitant official burial of "the Revolution" found their strongest expression in the negotiation of the North American Free Trade Agreement (NAFTA) Scheduled to begin on January 1, 1994, NAFTA tied Canada, the United States, and Mexico together in a trade pact that tore down tariff barriers and protectionist legislation. The Salinistas expected NAFTA to boost commerce and attract jobs to Mexico. It suited Salinas just fine that this treaty required significant revisions to the nationalist provisions of the revolutionary constitution, in particular the restrictions on foreign investments. Once again, as in the Díaz period, the Mexican government pursued laissez-faire economic policies — so much so that the old dictator would have probably turned over in his grave knowing that his successors could no longer award preferential treatment to capitalists of their choice. And just as during the Porfiriato, the impact of globalization would prove uneven across Mexico's regions. In the North and the major tourist centers, NAFTA provided a boost, as the majority of new investment poured into four northern states on the U.S. border. But NAFTA served to further divert attention from the problems of the agricultural economy in the heavily indigenous South, which stagnated with the elimination of federal subsidies.

The final piece of the Salinista strategy to reform "the Revolution" consisted of co-opting the opposition. This tactic intended to countervail the presidency's authoritarian propensities, which reminded many Mexicans even more of the ideological affinities between Salinas and Porfirio Díaz. The PRI's sharp neoliberal turn constituted a break with its own programmatic principles — ideas now more faithfully represented by Cuauhtémoc Cárdenas's new Partido de la Revolución Democrática (Party of the Democratic Revolution, or PRD). The PRI had become a center-right party. Not much now distinguished the PRI from the PAN, aside from the latter's pro-Catholic ideology; in Congress, both parties collaborated closely in approving neoliberal reforms. Following up on a gradual political opening that had occurred during de la Madrid's last years in office, Salinas and his allies promoted pluralism by allowing PAN candidates to win election to gubernatorial posts. Over time, this pluralism included the PRD as well. The victory of a PAN candidate in the gubernatorial elections in Baja California in 1989 marked the first such defeat for the official party since its founding; in subsequent years, the PRI allowed the PAN and the PRD to claim an increasing number of seats in Congress. Nonetheless Salinas and his allies kept a tight hold on their party's power in the executive branch.

The Salinato also sought to co-opt its critics by means of the president's signature, if rather moderate, antipoverty program, Solidaridad. The idea was to put a human face on the administration's market-driven capitalism, even as it was removing economic subsidies and social protections. Officially named the Programa Nacional de Solidaridad (PRONASOL), President Salinas's initiative enlisted states and communities in mobilizing a countrywide campaign to fight poverty and galvanize national pride in "social development." Throughout his sexenio, Salinas allocated millions of dollars to build and renovate schools, hospitals, health clinics, roads, and highways; provide poor Mexican communities with electricity and drinking water; and establish low-income credit unions, among other initiatives. Approximately 250,000 grassroots PRONASOL committees were charged with designing projects in collaboration with government bureaucrats to address the needs of communities and individuals at greatest risk. Despite undeniable achievements, critics contended that Solidaridad was merely a politicized repackaging of traditional welfare and public works projects—a short-term fix that did not address the root causes of poverty at a historical moment when inequalities were being exacerbated by neoliberalism. Moreover critics charged that it was not even clear if PRONASOL's resources ever significantly reached those in extreme poverty, given that funds were too often diverted into the hands of bureaucrats, politicians, and their favored clients. Salinas's defenders speculate that the president hoped eventually to replace the PRI with a more socially conscious party that would build on Solidaridad's incipient grassroots presence. Significantly Salinas's successor, President Ernesto Zedillo, modified the antipoverty program during his own neoliberal sexenio, although the concept did not catch on with the PRI's powerful dinosaur faction.

In 1993, with just a year to go in his administration, Salinas appeared to have much reason to rejoice. Mexico — and the rest of the world with it — seemed to be entering a new age. After the end of the Cold War, the political scientist Francis Fukuyama had proclaimed "the end of history,"[13] a new era without the ideologically driven wars and conflicts that had plagued the past. As Fukuyama saw it, global capitalism had triumphed over the narrow and repressive ideologies of the past, whether fascism, Communism, or nationalism. That certainly appeared to be the case in Mexico with the impending implementation of NAFTA, which created the largest free trade area in the world in terms of its geographic dimension. In a stunning turnaround, the Mexican government had agreed to end its eighty-year commitment to economic nationalism in exchange for the elimination of tariffs across North America. After several years of impressive growth, helped along by massive foreign investment, the nation was about to join the Organization for Economic Cooperation and Development, the exclusive club of the world's foremost capitalist nations.

ONE REVOLUTION IS BORN WHILE ANOTHER ONE DIES

On New Year's Day 1994, however — the day NAFTA took effect — it all fell apart. As Mexicans woke up from the festivities of ringing in the New Year, ski-masked rebels dashed through heavily indigenous central Chiapas. Shortly thereafter, the EZLN launched one of the world's first political manifestos disseminated with the help of the Internet. The manifesto called upon all Mexicans to rise up in revolt against a government that waged an "undeclared genocidal war against our people" and ignored the needs of ordinary Mexicans for the sake of globalization.[14] Yet the rebels shed relatively little blood as they seized the highland center of San Cristóbal and its surrounding areas. One of the EZLN's masked leaders, Rafael Guillén, a.k.a. Subcomandante Marcos, became an instant international celebrity. Even though he himself was from the northern state of Tamaulipas, middle class, and light-skinned, Marcos was designated as the principal spokesperson for the indigenous peoples of Chiapas — and, by extension, for all those left behind by globalization and neoliberalism. The EZLN waged a new kind of rebellion, more intent on winning the hearts and minds of its audience than winning a war. Though the government re-took most of the area seized by the EZLN, on January 12 the rebels and the government agreed on a cease-fire following the death of some 196 people. Over the next several years, the government attempted to encircle and eradicate the movement by means of a strategy of low-intensity warfare, which bore some similarities to the one that Echeverría had employed against the Marxist guerrillas of the 1970s. In 1997, for example, paramilitaries affiliated with the local PRI attacked a peaceful religious community in the highland village of Acteal, killing forty-five unarmed people, most of whom were women and children. This community, known as the Abejas ("The Bees" commune), had been organized by a radical priest but, owing to its tenacious pacifism, maintained a separate stance from the EZLN, even as it was sympathetic to the Zapatistas' social goals. Although some Zapatista supporters sought to reciprocate the violence, the EZLN leadership, ensconced in the remote jungles of Chiapas, increasingly committed itself to a peaceful strategy in civil society, and the movement remains a voice in Mexican politics and culture even today.

For example, on December 21, 2012 — the day many New Age enthusiasts were celebrating the alleged "end of the world" according to a flawed understanding of the ancient Maya calendar — thousands of masked Zapatistas marched silently into and briefly occupied the central plazas of the towns they had originally taken in 1994. Then, after marching peacefully through the streets of those Chiapanecan towns, they exited in the same precise formation with which they had entered. The message of their silent mobilization, apart from reiterating their ongoing protest against the abuses of the state and paramilitary forces, as well as the contradictions of neoliberalism, was unmistakable: "We are still here!"

Marcos and his allies had exposed Fukuyama's rhetoric as triumphalist and premature, as Mexico had clearly not reached the end of history nor exhausted the meanings of its historic revolution. Quite the contrary, Zapata had returned, demonstrating the powerful popular legacy of a revolution whose participants had died many decades earlier. The EZLN not only revived the Zapatistas' struggle for land but also fought for other abandoned ideas of the revolution. It demanded a return to revolutionary nationalism, an end to selling Mexican assets to foreign companies, and reforms to help protect the rights of the poor majority in general and indigenous peoples in particular. In the wake of centuries of indigenous resistance and the symbolic quincentennial of Columbus's 1492 voyage to the New World, the EZLN joined other indigenist movements in the Americas as an advocate of the preservation of indigenous culture. In 2003 Comandante Esther, a prominent EZLN leader, offered the following affirmation of indigenous identities: "We cannot stop being Indians [in order] to be recognized as Mexicans."[15] Congruent with indigenous and other ethnic movements throughout the hemisphere, the Zapatistas favored a policy of plurinationalism, a term frequently used to describe indigenous movements in the Andean region, which challenges the notion that Latin American states can be made up of only one nation, mestizos.

Congruent with earlier challenges to the hegemony of the PRI — left-wing guerrillas in the 1970s and the split of the ruling party in 1988 — Subcomandante Marcos reminded his followers that the Mexican Revolution remained alive as long as its symbols, ideas, and icons persisted. Separated by more than eighty years, Zapata's Plan of Ayala and the EZLN program coincided in three points: the demand for land, opposition to an authoritarian government that did not pay attention to the needs of rural Mexicans, and the call for a revalidation of local culture. Drawing on another early symbol of the revolution, the EZLN organized communities ruled from the grassroots which they labeled "Aguascalientes," a reference (in the plural) to the 1914 convention that resulted in the temporary ascendancy of Villa's and Zapata's popular factions. Finally, the references to Zapata and the epic revolution constituted only one way that the EZLN was inspired by and utilized history for its political purposes. Korda's iconic image of Che Guevara appeared on the movement's murals along with Zapata, the Flores Magón brothers, and Marcos.

This strong identification with history reflected the long road traveled by Mexico's indigenous peoples leading up to the EZLN rebellion. As we have seen, indigenous Mexicans played a role in the armed struggle of the 1910s, not just among Emiliano Zapata's army but also in the forces of each of the three major northern factions. But the end of the fighting had not brought significant improvements. To the contrary, the 1920s had featured Vasconcelos's educational crusade, a "Second Conquest" aimed at Hispanicizing Mexico's indigenous population, as well as the final defeat of the Yaquis of Sonora, Obregón's erstwhile allies who had revolted repeatedly against state and private encroachments upon their lands. In e 1930s Cardenista agrarian reform had returned some lands to indigenous communities but also made them dependent on the state rather than private landowners. Although radical Cardenista *indigenistas* advocated more than the incorporation of assimilated indigenous peoples, and many sought to adopt a true cultural pluralism for Mexico, President Cárdenas himself never departed from a position that saw indigenous peoples as "members of a social class taking part in the collective task of production." The solution to "our Indian problem," he maintained, "is not [to make] the Indian 'stay Indian,' nor [to] Indianize . . . Mexico, but [to] Mexican-ize the Indian himself": "If we respect his blood, and turn his emotional powers, his love of the soil to account, we shall root the national feeling more firmly in all, and enrich it with moral qualities that will strengthen the spirit of patriotism."[16] By the late 1930s, encouraged by the Cardenista regime, indigenous leaders did indeed speak as members of the Mexican nation, demanding the benefits of "the Revolution" for their communities. The last years of Cardenismo witnessed agrarian leagues and campesino and worker movements adopting the indigenous cause and claiming to represent indigenous interests and members. Still, indigenous voices were limited to those who identified their interests as synonymous with those of the Cardenista state. Compliance with the revolutionary project was rewarded with citizenship, while those who resisted, such as the Tarahu-maras, Cochimis, and Guaycuras, were portrayed as "nomads" and "sav-ages" — as irrational primitives.

In the 1940s official *indigenismo* fell out of favor, with the onset of World War II leading to renewed calls for national unity and cultural homo-geneity. The PRI's emergent bureaucracy now ignored or submerged in-digenous voices. As a result, indigenous resistance mounted against a government that, through the recently created Department of Indigenous Affairs, claimed to defend indigenous interests as its own but rarely de-livered on these claims. For example, for almost thirty years in Chihua-hua, the Tarahumara Regional Council held annual congresses to press its grievances; meantime, lacking faith in the regular political system, the Tarahumaras elected a parallel government to represent their interests before the PRI-led state. In 1968 largely urban-based indigenous leaders founded the Mexican Association of Indigenous Professionals and Intel-lectuals, adding their voices to the movement to democratize Mexico. Fif-teen years later, in Chiapas, Maoist organizers and progressive clergy — especially Samuel Ruiz, the bishop of San Cristóbal — became crucial

Spanish-speaking intermediaries for an indigenous population increasingly resentful of the exploitative conditions in which they lived. The Maya who subsequently formed the backbone of the clandestine EZLN in the late 1980s and early 1990s understood the part they played in five centuries of struggle against colonization, capitalism, and imperialism. For them, the Mexican Revolution also represented an indigenous uprising, followed by a postrevolutionary consolidation that kept Mexico on its capitalist path of internal colonialism.

Yet the EZLN looked forward as well as backward. Most significantly, it operated globally rather than in the national terms that had defined the revolution in Zapata's day. In particular the group had access to the Internet through its supporters in urban areas and aimed at reaching a sympathetic middle-class audience worldwide. Early on, the Mexican government was well aware of the reach of the new media. As one government official stated in a mixture of derision and fear, "If Marcos is equipped with a telephone modem and a cellular phone [he can] hook into the Internet [directly] even while on the run, as he is now."[17] The EZLN found its cyber audience among both critics of neoliberal free trade agreements and activists fighting for the rights of indigenous people. International support for the movement came in the form of volunteers, cash, food, medicine, and artistic expression; for example, the progressive rap metal band Rage against the Machine joined the fray on behalf of the Zapatistas.

Another indicator of the forward-looking orientation of the EZLN was its political sensibilities and platform. Although the movement invoked the iconic Che Guevara, it did not partake of the vanguardism that characterized the Cuban Revolution and other Marxist guerrilla movements that harked back to the Cold War. Indeed Subcomandante Marcos and other Zapatista leaders emphasized that their governing principle was "to lead by obeying," submitting all important initiatives to communal referenda. With some justification, then, the New York Times dubbed Marcos the "first post-modern guerrilla hero."[18] The Zapatistas preferred persuasion, propaganda, and negotiation to hierarchy and the use of brute force. They also featured two notable female leaders in Comandante Esther and Comandante Ramona, who (along with other women in the movement) drew up a manifesto containing basic guarantees for all women. In its ten provisions, the manifesto recognized the profound and deleterious consequences of machismo, demanding a series of basic rights:

1. Women, regardless of their race, creed, color, or political affiliation, have the right to participate in the revolutionary struggle as determined by their desire and capacity.
2. Women have the right to work and receive a fair salary.
3. Women have the right to decide the number of children they will have and care for.
4. Women have the right to participate in the matters of the community and take charge if they are freely and democratically elected.
5. Women and their children have the right to primary attention in their health and nutrition.
6. Women have the right to an education.
7. Women have the right to choose their partner and are not obliged to enter into marriage.
8. Women have the right to be free of violence from both relatives and strangers. Rape and attempted rape will be severely punished.
9. Women will be able to occupy positions of leadership in the organization and hold military rank in the revolutionary armed forces.
10. Women will have all the rights and obligations specified in the Revolutionary Laws and regulations.[19]

Finally, the EZLN program critiqued modernization itself rather than merely demanding a redistribution of resources. The Zapatistas called for ecological responsibility and drew attention to the destruction of the Lacandón rainforest, home to probably the poorest indigenous group in the nation (figure 8.1). They thus became the first Latin American rebellion to associate themselves with the global environmentalist movement.

The Zapatista rebellion inaugurated a terrible year for Carlos Salinas, the third president in a row to have his presidency end in disarray. In March 1994 a gunman assassinated Luis Donaldo Colosio, the PRI's presidential nominee. In a speech shortly before his death, Colosio had identified severe problems within the political system dominated by the PRI and promised to bring true democracy to Mexico. He had also visited EZLN representatives in Chiapas and advocated an open dialogue with the rebels. These plans far exceeded Salinas's paternalistic idea of co-opting the opposition by allowing them to hold a few governorships, and it is not surprising that many Mexicans blamed Salinas for the assassination of the man whom he had handpicked. The president proceeded to select another

FIGURE 8.1 Subcomandante Marcos addressing an EZLN meeting in the Lacandón jungle in August 2005. He is flanked by armed Zapatista troops and joined at the table by women leaders of the movement. Photo courtesy of Diane Rus.

nominee, the former education minister Ernesto Zedillo, then embarked on an election-year spending spree to pave the way for Zedillo's victory at the polls. Once again, both Cuauhtémoc Cárdenas and the PAN ran credible campaigns, and again the PRI won a narrow victory in a three-way race—this time with less than 49 percent of the vote. Many observers cited the *voto de miedo*, the "vote of fear," as a deciding factor in Zedillo's triumph, as many Mexicans feared adverse consequences for themselves and their families if they voted for the opposition. In September the assassination of PRI Secretary General José Francisco Ruiz Massieu, Salinas's former brother-in-law, chilled the nation. Neither Colosio's nor Ruiz's murders were ever solved. To make matters worse, with stunning predictability, an economic crisis accompanied the presidential transition. Political turmoil and the massive debt incurred by Salinas's excessive spending during his last year in office produced another massive capital flight and a 65 percent devaluation of the peso. Although U.S. President Bill Clinton put together a loan package of fifty billion dollars in order to stop the peso's slide and rescue the recently privatized banking system, the consequences were disastrous. In 1995 the economy contracted at a rate of 6.2 percent, which effectively wiped out the economic growth of the entire Salinas sexenio.

The peso crisis constituted a new setback for ordinary Mexicans. One popular joke sarcastically made light of Zedillo's expertise as a trained economist with a Ph.D. from Yale University. A woman encounters a friend on the street, and the two women sustain the following conversation:

> "You have lost a lot of weight."
> "Well, my doctor made me give up meat."
> "Still, you are really skinny, almost too thin!"
> "My doctor also made me give up cheese and milk."
> "What's the name of your doctor?"
> "Doctor Zedillo!"[20]

The crisis also spawned the development of new conservative grassroots movements. One of them, El Barzón (referring to the hitch ring for a team of oxen pulling a plow), represented a movement of small business owners and farmers who struggled to repay dollar-denominated debts. The crisis had also made it difficult for small-scale entrepreneurs to obtain credit, as the devaluation contributed to higher interest rates for new loans. Like the EZLN, El Barzón resuscitated revolutionary-era slogans, most famously, *Debo, no niego, pago lo justo* (I owe, I do not deny it; I will pay what is fair). Unlike the Zapatistas, however, El Barzón did not take military action, limiting itself to random protests. In the central Mexican state of Zacatecas, members of El Barzón organized road blocks using farm vehicles. Along with the postearthquake fallout, the emergence of groups such as this one indicated that the PRI had lost much of its remaining support among the middle class.

Zedillo confronted these challenges by assuaging the formal opposition and repressing the EZLN. Aware that his own mandate was weak, having been elected only after the assassination of a popular nominee, he continued Salinas's practice of allowing PAN candidates to win governorships.

By 1998 PAN governors ruled in six northern and central states, and Cuauhtémoc Cárdenas served as mayor of Mexico City. Meantime Zedillo was far less generous with the EZLN. In February 1995 he deployed the army for a surprise raid against the Zapatistas, and the government quickly recaptured most of the rebel-held territory. Army checkpoints controlled most major roads in the highlands and throughout the state, but the military failed to capture Marcos, Ramona, or any of the other leading EZLN commanders. The movement again took to the Internet to make its case, and Zedillo faced an international outcry over his unilateral decision to end the prevailing cease-fire. In short order, the president resumed negotiations with the EZLN, leading to the San Andrés Accords of 1996, which stipulated special rights and autonomy for Mexico's indigenous people. Nonetheless tensions persisted, and Zapatista sympathizers strongly suspected federal government involvement in the massacres of EZLN supporters in the communities of Aguas Blancas and Acteal. Violent clashes with insurgent groups in Guerrero and Oaxaca further accentuated the sense that the Zedillo government had chosen confrontation over negotiation in its approach to conflict in indigenous southern Mexico. Apart from those working in exclusive tourist enclaves like Huatulco and Cancún, the inhabitants of that region stood to lose the most from NAFTA, especially campesino maize producers who now had little protection against large agribusiness interests.

By 1997, however, the rest of the country fared somewhat better after weathering the latest economic crisis. Multinational corporations relocated production from the United States to Mexico, prompting the U.S. independent presidential candidate Ross Perot and others to complain about the loss of U.S. manufacturing jobs to plants south of the border. Wages rebounded, and export-oriented entrepreneurs reaped the benefits of a U.S. economic expansion that averaged 4.5 percent per year. By the end of Zedillo's term, Mexico's exports surpassed those of Brazil, making the nation the leading exporter in Latin America.

Despite this economic rebound, the PRI found itself at a crossroads in the years leading up to the 2000 presidential elections. Recent changes to the electoral law had made elections relatively fair and impartial, and in 1994 international observers had ensured the proper reporting of results in Zedillo's narrow victory. The PRI could not continue the authoritarian practices of the past; now it needed to win fair and square if it desired to rule into the new millennium. In 2000 that was a tall task. To be sure, the party still enjoyed a considerable advantage over the opposition due to its corporatist control of mass organizations and the fact that it held a monopoly over the use of the national colors, red, white, and green (the PAN's colors were blue and white, and those of the PRD, yellow and black). But two powerful opposition candidates opposed the PRI: Cuauhtémoc Cárdenas of the PRD and Vicente Fox Quesada, a former rancher and Coca-Cola executive, of the PAN. In many ways, Fox was attractive to much of the PRI leadership. The son of Irish and Spanish immigrants, the strapping, charismatic Fox stood six-five in his trademark cowboy boots. He had become eligible to run for the presidency after a constitutional amendment eliminated the requirement that both parents of a presidential candidate be native-born Mexicans. Indeed rumors circulated that Fox was the preferred candidate of the now-displaced ex-president Salinas. He enjoyed the backing of the millionaires of Monterrey and the multinational corporations, and his Catholic faith and social conservatism earned him substantial middle-class support. Fox also advocated open dialogue with the Zapatistas and other opposition groups. The PRI went into the campaign against Cárdenas and Fox with a singularly bland candidate, Francisco Labastida from the northern state of Sinaloa.

On July 2, 2000, voters went to the polls, and the unthinkable happened: Fox won the election with 42 percent of the vote, 7 percent more than Labastida. After seventy-one years, the Institutional Revolutionary Party had lost its hold on the executive branch. Significantly the PRI remained the largest party in Congress and thus retained the ability to stop any reforms that Fox might propose that required legislative approval. Nonetheless Fox's victory seemed to signal the official demise of the PRI.

It was the dawn of a new day, and once again Mexicans wondered if their revolution had ended — this time by means of the victory of the conservative PAN. It certainly appeared that way for those who dreamed of reviving social reforms or, at the very least, the social compact that had dissolved under the onslaught of economic crisis and neoliberal globalization in the 1990s. In one important way, however, the 2000 elections had vindicated a significant goal of the 1910 revolution: Madero's struggle for democracy and local autonomy. As the nation entered a new millennium, it featured divided government at the federal level, an assortment of PRI, PRD, and PAN governors at the state level, and a patchwork of municipal governments chosen by local people. In addition, the EZLN reminded Mexicans that it would not go away under the Fox administration; in 2001 the Zapatistas organized a huge demonstration in Mexico City.

Those who took their cues from nature remained hopeful that the cycles of history would again favor revolutionary change. No sooner was Fox inaugurated than the majestic volcano Popocatépetl blew its top. As some indigenous campesinos believed, the ancient fire god residing inside the volcano was angry, either because the Mexican people had abandoned the revolution or because "the Revolution" had forsaken its people.

"The Revolution is dead."—the PRI
"The PRI is dead."—the Revolution

— GRAFFITI ON A BARRIO WALL IN
 SAN CRISTÓBAL DE LAS CASAS, 1994

Conclusions
A REVOLUTION WITH LEGS | 9

In the epigraph that launched this volume, the young journalist and revolutionary participant Martín Luis Guzmán expressed a central, bitter truth about the revolution of 1910, namely, the moral impossibility of not supporting it, yet the material impossibility of achieving through it the national regeneration that would justify so much death and destruction. Between 1910 and 1920, in one form or another, millions of men and women, divided along lines of region, class, ethnicity, and generation—not to mention the array of factions and bands in which they affiliated—participated in the epic revolution. One would have to go back to Mexico's first celebrated cycle of violence, the independence insurgencies of the early nineteenth century, to find comparably protracted and far-flung episodes of mass mobilization and social upheaval. Yet a hundred years of advances in military technologies and national communications render this earlier cycle of violence almost quaint by comparison. As the revolutionaries first fought *federales* and then, in the struggle's bloodiest phase, one another, approximately one million people lost their lives, and others saw their home villages erased from the map. No doubt a good many of these participants merely sought the best means to survive the fiesta of bullets, expediently changing sides and ultimately fleeing *la bola*'s carnage and chaos at the first real opportunity. Still, many more made active choices in a ragged revolutionary process they came to embrace. While individual motivations differed and often overlapped, some sought to raise up themselves and their families, improving their socioeconomic and political positions and exacting a greater measure of dignity by lashing out at their class and ethnic antagonists, neighborhood rivals, or the local political boss. Others saw the revolution as a means of collective political empowerment, mobilizing to preserve or increase the autonomy of their communities and regions. Still others saw beyond such personal or local logics of revolution, glimpsing junctures (such as the U.S. occupation of Veracruz, or the "Punitive Expedition") when larger national stakes were involved, such as restoring pride and honor to the *patria*, and increasing the jurisdictional capacity of a socially revindicationist state.

By 1920 the worst paroxysms of military violence — the "wind that swept Mexico," as the writer Anita Brenner put it — had subsided, not least owing to attrition and exhaustion. Still, throughout the ensuing decades, the revolution reverberated in local contests over land, labor rights, political office, the control of markets and natural resources, and the shape that ethnic and gender relations, and citizenship itself, would take. As the winning Constitutionalists, embodied after 1920 by the so-called Sonoran Dynasty of Obregón and Calles, consolidated the state, these various local contests became imbricated in official projects of state and nation formation and were often affected by the imperatives of interstate relations as well. Local manifestations of revolution and their leaders were institutionalized into "the Revolution," first under the clientelist proto-corporatism of the Sonorans and then under Cárdenas's more fully realized state mechanism of corporatist inclusion and vertical control. In the process, the incipient official party — first the National Revolutionary Party, then the Party of the Mexican Revolution — seeking to legitimate its grip on the new revolutionary regime, finally began to make good on the deferred social reform and economic and cultural "regeneration" to which Guzmán had alluded, absent a modicum of which long-term social peace could not plausibly be guaranteed.

Thus in the 1920s and 1930s the business of the Mexican Revolution was political incorporation, commitment to social reform, and the cultural politics of nation building (*forjando patria*) as the state sought to build itself up in the hearts and minds of Mexicans. But as the high tide of social revolution receded in the waning years of President Cárdenas's *sexenio*, and as the revolution increasingly moved to the right during World War II and the early years of the Cold War, the business of the revolution literally became business. Under Miguel Alemán's developmentalist regime, *modernización y justicia social* became an empty catch phrase, as the ruling party realized its final incarnation in 1946 with the PRI, whose colors were identical to those on the tricolored national flag. To be a patriotic Mexican now meant to be a good consumer, as Mexico took its rightful place as a bulwark of the Free World and its New Economic Order. Under Alemán and his successors, the government repressed independent workers and persecuted the Communist Party; agrarian reform became an afterthought; and dissidents of most stripes found themselves ridiculed and red-baited. Still, the economic miracle (fueled by import-substitution industrialization [ISI]), the oil boom, and the PRI's timely alternation from right to center-left tendencies (witness the populist administrations of López Mateos, Echeverría, and López Portillo) permitted the official party to commit enough social spending and bestow enough patronage to cling to its reputation as el *Estado Educador, Protector y Constructor*, even in the wake of its debacle at Tlatelolco Plaza. Moreover, for many years after the massacre, the PRI continued to tout its credentials as the steward of "the Revolution" and its legacies.

Sadly, one of the PRI's unacknowledged revolutionary legacies was the degradation of Mexico's environment. It is only within the past ten to fifteen years, with the beginnings of a new environmental history of twentieth-century Mexico, that scholars have joined environmental activists in documenting the ecological costs of ISI and market-driven developmentalism. This darker side of the revolutionary inheritance includes PEMEX's negligence in failing to prevent a number of horrific accidents (such as the 1992 gasoline explosions caused by PEMEX pipe leaks into Guadalajara's sewer system, which killed more than two hundred people and left craters fifty-five yards wide) and its poisoning of countless estuaries along the Gulf Coast. From the onset of the Border Industrialization Program in the early 1960s, maquiladora-led development has spawned chemical pollution that has degraded air and water resources on both sides of the border, and increasingly in interior industrial zones as well. The chronic levels of toxicity in the air and water of the Federal District and surrounding states, while they reflect the failures of hydraulic and industrial policies dating back to the Porfiriato and even the colony, have been compounded exponentially by the lack of adequate environmental planning since the ISI-fueled economic miracle. Much the same could be said about the soil degradation, pesticide pollution, and other unsavory agricultural consequences that accompanied the advance of the "green revolution" and ranching economies in tropical regions such as the Pacific coastal lowlands and the canyons and forests of Chiapas.

The PRI, as we have seen, abandoned its posture of revolutionary stewardship with the economic crisis of 1982, the IMF-mandated austerity regimes that ensued, and Mexico's subsequent commitment to "reform the Revolution" and jettison the revolutionary social compact enshrined in the 1917 Constitution. The neoliberal PRI's fire sale of nationalized enterprises, including telecommunications and the Mexican national bank, to private investors, as well as its agrarian "reform" (read "termination") rooted in Article 27, eloquently attested to its repudiation of revolutionary legacies. The PRI's neoliberal reforms left little distinction between it and the National Action Party (PAN), except for the latter's pronounced Catholicism and rejection of historical Liberalism. (Not for nothing, then, did pundits begin to joke about the appearance of a new political entity: the "PRIPAN"). Interestingly, although Salinas made it clear that the national oil monopoly PEMEX was in drastic need of reform, which would open up the corrupt and inefficient energy behemoth to foreign investment, neither he nor his successor, Ernesto Zedillo, ever felt strong enough to seriously challenge the iconic symbol of Cárdenas's historic nationalist expropriation—a trend that continued under the PANista Presidents Vicente Fox and Felipe Calderón.

HEGEMONY AND ITS DISCONTENTS: THE LEGACY OF A REVOLUTIONARY STATE COMMUNITY

As the PEMEX issue suggests, the unprecedented seven decades of PRI rule owed to much more than authoritarian rule, whether of the *mano dura* or *dictablanda* varieties. To be sure, the party did not shrink from coercion and even liquidation of its enemies, and a case could be made that, in the final instance, its extended rule always depended upon it. Yet one should also not minimize the significance of the PRI's far-flung cultural project. The official party had harnessed education, the plastic arts, music, archaeological sites, and museums since its inception; and beginning in the 1930s, the state expanded its sizable investment into radio, film, newspapers, comic books, roads, and tourism. By the 1950s its efforts embraced television and evocative national spectacles of folkloric dance.

Whether directly controlled (e.g., public education and national monuments and museums) or regulated through subsidization and often subtle regimes of censorship (the electronic and print media), few areas of cultural production escaped the state's attention prior to the onset of the neoliberal reforms of the late 1980s and 1990s. It was through this cultural project bridging state and private sector—which many have judged to be the most sophisticated and best funded in the western hemisphere during the mid-twentieth century—that the PRI leadership exhorted Mexicans across class, regional, ethnic, race, gender, and generational lines to feel connected to the "revolutionary family" that spoke in their name. In the decades following World War II, the official party's campaign to unify the nation as never before deployed a shared mythology drawing on a pantheon of popular icons. These included historic military and political heroes as diverse as Benito Juárez and Emiliano Zapata; figures from mass consumer culture such as the singer and actor Pedro Infante, the everyman comic Cantinflas, and the masked wrestler El Santo; stock villains like La Malinche; and, above all, the nation's beloved patroness, the Virgin of Guadalupe.

In its advancement of this cultural project, the PRI enjoyed an extraordinarily close partnership with the private sector in the critically burgeoning field of electronic media. Indeed in the postwar decades the media empire Televisa, which exercised a virtual monopoly on TV and other media, functioned as a veritable Ministry of Propaganda for the PRI and was recognized as such by most Mexicans. The origins of Televisa can be traced to the formation of the Telesistema Mexicano in 1955, a mass-media conglomerate that was the result of a merger between two of Mexico's most powerful media moguls, Rómulo O'Farrill, a confidant of Miguel Alemán, and Emilio Azcárraga Vidaurreta, whose dominance over commercial radio paved the way for his control and—more important—that of his son Emilio ("El Tigre") Azcárraga Milmo, over television. The Azcárragas quickly came to dominate the new relationship, galvanizing a mass-media dynasty centered on the renamed Televisa, which came to dictate commercial production of culture in Mexico and throughout parts of Latin America for the next four decades.

Of course, putative hegemonies must always be regarded as fragile and contested processes rather than inevitable outcomes. Beneath the smooth surface of PRI rule, with its multiple symbols of a prosperous and uni-

mexicanidad, there had always been unmistakable signs of fragmentation and discontent. As we have seen, the cultural and political symbols of Mexicanness also underwrote movements and protests against the PRI's long-running regime. In the 1950s and 1960s the Morelos-based Jaramillistas dusted off the historic revolutionary Zapata in their struggles with PRI power holders who controlled the region's sugar industry. In 1968 a student-led coalition in civil society harnessed both Mexican revolutionary and transnational countercultural symbols (Pancho Villa and Che Guevara, among others), to press democratization on the politically sclerotic regime. A quarter century later, on the very day the North American Free Trade Agreement went into effect, Zapata was again reclaimed, this time by rebellious Mayan peasants in Chiapas whose lands and commodity production had been targeted by neoliberalism and who hoped to restore the Mexican Revolution's social compact.

By invoking such potent revolutionary symbols as Zapata, Ricardo Flores Magón, and the Aguascalientes Convention in their movement's name and justifying proclamations, as well as in their mural art and local self-governing institutions, the Zapatista National Liberation Army (EZLN) was endorsing what the Mexican historian and activist Adolfo Gilly has referred to as perhaps the Mexican Revolution's most enduring legacy: the notion of a "state community." In a seminal essay analyzing the 1994 rebellion, Gilly points out that since colonial times, the legitimacy and authority of the nation's rulers was "not constituted in a vacuum." Rather authority and rule were always fashioned "by taking into account . . . the active or passive resistance of the ruled, not their inert subordination." Particularly since the revolution of 1910, he argues, "the established rule in Mexico [has been] the permanent negotiation of authority, case by case and space by space, within frameworks recognized by all."[1] Indeed it was the debate about Article 27 and subsequent legislation that served to enlarge these spaces in the popular imaginary. The result, in the words of Alan Knight, was a new revolutionary hegemony, "more durable than the [failed hegemonies] of the past" because it was "the work not only of elite architects but also of the calloused hands of common peons."[2] The fact that the PRI state did not quash the EZLN in the wake of its occupation of San Cristóbal (the old Ciudad Real) and other provincial towns owed much more to the fact that the rebellion had fired the nation's popular imagination than to the military equation on the ground.

Indeed, the state and the rebels invoked two different appropriations of Emiliano Zapata's legacy—one "official," and the other, grassroots— and the popular version proved far more powerful than the official one. The state connected Zapata's image with the neoliberal reform of Article 27 that stripped it of its original intent and facilitated Mexico's passage into NAFTA. As the reform was being deliberated, its proponents justified their proposal by invoking Zapata's memory as a defender of law. Most Mexicans, however, did not buy this bald attempt to harness revolutionary imagery for the purposes of dismantling one of the most salient laws that came out of the revolutionary struggle. Instead, Mexicans seemed more captivated by the second coming of a more revolutionary Zapatismo, which fought to protect "land and liberty" from the encroachment of modernizing agribusiness. In truth, the Mexican people would not permit the rebellion to be crushed, testament to the residual notions of a state community and the revolutionary social compact that underwrote it. The EZLN had dictated a body of "revolutionary laws" for the Chiapanecan territory it held, just as Zapata's Liberating Army of the South had done eight decades earlier in Morelos. These gestures, tied to a historical reality and not just newly issued proclamations, "addressed both the present and Mexican [collective] memory."[3]

If the rebellion was perceived to be legitimate, Gilly observes, the PRI state was obliged to negotiate:

> One doesn't negotiate because one has the right to, but because one has the *force* to make that *right* be recognized. These ideas [were] rooted in the common culture within which the Mexican state community has sustained itself . . . since the revolution of 1910 and its aftermath, the *cardenista* reforms. Of course that doesn't guarantee that a rebellion or movement won't be repressed, and ferociously, as occurred many times before and since. But it does permit the State, when events or convenience oblige it, to *negotiate without losing* face. . . . [The Mexican state] knows when public opinion demands truce and negotiation.[4]

The EZLN rebels realized that they had to be organized to negotiate effectively, and that their campaign to negotiate would fail without effective resistance. In other words, no one would care about them until they took San Cristóbal. But from the outset, they also made it abundantly clear to the Mexican state and people that their purpose was to reestablish the

lutionary constitution, not to subvert it. Gilly concludes, "The cen-
ᴛ.ᴀ..ᴄy of the Constitution in the discourse of the rebel communities says
much about the historical thread of that state community to which the
[EZLN] rebels [were] demanding entrance as Indians with rights. All who
had entered before did so by knocking down the doors, in the revolution
of 1910 or in the 1930s."[5] The EZLN's high-profile rebellion at the end of
the twentieth century thus casts in bold relief a fundamental conclusion
regarding the nation's revolutionary legacy: that the revolution forever
changed the terms by which the Mexican state would be formed. It has
been the revolutionary state's partial incorporation of insistent popular
demands that helps to distinguish Mexico from countries like Peru and
Guatemala today. One has only to juxtapose the contrasting images of
Chiapas's Zapatista rebels and Peru's Sendero Luminoso to appreciate the
point. For Mexico's latter-day Zapatistas, their struggle has consistently
been circumscribed within the framework of the revolution, the nation-
state, and the revindicative constitution the revolution bequeathed; for
the Senderistas, it has been about the bankruptcy of the state and the absence of an inclusive national imaginary.

It has become fashionable among theorists of revolutionary change in
Latin America to conceive of state formation as cultural revolution over
a medium or long *durée*. In the process, scholars have conjured up archi-
tectonic images of a "great arch," à la Philip Corrigan and Derek Sayer's
classic formulation of the development of the triumphant English capitalist state, which skillfully managed to integrate regimes of domination
and forms of resistance over centuries.[6] Thus rule became sedimented in
laws, institutions, routines, rituals, and symbols that regulated quotidian
life and, more often than not, preempted alternatives.

But if history teaches us anything, it is that nation-state formation is a
sui generis process, and we should be leery of applying ready-built theoretical models. Responding to Eurocentric notions of "great arches" and
stately viaducts spanning centuries of Mexican state formation, Gilly conjured up the quintessentially Mexican image of the Tule Tree, the mam-
moth Montezuma cypress tree located in a small indigenous barrio nine
kilometers east of Oaxaca City, judged to have the stoutest trunk of any
tree in the world, surpassing even the largest of California's giant sequoias.
The tree has been around for centuries, even millennia, and its spreading
subterranean root network is labyrinthine and immense. Frequently nick-

named the "Tree of Life," owing to the images of animals and people are reputedly visible in the tree's gnarled trunk, the Tule Tree conjures the durability, adaptability, and transitivity of the revolution's popular traditions and symbols, through which both the state and its opponents have sought to negotiate and legitimate their contests and struggles.[7] This ongoing process, a state of play that articulates nation-state formation and grassroots political cultures, with each connected to as well as expressed in the other, lies at the heart of this volume, and to our knowledge distinguishes the Mexican revolutionary process from that of other twentieth-century social movements.

REVOLUTIONARY LEGACIES IN THE NEW MILLENNIUM

Has the revolutionary legacy extended into the new millennium? To a certain extent it has, although those on the Left who awaited the detonation of yet another revolutionary cycle in 2010 were bound to be disappointed. (This is hardly surprising, since true revolutions are rare events in human history, and nations that survive upheavals as bloody and destructive as Mexico's tend to regard revolution, whatever the social benefits, as a drastic and final resort.) Since the PRI's watershed defeat at the polls in 2000, the revolution's legacy has surfaced in a variety of political and cultural contests. In March 2001 the new Fox administration was forced to contend with a boisterous "Zapatour" mounted by the EZLN, a large consciousness-raising caravan that frequently doubled as a merchandising event and pop concert. The caravan wended its way through Mexico's indigenous regions and culminated in an occupation of Mexico City's central plaza, threatening not to leave until the PAN- and PRI-dominated Congress passed a long-awaited bill on indigenous rights.

In 2006 Mexico City's charismatic former mayor, Andrés Manuel López Obrador (popularly known by his initials as AMLO) launched a wildly popular Party of the Democratic Revolution (PRD) candidacy against the incumbent PAN and its presidential candidate Felipe Calderón, ultimately losing a fraud-plagued election by the razor-thin margin of 0.5 percent of the vote. AMLO invoked the economic nationalism of the revolutionary icon Lázaro Cárdenas to combat the "savage capitalism" of neoliberalism, and he refused to recognize the Federal Electoral Tribunal's verdict that Calderón had won fairly; eventually he was symbolically sworn in by his supporters, appropriately on November 20, the Día de la Revolución.

Prior to that, for weeks in August 2006, AMLO supporters had occupied twelve kilometers of the Paseo de la Reforma, Mexico City's most bustling thoroughfare. In effect, they convened a massive popular fair and parallel tent society (*el plantón*) along the Paseo, paralyzing corporate businesses and luxury hotels and staging popular *fútbol* matches outside the Mexican Stock Exchange. AMLO's intent was to emphasize the hijacking of Mexico's new democracy and the nation's subordination to big domestic and foreign business and media interests. Ultimately, however, the plantón produced opposition from many of AMLO's own supporters who resented the authoritarian manner in which he was interfering in the social and economic life of the capital, inconveniencing many poor and middle-class residents in the process.

In April 2008 López Obrador's PRD supporters and allies from other left and environmental parties took over both houses of Congress: they chained shut the doors of the chambers and barricaded themselves behind chairs and tables to protest the ruling PAN's attempt to modify the nation's energy policy and privatize the national oil monopoly, PEMEX, a violation of the 1917 Constitution. Many of the men were dressed in white oil workers' overalls and hard hats; women protesters proclaimed themselves the Adelita Brigade, twenty-first-century *soldaderas* who would not relinquish hard-won revolutionary rights to the national patrimony. The Adelitas dressed in long period skirts, with homemade bandoleers across their blouses, and sang and danced to revolutionary *corridos* and popular *cumbias* about oil and nationalism. The protesters camped out in pup tents arranged around the Senate podium for well over a week, paralyzing legislative debate and ultimately triggering an extended national dialogue on President Calderón's plans to open up PEMEX to transnational investment.

A debate continues regarding whether AMLO's wing of the PRD actually has revolutionary politics or, since many of them are former PRIistas, harks back to the postwar corporatism of the Institutional Revolutionary Party. Certainly AMLO's bloc includes some radical reformers from new social movements or the independent and labor Left. Others are significantly less progressive and likely would advocate little more than the partial social compact that the PRI espoused during the sexenios of López Mateos, Echeverría, and López Portillo, under the auspices of a strong, centralized corporatist machine.

In the presidential elections of July 1, 2012, AMLO once again mounted a stiff electoral challenge, ultimately losing to the standard-bearer of the PRI, Enrique Peña Nieto, the former governor of the Estado de México. Amid accusations of fraud and vote-buying on the part of the PRI, López Obrador lost by a little more than 6 percent, with the PAN candidate, Josefina Vázquez Mota, finishing third. While Mexico's once-official revolutionary party has thus recently regained the presidency (with the jury still out on whether the "PRI 2.0" will be an improvement or even markedly different from its "dinosaur"-led predecessor), the left-wing opposition spearheaded by AMLO and the PRD remains vibrant. Less than two months before the vote, Peña Nieto confronted unexpected criticism at the Universidad Iberoamericana, a Catholic private university in the western suburbs of Mexico City. When the candidate and his staffers suggested that López Obrador and what they called his paid protesters (*porros*) had staged the protests, 131 students posted a video on YouTube in which they brandished their university credentials. This video went viral, prompting thousands of messages on Twitter in which citizens claimed, "Yo soy 132" (I am number 132). Thus was born the Yo Soy 132 movement, one that exemplifies the ongoing resistance to Mexico's neoliberal policies and a critique of undemocratic practices by the PRI and the PAN (figure 9.1).

An underexamined dimension of the PRD coalition—and to date an underappreciated group in the nation's historical experience more generally—are lesbian, gay, bisexual, and transgender (LGBT) Mexicans. (This is about to change, with the imminent appearance of several dissertations and books.) Participation by sexual minorities has been widely accepted in the PRD, which in 1997 celebrated the election of Patria Jiménez, the first openly lesbian member of the Federal Congress, and has since spearheaded a raft of progressive legislation in Mexico City and several states that legalizes same-sex unions and protects their adoption and inheritance rights. Still, the LGBT community has hitherto been the focus of only a few footnotes and anecdotes in the recounting of Mexico's modern past. Most notable perhaps is Carlos Monsiváis's and others' recounting of a sensationalized episode known as "El Baile de los Cuarenta y Uno" (the Dance of the Forty-One). The incident triggered a scandal in Porfirian high society in 1901, when police raided a tony drag ball, arresting forty-two cross-dressed men, and then releasing one, who was allegedly the son-in-law of Porfirio Díaz. (Two weeks later, in December 1901, the

FIGURE 9.1 Demonstration of Yo Soy 132 protest movement on the Paseo de la Reforma, Mexico City, May 2012. Wikimedia Commons, http://en.wikipedia.org /wiki/File:MarchaYoSoy132.jpg.

police carried out a similar raid on a group of lesbians, but the incident received substantially less fanfare.) The raid that apprehended *los 41 maricones* (homosexuals) received a wave of press coverage and quickly drew the attention of *corridistas* and popular artists (including José Guadalupe Posada), as well as satirists, playwrights, and novelists. Eventually it was featured in Televisa's lavish 1994 historical telenovela on the Porfiriato, *El vuelo del águila* (The Flight of the Eagle). So scandalous was the affair that the number 41 quickly became taboo in Mexican culture: no division or regiment bore the number, and it was typically eschewed in enumerating house addresses, hotel and hospital rooms, and license plates — even in the celebration of birthdays.

Mexican history, especially the trajectory of its revolutionary and post-revolutionary past, provides an interesting context for appreciating LGBT struggles. The ideological and cultural influence of the French Revolution and also of the French occupation of the 1860s resulted in the adoption of the Napoleonic Code, which decriminalized homosexuality in 1871. Nevertheless prevailing laws against public immorality or "lurid," "indecent" behavior, rooted in a fiercely patriarchal and masculinist culture, have routinely been deployed to prosecute homosexual behavior over generations. Similarly, homophobic hate crimes and the murder of homosexuals have been a tragic fact of modern Mexican life, proliferating in the nation's capital and major cities, often with impunity. Not surprisingly Mexico City, which possesses the greatest number of openly LGBT communities in the country, also has the worst record of homophobic hate crimes. As transnational influences have changed the tenor of Mexican cultural life and popular politics, patriarchal and sexual attitudes have begun to change, most quickly in the larger metropolitan areas, where access to foreign cultural and political trends are greatest. Although the historical roots of LGBT communities' claims on citizenship date back at least to Cardenismo in the 1930s, developments in the tumultuous 1960s and 1970s, especially the rise of the U.S. gay movement, fallout from the Tlatelolco massacre, and democratizing trends since then, have transformed the prospects of the LGBT movement. Since the late 1990s LGBT organizations have mobilized mass demonstrations, pride marches, and AIDS awareness events, some of which, harnessed to left-wing parties such as the PRD, the Labor Party, and the now-defunct Social Democratic Party, have turned out tens and even hundreds of thousands of people.

Tlatelolco's symbolic importance to this trajectory cannot be minimized. Gone in the wake of the student massacre was any willingness to accept the PRI's rhetoric of revolutionary partnership with a broad spectrum of the Mexican people. Equally important, the students' challenge to the state's patrimonial authority and the latter's brutal response — with the head of the revolutionary family effectively ordering the slaughter of his own children — dealt a fatal blow to the *patriarchal* culture that underpinned the state's authority. Reassembling the patriarchal ideal of the Revolutionary Family would prove impossible in the decades that followed. Cultural critics such as Monsiváis and social scientists such as the anthropologist Matthew Gutmann have argued provocatively that the disintegration of the revolutionary family model coincided with a whole complex of changes in daily behavior, including the discrediting of the *casa chica* (a second, informal household for men who could afford to keep mistresses), greater participation by women in feminist organizations, broader constructions of the composition of family and household, and the firm institutionalization of a gay and lesbian movement. Other scholars agree that recent changes in discourses about love, sex, family, and gender roles and identities have been impressive, but they are less sure that

actual behavior follows discourse in any predictable pattern. Nevertheless it seems clear that the demise of the revolutionary family metaphor,
which casts the state and president as the alternately gentle and macho,
all-providing father, was congruent with the end of the ideal of such a
patriarch in Mexican families too. No doubt the activism engineered by
leaders of the gay and lesbian communities was made possible in part by
the crumbling myths of the macho revolutionary that accompanied the
PRI's decline. In the new cultural and social spaces that have appeared in
recent decades, charismatic (and undeniably *Mexican*) singers like Juan
Gabriel have demonstrated the presence of gendered alternatives to traditional macho icons like Pedro Infante.

Another social movement that has elicited regional comparison with
Chiapas's EZLN is the the Asamblea Popular de los Pueblos de Oaxaca
(Popular Assembly of the Peoples of Oaxaca, or APPO). Initially organized
in June 2006 in support of the state's repressed teachers' union, the Popular Assembly began as a broad-based movement whose initial goal was the
removal of the PRI's corrupt and brutal governor, Ulises Ruiz Ortiz. At
its core, the APPO bore many similarities to Chiapas's Zapatistas: it was
a consensus-driven, horizontally configured movement rooted in the tradition of popular assemblies, which draws from both the practice of new
social movements and indigenous traditions that go back centuries. Like
the EZLN, the APPO initially included members of the old Marxist Left,
who eschewed a vanguardist strategy; representatives of new social movements (e.g., women, students, neighborhood and environmental groups)
who opposed neoliberalism; broad support from the state's indigenous
communities; and a sprinkling of countercultural and fringe elements
(like anarchopunks). For more than five months in 2006, the APPO barricaded and controlled the city of Oaxaca and held sway over much of the
state. Not until Vicente Fox, in one of his final acts as president, sent in
federal security forces on November 25 did Ruiz regain control. There is
an abundant literature produced by the movement and its national and
international supporters about the "days of freedom" under APPO "rule."
Although it never constituted a military force like the Zapatistas, Oaxaca's
Popular Assembly was hailed by the triumphalist Left as the catalyst of
another centennial revolutionary cycle (1810, 1910, 2010), and parallels to
former radical precursor movements like the Magonistas were frequently
drawn.

The movement has fragmented and waned in recent years, with significant internal discussion regarding whether APPO should engage in the formal political arena or remain a social movement more focused on the autonomy of self-governing indigenous communities. In the process, some of APPO's original leaders have defected and the movement has suffered internecine squabbles. Disturbing revelations have surfaced that some members of the leadership have maintained strong ties to the anti-Ruiz faction of the Oaxacan PRI and even links to the powerful national and regional oligarch Alfredo Harp Helú, the cousin of Carlos Slim. Critics have observed sardonically that APPO could not barricade the exclusive hillside neighborhoods of Oaxaca City, where Ruiz's cronies resided, because several of APPO's own leaders lived there too.

At the same time, the state's indigenous population — the largest segment of Oaxacan society — has assumed a higher profile in the residual movement. The debate among indigenous APPO communities in recent years has been how to gain greater protection against the caciques and economic elites who have historically preyed upon them. One option, espoused in the traditionally militant (and now PRD-aligned) center of Juchitán, in the Isthmus of Tehuantepec, is the need to form a strong regional alliance. Another, epitomized by Sierra Norte villages like Guelatao (Benito Juárez's birthplace), is to maximize each community's autonomy, negotiating arrangements when necessary with the authorities in Oaxaca City. Even in formerly isolated parts of the sierra there has been an effort in recent years to link up villages through the medium of community radio, which has extended participation in APPO. Still, as in Chiapas, local organization remains the hallmark of the movement, and hundreds of organizations at the indigenous base of society currently exist.

Although, as we have seen, a variety of protests and mobilizations are ongoing, a second Mexican Revolution does not appear remotely on the horizon in our era of globalization and instantaneous communication. Indeed, throughout its twelve-year rule, the PAN, often aided by the PRI, waged an unremitting campaign to erode the constitutional underpinnings of the revolution of 1910. Nevertheless the concept of revolution itself remains fraught with meaning. Presidents Fox and Calderón frequently characterized the PAN's market-driven agenda, complete with a shrunken state and tighter relations with the United States, as a "second Mexican revolution" meant to rectify the economic and ideological shortcomings of its predecessor. It is too early to tell whether the new president, Enrique Peña Nieto of the PRI, will attempt to resuscitate any of the old discourse of the Institutional Revolutionary Party. So far, Peña Nieto has insisted that his party lives in the future rather than in the past, and his inaugural discourse on December 1, 2012, focused on the need to bring peace to a nation ravaged by six years of drug wars.

Likewise, the 2010 bicentennial and centennial celebrations of independence and the revolution showcased the decreased significance of the revolution in official discourse. The government, not to mention the Church, clearly put more effort into commemorating the bicentennial of independence. For example, President Felipe Calderón announced that the government of Mexico City would construct an arch to mark the bicentennial. Many PAN leaders saw the revolution at best as a political movement of liberation against an oppressive dictator, and at worst as an inconvenient artifact, an upheaval of limited, even negative significance — *lo de Pancho Villa*. Significantly the PAN modestly celebrated the democratic credentials of Francisco Madero; not surprisingly most of the members of the Madero family who are still active in politics operate as PANistas in the party's northern heartland. By contrast, the PAN-led national government elevated independence as a major watershed imbued with both Catholic and social significance: the birth of the Mexican nation under the aegis of Guadalupanismo. Indeed, for some right-wing commentators, the Catholic birthmark of independence established it as a wholesome counterweight to the anticlerical chaos that was the revolution.

President Calderón's New Year's speech commemorating the double anniversary in 2010 eloquently shows his regime's efforts to lionize the independence heroes and to downplay both the social goals of "the Revolution" and its protagonists. In light of the ongoing significance of revolutionary imagery, Calderón could ill afford to denigrate "the Revolution," but his words reveal his preference for a narrowly political legacy: "2010 will be the year of the *patria*; this year, we are celebrating the beginning of the independence movement, thanks to which our country conquered its liberty and sovereignty." After naming Hidalgo and Morelos as iconic figures in that movement, Calderón continued: "In 2010 we are also celebrating the centennial of the Revolution, an era in which we Mexicans revindicated the right of suffrage and individual guarantees, in addition to social rights and the nation's sovereignty over national resources."[8] No revolutionary leader—not even Madero—was mentioned in this speech, and the president closed his remarks with a call for national reconciliation: a message to Mexicans to abandon messy resistance movements such as the EZLN and APPO in favor of the official political process.

It remains to be seen how the Mexican revolutionary legacy will fare in the wake of the 2012 elections. In the last few months before the elections, the PRI—once the custodian of "the Revolution" and now more consciously a neoliberal option to the PAN—saw a 20-point lead in the polls virtually evaporate, but it eventually managed to prevail over the PRD and the PAN, which had been badly discredited by Calderón's disastrous and costly War on Drugs. AMLO's PRD continues to tout its revolutionary credentials, yet his party and the political Left in general appear to be in institutional disarray, often seemingly disconnected from the nation's new social movements, like the emergent, student-led Yo Soy 132. With the PRI distancing itself from "the Revolution" in every respect but its name, and once again discredited by charges of electoral fraud, the party's best means to consolidate its shaky 2012 electoral triumph may lie in its former reputation for smooth (if obscenely corrupt) dealings with the drug lords, in combination with renewed efforts to propitiate the U.S. government, which may well insist on tougher relations with the cartels. Ironically the narcos themselves seem more apt to use revolutionary and revindicationist imagery than the spanking new leaders of the PRI, often boasting of their philanthropy and "social mission" to the poor.

Finally, as the burgeoning literature on the U.S.-Mexican borderlands illustrates, the Mexican Revolution, epitomized by such telluric leaders as Pancho Villa and Pascual Orozco, who operated defiantly on both sides of the border, contributes powerful symbols for social and political movements that seek to advance transborder migrants' rights and combat the Mexican and U.S. states' ineffectual response to narcoviolence in border communities (figure 9.2). Borderlands scholars and activists have revalued the transnational *frontera*'s pivotal participation in the epic revolution and emphasized the importance of revolutionary events and heroes in contemporary "border thinking." Thus, for one activist scholar, Villa's and Orozco's capture of Ciudad Juárez in 1911 has "an elective affinity" with present-day *fronterizos'* border crossing as a strategy of resistance and survival. Villa in particular represents a specter whose example continues to haunt the border and the states that attempt to regulate it, ignoring

FIGURE 9.2 The Mexican revolution's symbols and visual imagery continue to exert a powerful hold on popular culture north of the border. The Chicago History Museum recently exhibited a low-rider car tricked out with a mural of Mexican revolutionary heroes on its hood. Photo courtesy of Christopher Moore and the Chicago History Museum.

the unfulfilled social promises of the revolution for which he fought. For some contemporary border activists, undocumented migration represents a "strange new revolution," an act whereby impoverished Mexicans attempt to fashion a future. In this movement from below against would-be hegemons on both sides of the Río Bravo/Rio Grande, "Ciudad Juárez, the city of immigrants . . . the vestibule to the United States and the American dream, the natural environment for the trafficking of drugs, arms, and people, is still the location of Villa's revolution."[9]

The epigraph that launched this chapter appeared as graffiti on a wall in San Cristóbal de las Casas shortly after the PRI had retaken the city from the Zapatista rebels after only a few days in January 1994. Apart from representing something of a play on the old joke about God and Nietzsche, it is a fine illustration of the popular brand of Mexican humor known as *la venganza del pueblo* (the people's revenge), which we have encountered frequently in this volume. More relevant for our closing discussion, the conflictual juxtaposition of ruling party and revolution in the graffiti reminds us that the long history of the Mexican Revolution and its enduring legacy can never be reduced to the official history and rhetoric of the ruling state or party, or to triumphalist depictions of popular resistance from below. Indeed it is the historical dynamic that connects both registers in a complex state of play, producing different outcomes at different junctures, which we have attempted to evoke in this volume. What has made the Mexican Revolution such an intriguing problem over several generations — and what has given it such sturdy legs — is the capacity of state rulers and local rebels and dissidents, more often than not, to contest and negotiate politics within a discursive framework that embraces the legitimacy of revolution within the context of the modern nation-state.

CHAPTER 1: INTRODUCTION

1. Martín Luis Guzmán, *The Eagle and the Serpent*, trans. Harriet de Onís (1928; Garden City, N.Y.: Doubleday, 1965), 163.

2. Luis Cabrera, "La revolución es la revolución," in *Obras Completas* (1911; Mexico City: Ediciones Oasis, 1975), 274.

3. John Mason Hart, *Revolutionary Mexico: The Coming and Process of the Mexican Revolution* (Berkeley: University of California Press, 1987).

4. Alan Knight, "The Mexican Revolution: Bourgeois? Nationalist? or Just a 'Great Rebellion,'?" *Bulletin of Latin American Research* 4.2 (1985): 1–37. The argument that the revolution was merely a "great rebellion" comes from Ramón Eduardo Ruiz, *The Great Rebellion: Mexico, 1905–1924* (New York: Norton, 1980).

5. Alan Knight, *The Mexican Revolution*, 2 vols. (Cambridge, U.K.: Cambridge University Press, 1986), 1:5 and passim.

6. See, for example, the popular history of the struggle by the cartoonist Eduardo del Río, known as RIUS, *La revolucioncita Mexicana* (Mexico City: Editorial Posada, 1978), 163.

7. See, for example, Jocelyn Olcott, Mary Kay Vaughan, and Gabriela Cano, eds., *Sex in Revolution: Gender, Politics, and Power in Modern Mexico* (Durham: Duke University Press, 2006).

8. Mario Vargas Llosa, "México es la dictadura perfecta," *El País* (Madrid), Sept. 1, 1990.

9. Paul Gillingham and Benjamin Smith, eds., *Dictablanda: Soft Authoritarianism in Mexico* (Durham: Duke University Press, 2013), forthcoming.

10. A variety of monographs, collections, political tracts, and documentary films have explicitly raised these questions. See, for example, Stanley Ross, ed., *Is the Mexican*

Revolution Dead? (New York: Knopf, 1966); Adolfo Gilly, *La revolución interrumpida: México, 1910–1920* (Mexico City: El Caballito, 1971), English trans., *The Mexican Revolution* (London: New Left Books, 1983); Gilbert M. Joseph and Daniel Nugent, eds., *Everyday Forms of State Formation: Revolution and the Negotiation of Rule in Modern Mexico* (Durham: Duke University Press, 1994); and the powerful 1972 documentary by Raymundo Gleyzer, *México, la revolución congelada* (Mexico, the frozen revolution).

11. Friedrich Katz, "Rural Uprisings in Mexico," paper presented at the Social Science Research Council Conference on Rural Uprisings in Mexico, New York, 1981; also see Katz's contributions to his edited collection, *Riot, Rebellion, and Revolution* (Princeton: Princeton University Press, 1988).

12. Luis González y González, *Invitación a la microhistoria* (Mexico City: SepSetentas, 1973).

13. Luis González y González, "Microhistory, *Terruño*, and the Social Sciences: A Prefatory Note," in *Regional Impacts of U.S.-Mexican Relations*, ed. Ina Rosenthal-Urey (La Jolla, Calif.: Center for U.S.-Mexican Relations, 1986), ix.

14. Knight, *The Mexican Revolution*, 1:xi.

15. The following discussion draws upon Gilbert M. Joseph, "Latin America's Long Cold War: A Century of Revolutionary Process and U.S. Power," in *A Century of Revolution: Insurgent and Counterinsurgent Violence during Latin America's Long Cold War*, ed. Greg Grandin and Gilbert M. Joseph (Durham, N.C.: Duke University Press, 2010), 397–414; and Jaime Marroquín, Adela Pineda Franco, and Magdalena Mieri, eds., *Open Borders to a Revolution: Culture, Politics, and Migration* (Washington, D.C.: Smithsonian Institution Scholarly Press, 2013).

16. Paco Ignacio Taibo II, *Four Hands*, trans. Laura Dail (New York: St. Martin's Press, 1994); Mauricio Tenorio-Trillo, "Viejos gringos: Radicales norteamericanos en los años treinta y su visión de México," *Secuencia* 21 (Sept.–Dec. 1991): 95–116; Helen Delpar, *The Enormous Vogue of Things Mexican: Cultural Relations between the United States and Mexico* (Tuscaloosa: University of Alabama Press, 1992); John A. Britton, "From Antagonism to Accord: The Controversy over the Mexican Revolution in the Political Culture of the United States," and Rick López, "Anita Brenner and the Jewish Roots of Mexico's Postrevolutionary National Identity," both in Marroquín et al., *Open Borders to a Revolution*.

17. Greg Grandin, "The Liberal Tradition in the Americas: Rights, Sovereignty, and the Contestations of Informal Empire," *American Historical Review* 117.1 (February 2012): 88; Christy Thornton, "Revolutionary Internationalism: Mexico and the Creation of the Multilateral System, 1919–1948," paper presented at Yale University, April 2011.

18. In this regard, see Gilbert M. Joseph, Anne Rubenstein, and Eric Zolov, "Assembling the Fragments: Writing a Cultural History of Mexico Since 1940," in *Fragments of a Golden Age: The Politics of Culture in Mexico Since 1940*, ed. Gilbert M. Joseph, Anne Rubenstein, and Eric Zolov (Durham: Duke University Press, 2001), 3–22.

CHAPTER 2: PORFIRIAN MODERNIZATION AND ITS COSTS

1. The episode is recounted in a variety of popular histories.
2. Gilbert Joseph, personal communication with the late Hernán Menéndez Rodrí-guez, a historian of Porfirian Yucatán, June 10, 1997.
3. Lesley Byrd Simpson, *Many Mexicos*, 4th ed. (Berkeley: University of California Press, 1974), 260.
4. Root quoted in Simpson, *Many Mexicos*, 262.
5. Quoted in John Womack Jr., *Zapata and the Mexican Revolution* (New York: Knopf, 1968), 63.

CHAPTER 3: THE REVOLUTION COMES (AND GOES)

1. Quoted in Friedrich Katz, *The Life and Times of Pancho Villa* (Stanford, Calif.: Stanford University Press, 1996), 105.
2. John Womack Jr., *Zapata and the Mexican Revolution* (New York: Knopf, 1968), 1.
3. Rosa King, *Tempest over Mexico* (Boston: Little, Brown, 1935), 62–63.
4. Quoted in Michael Meyer, William Sherman, and Susan Deeds, *The Course of Mexican History*, 9th ed. (New York: Oxford University Press), 372.
5. Mariano Azuela, *Las moscas: Domitilo quiere ser diputado* (Mexico City: Tip. de A. Carranza e hijos, 1918), 17.
6. Quoted in Charles C. Cumberland, *Mexican Revolution, Genesis under Madero* (Austin: University of Texas Press, 1952), 151.
7. Womack, *Zapata and the Mexican Revolution*, 67.
8. Frank Tannenbaum, *Peace by Revolution: Mexico after 1910* (New York: Columbia University Press, 1933), 115–19.
9. Quoted in Moisés González Navarro, "El maderismo y la reforma agraria," *Historia Mexicana* 37.1 (1987): 6.
10. Personal communication with Hernán Menéndez Rodríguez, August 28, 1998.
11. Luis Cabrera, "The Restoration of the *Ejido*," in *The Mexico Reader: Culture, Society, and Politics*, ed. Gilbert M. Joseph and Timothy Henderson (Durham, N.C.: Duke University Press, 2002), 349.
12. Quoted in Enrique Krauze, *Mexico: Biography of Power*, trans. Hank Heifetz (New York: HarperCollins, 1997), 392.
13. Alan Knight, *The Mexican Revolution*, vol. 1 (Cambridge, U.K.: Cambridge University Press, 1986).

CHAPTER 4: THE VIOLENT CLIMAX OF THE REVOLUTION

1. Plutarco Elías Calles, quoted in *Pensamiento político y social: Antología, 1913–1936*, ed. Carlos Macías Richard (Mexico City: Fondo de Cultura Económica, 1988), 28–31.
2. "Do *You* Think the Glory of America Would Be Enhanced by a War of Conquest in Mexico," address delivered by President Woodrow Wilson at the 44th annual dinner of the New York Press Club, offprint, June 30, 1916, 5.

3. Michael C. Meyer, *Huerta: A Political Portrait* (Lincoln: University of Nebraska Press, 1972).

4. Archivo Boker, Mexico City, Fondo Memorias, Franz Böker, "Ein Versuch, über den Verlauf meines Lebens etwas aufzuzeichnen," 37.

5. Quoted in Alfredo Breceda, *México revolucionario, 1913–1917* (Madrid: Tipografía Artística, 1920–41), 2:195.

6. Villa quoted in Benjamin Keen and Mark Wasserman, eds., *A Short History of Latin America* (Boston: Houghton Mifflin, 1980), 278.

7. Quoted in Jocelyn Olcott, "The Center Cannot Hold: Women on Mexico's Popular Front," in *Sex in Revolution: Gender, Politics, and Power in Modern Mexico*, ed. Jocelyn Olcott, Mary Kay Vaughan, and Gabriela Cano (Durham, N.C.: Duke University Press, 2006), 223.

8. Elizabeth Salas, *Soldaderas in the Mexican Military: Myth and History* (Austin: University of Texas Press, 1990), 38–47.

9. John Womack Jr., *Zapata and the Mexican Revolution* (New York: Knopf, 1968), 7.

10. Gonzalo de la Parra, *De cómo se hizo revolucionario un hombre de buena fe* (Mexico City: n.p., 1915), 98, 114–16, 122–24.

11. "Pacto de Xochimilco," in *Fuentes para la historia de la Revolución Mexicana, I: Planes politicos y otros documentos*, ed. Manuel González Ramírez (Mexico City: Fondo de Cultura Económica, 1954), 113, 116–17.

12. Alan Knight, *The Mexican Revolution*, 2 vols. (Cambridge, U.K.: Cambridge University Press, 1986), 2:26.

13. U.S. consul in Progreso to the secretary of state, quoted in Gilbert M. Joseph, *Revolution from Without: Yucatán, Mexico, and the United States, 1880–1924*, rev. ed. (Durham, N.C.: Duke University Press, 1988), 93.

14. Excerpts from Article 27 of the Mexican Constitution of 1917, quoted in *The Mexico Reader: History, Culture, Politics*, eds. Gilbert M. Joseph and Timothy Henderson (Durham, N.C.: Duke University Press, 2002), 400.

CHAPTER 5: FORGING AND CONTESTING A NEW NATION

1. Anita Brenner and George R. Leighton, *The Wind That Swept Mexico* (New York: Harper, 1943), 62.

2. Quoted in Jürgen Buchenau, *The Last Caudillo: Alvaro Obregón and the Mexican Revolution* (Chichester, U.K.: Wiley Blackwell, 2011), 2.

3. Quoted in Buchenau, *The Last Caudillo*, 109.

4. Quoted in Brígido Caro, *Plutarco Elías Calles, dictador bolcheviki de México: Episodios de la revolución mexicana desde 1910 al 1924* (Los Angeles: n.p., 1924), 13.

5. Quoted in Héctor Aguilar Camín and Lorenzo Meyer, *In the Shadow of the Mexican Revolution* (Austin: University of Texas Press, 1993), 80.

6. Quoted in Robert F. Smith, *The United States and Revolutionary Nationalism in Mexico, 1916–1932* (Chicago: University of Chicago Press, 1972), 234.

7. Quoted in Daniela Spenser, *The Impossible Triangle: Mexico, Soviet Russia, and the United States in the 1920s* (Durham, N.C.: Duke University Press, 1999), 76.

8. Quoted in Ernest Gruening, *Mexico and Its Heritage* (New York: D. Appleton, 1928), 275.

9. Plutarco Elías Calles, quoted in *Pensamiento político y social: Antología, 1913–1936*, ed. Carlos Macías (Mexico City: Fondo de Cultura Económica, 1988), 122.

10. Quoted in Enrique Krauze, *Mexico: Biography of Power*, trans. Hank Heifetz (New York: Harper Collins, 1997), 421.

11. Jean Meyer, *La cristiada: Los cristeros* (Mexico City: Siglo Veintiuno Editores, 1973), 305.

12. Quoted in Gilbert M. Joseph and Timothy J. Henderson, eds. and trans., *The Mexico Reader: History, Culture, Politics* (Durham, N.C.: Duke University Press, 2004), 422.

13. Luis Javier Garrido, *El Partido de la Revolución Institucionalizada: La formación del nuevo estado en México (1928–1945)* (Mexico City: Siglo Veintiuno Editores, 1982), 103.

14. Manuel Gamio, *Forjando patria: Pro-nacionalismo* (Mexico City: Porrúa Hermanos, 1916).

15. Quoted in Lorenzo Meyer, Rafael Segovia, and Alejandra Lajous, *Historia de la Revolución Mexicana, 1928–1934: Los inicios de la institucionalización* (Mexico City: El Colegio de México, 1978), 178.

16. Daniel Cosío Villegas, *Memorias* (Mexico City: Joaquín Mortiz, 1976), 91.

17. Quoted in Ramón Eduardo Ruiz, *Triumph and Tragedy: A History of the Mexican People* (New York: W. W. Norton, 1993), 379.

18. José Vasconcelos, *La raza cósmica: Misión de la raza Iberoamericana, Argentina y Brasil* (Mexico City: Espasa-Calpe, 1966).

19. Rick López, *Crafting Mexico: Intellectuals, Artisans, and the State after the Revolution* (Durham, N.C.: Duke University Press, 2010), 74.

20. Samuel Ramos, *Perfil del hombre y la cultura en México* (Mexico City: Espasa-Calpe, 1965).

21. Verna Millán, *Mexico Reborn* (Boston: Houghton Mifflin, 1937), 160–61.

22. Carlos Monsiváis, foreword to *Sex in Revolution: Gender, Politics, and Power in Modern Mexico*, ed. Jocelyn Olcott, Mary Kay Vaughan, and Gabriela Cano (Durham, N.C.: Duke University Press, 2006), 11.

CHAPTER 6: RESURRECTING AND INCORPORATING
THE REVOLUTION

1. Quoted in Ben Fallaw, "The Life and Deaths of Felipa Poot: Women, Fiction, and Cardenismo in Postrevolutionary Mexico," *Hispanic American Historical Review* 82.4 (2002): 645–83.

2. Gonzalo N. Santos, quoted in Enrique Krauze, *Mexico: Biography of Power* (New York: Harper, 1998), 454.

3. Lorenzo Meyer, Rafael Segovia, and Alejandra Lajous, *Historia de la Revolución Mexicana, 1928–1934: Los inicios de la institucionalización* (Mexico City: Colegio de México, 1978), 158.

4. National Archives, College Park, Md. (hereafter NA), RG 59, 812.00/29828, Robert Cummings, G-2 Report, Jan. 1933.

5. NA, RG 59, 812.00/29926, Daniels to Secretary of State, Sept. 29, 1933.

6. Quoted in Michael J. Gonzales, *The Mexican Revolution, 1910–1940* (Albuquerque: University of New Mexico Press, 2002), 244.

7. Quoted in John W. F. Dulles, *Yesterday in Mexico: A Chronicle of the Revolution, 1919–1936* (Austin: University of Texas Press, 1961), 630.

8. Anita Brenner and George R. Deighton, *The Wind That Swept Mexico: The History of the Mexican Revolution, 1910–1942* (New York: Harper, 1943), 91.

9. "Sensacionales Declaraciones del General Calles," *El Universal*, June 12, 1935.

10. Brenner and Deighton, *The Wind That Swept Mexico*, 91.

11. Quoted in Gonzales, *The Mexican Revolution*, 229.

12. Evelyn Waugh, *Robbery under Law: The Mexican Object-Lesson* (London: Chapman and Hall, 1939), 59–60.

13. Alan Knight, "Cardenismo: Juggernaut or Jalopy?" *Journal of Latin American Studies* 26 (1994): 81.

14. Quoted in James M. Cypher, *State and Capital in Mexico* (Boulder, Colo.: Westview Press, 1990), 10–11.

15. Angeles Mastretta, *Arráncame la vida* (Mexico City: Ediciones Océano, 1985), which first appeared in English translation as *Mexican Bolero* (New York: Viking, 1990).

16. Gregory S. Crider, "Material Struggles: Workers' Strategies during the 'Institutionalization of the Revolution' in Atlixco, Puebla, Mexico, 1930–1942," Ph.D. diss., University of Wisconsin-Madison, 1996, 228–29.

CHAPTER 7: THE "PERFECT DICTATORSHIP"

1. Stanley Ross, ed., *Is the Mexican Revolution Dead?* (New York: Knopf, 1966).

2. Howard Cline, *Mexico: From Revolution to Evolution, 1940–1960* (New York: Oxford University Press, 1962).

3. Quoted in Donald C. Hodges and Daniel R. Gandy, *Mexico: The End of the Revolution* (Westport, Conn.: Greenwood Press, 2002), 86.

4. Fideicomiso Archivos Plutarco Elías Calles y Fernando Torreblanca (hereafter FAPEC), Fondo Alvaro Obregón (hereafter FAO), series 060400, exp. 13, inv. 5140, Alfonso Romandía Ferreira, "Discurso," July 18 [sic], 1941.

5. John W. Sherman, "The Mexican Miracle and Its Collapse," in *The Oxford History of Mexico*, ed. Michael C. Meyer and William H. Beezley (Oxford: Oxford University Press, 2000), 576.

6. Daniel Cosío Villegas, "Mexico's Crisis," in *The Mexico Reader: History, Culture, Politics*, ed. Gilbert M. Joseph and Timothy Henderson (Durham, N.C.: Duke University Press, 2002), 470.

7. Enrique Krauze, quoted in "Vargas Llosa, el provocador," *El Economista*, Oct. 7, 2010. The original usage comes from Spain in the early 1930s. Our discussion of local power draws on insights provided by Ray Craib.

8. Mary Kay Vaughan, *Cultural Politics in Revolution* (Tucson: University of Arizona Press, 1997), 23.

9. Claudio Lomnitz, "Elusive Property: The Personification of Mexican National Sovereignty," in *The Empire of Things: Regimes of Value and Material Culture*, ed. Fred R. Myers (Santa Fe, N.M.: School of American Research Press, 2001), 128.

10. FAPEC, FAO, f. 11. s. 060400, gav. 33, exp. 22, inv. 5149, "Discurso pronunciado por el Sr. Ing. Luis L. León . . . ," 12–13.

11. FAPEC, FAO, f. 11. s. 060400, gav. 33, exp. 22, inv. 5149, Humberto Obregón to Aarón Sáenz, Mexico City, June 7, 1950.

12. Jeffrey M. Pilcher, *Cantinflas and the Chaos of Mexican Modernity* (Wilmington, Del.: Scholarly Resources, 2001), xvii.

13. Franz Böker, "The Downside of the Miracle," in *Mexico OtherWise: Modern Mexico in the Eyes of Foreign Observers*, ed. Jürgen Buchenau (Albuquerque: University of New Mexico Press, 2005), 217–18.

14. Böker, "The Downside of the Miracle," 219; Michael N. Miller, *Red, White, and Green: The Maturing of Mexicanidad* (El Paso: Texas Western Press, 1998), 1.

15. Quoted in Manuel López Gallo, *Economía y política en la historia de México* (Mexico City: Ediciones Solidaridad, 1965), 581.

16. Arthur K. Smith, "Mexico and the Cuban Revolution: Foreign Policy-Making in Mexico under President Adolfo López Mateos (1958–1964)," Ph.D. diss., Cornell University, 1970, 46.

17. Archivo Histórico de la Secretaría de Relaciones Exteriores, III-2145-17, Bosques to secretary, Havana, July 15, 1959.

18. Archivo General de la Nación, Mexico City (hereafter AGN), Archivo Personal Lázaro Cárdenas (hereafter APLC), 5:2, Cárdenas to Arévalo, Pátzcuaro, Michoacán, Oct. 20, 1945.

19. AGN, APLC, 5:2, Cárdenas to Arévalo, Morelia, Michoacán, Apr. 6, 1949.

20. Olga Pellicer de Brody and Esteban L. Mancilla, *Historia de la Revolución Mexicana, 1952–1960: El desarrollo estabilizador y el entendimiento con los Estados Unidos* (Mexico City: Colegio de México, 1978), 104.

21. Eric Zolov, "Cuba sí, Yanquis no! The Sacking of the Instituto Cultural México-Norteamericano en Morelia, Michoacán, 1961," in *In from the Cold: Latin America's New Encounter with the Cold War*, ed. Gilbert M. Joseph and Daniela Spenser (Durham, N.C.: Duke University Press), 216.

22. Olga Pellicer de Brody, *México y la revolución cubana* (Mexico City: El Colegio de México, 1972), 19–21.

23. Zolov, "Cuba sí, Yanquis no," 214–52.

24. FAPEC, Fondo Plutarco Elías Calles, serie 010400, "Homenajes 1971," Plutarco Elías Calles Chacón, "Discurso."

CHAPTER 8: THE EMBERS OF REVOLUTION

1. Personal recollections of conversations with Alejandra García Quintanilla in July 1995.
2. Echeverría quoted in John Womack Jr., "The Spoils of the Mexican Revolution," *Foreign Affairs* 48.4 (1970): 685.
3. Elena Poniatowska, "The Student Movement of 1968," in *The Mexico Reader: History, Culture, Politics*, ed. Gilbert M. Joseph and Timothy Henderson (Durham: Duke University Press, 2002), 568.
4. Quoted in Alexander Aviña, "'We Have Returned to Porfirian Times': Neopopulism, Counterinsurgency, and the Dirty War in Guerrero, Mexico, 1969–1976," in *Populism in 20th-Century Mexico: The Presidencies of Lázaro Cárdenas and Luis Echeverría*, ed. Amelia M. Kiddle and María L. O. Muñoz (Tucson: University of Arizona Press, 2010), 106.
5. Quoted in Alan Knight, "Cárdenas and Echeverría Compared," in Kiddle and Muñoz, *Populism in 20th-Century Mexico*, 33.
6. Quoted in George W. Grayson, *Mexico: Narco-Violence and a Failed State* (New York: Transaction, 2010), 42.
7. Alan Riding, *Distant Neighbors: A Portrait of the Mexicans* (New York: Knopf, 1985), 121.
8. Quoted in "Corruption, Mexican Style," *New York Times*, Dec. 16, 1984.
9. Quoted in Wayne A. Cornelius, "The Political Economy of Mexico under De la Madrid: Austerity, Routinized Crisis, and Nascent Recovery," *Mexican Studies/Estudios Mexicanos* 1.1 (1985): 92–93.
10. Quoted in Louise Walker, "Economic Fault Lines and Middle-Class Fears: Tlatelolco, Mexico City 1985," in *Aftershocks: Earthquakes and Popular Politics in Latin America*, ed. Jürgen Buchenau and Lyman L. Johnson (Albuquerque: University of New Mexico Press, 2009), 192.
11. Quoted in Donald Hodges and Ross Gandy, *Mexico: The End of the Revolution* (New York: Greenwood Press, 2002), 126.
12. "Letters to Cuauhtémoc Cárdenas," in Joseph and Henderson, *The Mexico Reader*, 597.
13. Francis Fukuyama, "The End of History?," *National Interest*, Summer 1989.
14. "La fiesta de los caracoles," *La Jornada*, Aug. 10, 2003.
15. Quoted in Philip L. Russell, *The History of Mexico: From Pre-Conquest to Present* (New York: Routledge, 2010), 501.
16. Quoted in Alexander Dawson, *Indian and Nation in Revolutionary Mexico* (Tucson: University of Arizona Press, 2004), 85–86.
17. Quoted in Jerry W. Knudson, "Rebellion in Chiapas: Insurrection by Internet and Public Relations," *Media, Culture, and Society* 20 (1998): 509.
18. "The Voice of the Revolution Has Mexicans in His Spell," *New York Times*, Feb. 8, 1994.

19. Published in *El Despertador Mexicano*, Jan. 1, 1994.

20. Related to Jürgen Buchenau by Pablo Pellat, May 1998.

CHAPTER 9: CONCLUSIONS

1. Adolfo Gilly, "Chiapas and the Rebellion of the Enchanted World," in *Rural Revolt in Mexico: U.S. Intervention and the Domain of Subaltern Politics*, ed. Daniel Nugent (Durham, N.C.: Duke University Press, 1998), 273.

2. Alan Knight, "Weapons and Arches in the Mexican Revolutionary Landscape," in *Everyday Forms of State Formation: Revolution and the Negotiation of Rule in Modern Mexico*, ed. Gilbert M. Joseph and Daniel Nugent (Durham, N.C.: Duke University Press, 1991), 54.

3. Gilly, "Chiapas and the Rebellion of the Enchanted World," 309.

4. Gilly, "Chiapas and the Rebellion of the Enchanted World," 309–10.

5. Gilly, "Chiapas and the Rebellion of the Enchanted World," 310.

6. Philip Corrigan and Derek Sayer, *The Great Arch: English State Formation as Cultural Revolution* (Oxford: Basil Blackwell, 1985). For a discussion of their work in the context of Mexico, see Joseph and Nugent, *Everyday Forms of State Formation*.

7. Gil Joseph's personal communications with Adolfo Gilly in 1991 and thereafter.

8. Felipe Calderón, New Year's address to the nation, January 6, 2010, http://www .bicentenario.gob.mx/index.php?option=com_content&view=article&id=259 :discurso-del-presidente-felipe-calderon-hinojosa&catid=68:arco-bicentenario (accessed Mar. 9, 2012).

9. Oswaldo Zavala, "On the Banks of the Future: Ciudad Juárez and El Paso in the Mexican Revolution," in *Open Borders to a Revolution: Culture, Politics, and Migration*, ed. Jaime Marroquín, Adela Pineda Franco, and Magdalena Mieri (Washington, D.C.: Smithsonian Institution Scholarly Press, 2013).

Bibliographical Essay

The historical literature on Mexico during the nineteenth and twentieth centuries is vast and growing at a dizzying pace. This brief essay lists some of the most important scholarly works in English. The references and bibliographies contained in these works provide points of departure for further research.

Useful general histories include John Sherman, Michael C. Meyer, and Susan Deeds, *The Course of Mexican History*, 9th ed. (New York: Oxford University Press, 2010); Jürgen Buchenau, *Mexican Mosaic: A Brief History of Mexico* (Wheeling, Ill.: Harlan Davidson, 2008); Alicia Hernández Chávez, *Mexico: A Brief History*, trans. Andy Klatt (Berkeley: University of California Press, 2006); Enrique Florescano, *National Narratives in Mexico: A History* (Norman: University of Oklahoma Press, 2006); Colin MacLachlan and William H. Beezley, *El Gran Pueblo: A History of Greater Mexico*, 3rd ed. (Upper Saddle River, N.J.: Prentice Hall, 2003); Douglas W. Richmond, *The Mexican Nation: Historical Continuity and Modern Change* (Upper Saddle River, N.J.: Prentice Hall, 2001); Michael C. Meyer and William H. Beezley, eds., *The Oxford History of Mexico* (Oxford, U.K.: Oxford University Press, 2000); Enrique Krauze, *Mexico: Biography of Power*, trans. Hank Heifetz (New York: Harper Collins, 1997); Ramón Eduardo Ruiz, *Triumph and Tragedy: A History of the Mexican People* (New York: W. W. Norton, 1993); and Leslie Bethell, ed., *Mexico Since Independence* (Cambridge, U.K.: Cambridge University Press, 1991). Interesting vignettes of individual Mexicans during the period since 1750 can be found in Jeffrey Pilcher, ed., *The Human Tradition in Mexico* (Wilmington, Del.: Scholarly Resources, 2004).

For primary source collections, see Gilbert M. Joseph and Timothy J. Henderson, eds., *The Mexico Reader: History, Culture, Politics* (Durham, N.C.: Duke University Press, 2002); Jürgen Buchenau, ed. and trans., *Mexico OtherWise: Modern Mexico in the Eyes of Foreign Observers* (Albuquerque: University of New Mexico Press, 2005);

W. Dirk Raat, ed., *Mexico from Independence to Revolution, 1810–1910* (Lincoln: University of Nebraska Press, 1982); and W. Dirk Raat and William H. Beezley, eds., *Twentieth-Century Mexico* (Lincoln: University of Nebraska Press, 1986).

The historical literature on the Reforma era includes Guy P. C. Thomson and David LaFrance, *Patriotism, Politics, and Popular Liberalism in Nineteenth-Century Mexico: Juan Francisco Lucas and the Puebla Sierra* (Wilmington, Del.: Scholarly Resources, 2002); Florencia E. Mallon, *Peasant and Nation: The Making of Postcolonial Mexico and Peru* (Berkeley: University of California Press, 1995); Charles R. Berry, *The Reform in Oaxaca, 1856–1876: A Microhistory of the Liberal Revolution* (Lincoln: University of Nebraska Press, 1981); and Richard N. Sinkin, *Mexican Reform, 1855–1876* (Austin: University of Texas Press, 1980). A good biography of Benito Juárez is Brian Hamnett, *Juárez* (London: Longman, 1994). For Juárez's legacy, see Charles Weeks, *The Juárez Myth in Mexico* (Tuscaloosa: University of Alabama Press, 1987). Works examining the role of the United States include Donathon C. Olliff, *Reforma Mexico and the United States: The Search for Alternatives to Annexation* (Tuscaloosa: University of Alabama Press, 1981); and Thomas D. Schoonover, *Dollars over Dominion: The Triumph of Liberalism in Mexican–United States Relations* (Baton Rouge: Louisiana State University Press, 1978).

For studies examining the French Intervention and Emperor Maximilian, see Erika Pani, "Dreaming of a Mexican Empire: The Political Projects of the 'Imperialistas,'" *Hispanic American Historical Review* 82.1 (2002): 1–31; and Bertita Harding, *Phantom Crown: The Story of Maximilian and Carlota of Mexico* (Mexico City: Ediciones Tolteca, 1960).

Among the growing scholarship on the social and cultural history of nineteenth-century Mexico, see Mark Wasserman, *Everyday Life and Politics in Nineteenth-Century Mexico: Men, Women, and War* (Albuquerque: University of New Mexico Press, 2000); Matthew O'Hara, *A Flock Divided: Race, Religion, and Politics in Mexico, 1749–1857* (Durham, N.C.: Duke University Press, 2010); Edward Wright-Rios, *Revolutions in Mexican Catholicism: Reform and Revelation in Oaxaca 1887–1934* (Durham, N.C.: Duke University Press, 2009); and Kathryn A. Sloan, *Runaway Daughters: Seduction, Elopement, and Honor in Nineteenth-Century Mexico* (Albuquerque: University of New Mexico Press, 2008).

For regional studies, see Terry Rugeley, *Rebellion Now and Forever: Mayas: Hispanics, and Caste War Violence in Yucatán, 1800–1880* (Stanford: Stanford University Press, 2009); Marie E. Francois, *A Culture of Everyday Credit: Housekeeping, Pawnbroking, and Governance in Mexico City, 1750–1920* (Lincoln: University of Nebraska Press, 2007); Peter Guardino, *The Time of Liberty: Popular Political Culture in Oaxaca, 1750–1850* (Durham, N.C.: Duke University Press, 2005); Michael T. Ducey, *A Nation of Villages: Riot and Rebellion in the Mexican Huasteca, 1750–1850* (Tucson: University of Arizona Press, 2004); Peter Guardino, *Peasants, Politics, and the Formation of Mexico's National State: Guerrero, 1800–1857* (Stanford: Stanford University Press, 2002); Silvia M. Arrom, *Containing the Poor: The Mexico City Poor House, 1774–1871* (Durham, N.C.: Duke University Press, 2000); Margaret Chowning, *Wealth and*

Power in Provincial Mexico: Michoacán from the Late Colony to the Revolution (Stanford: Stanford University Press, 1999); Don E. Dumond, *The Machete and the Cross: Campesino Rebellion in Yucatán* (Lincoln: University of Nebraska Press, 1997); and Evelyn Hu-Dehart, *Yaqui Resistance and Survival: The Struggle for Land and Autonomy, 1821–1910* (Madison: University of Wisconsin Press, 1984).

There are many fine studies on the Liberal modernization project. On the Mexican state and its protagonists, see Laurens B. Perry, *Juárez and Díaz: Machine Politics in Mexico* (DeKalb: Northern Illinois University Press, 1979); and Don M. Coerver, *The Porfirian Interregnum: The Presidency of Manuel González of Mexico, 1880–1884* (Fort Worth: Texas Christian University Press, 1979). A good general biography of General Porfirio Díaz is Paul Garner, *Porfirio Díaz* (London: Longman, 2001). On the *científicos* and Mexican positivist thought, see Charles Hale, *The Transformation of Liberalism in Late Nineteenth-Century Mexico* (Princeton: Princeton University Press, 1989); and Dirk W. Raat, "Ideas and Society in Don Porfirio's Mexico," *The Americas* 30.1 (1973): 32–53. For foreign relations and the international image of Mexico in the Porfirian era, see Mauricio Tenorio Trillo, *Mexico at the World's Fairs: Crafting a Modern Nation* (Berkeley: University of California Press, 1996); and Jürgen Buchenau, *In the Shadow of the Giant: The Making of Mexico's Central America Policy, 1876–1930* (Tuscaloosa: University of Alabama Press, 1996).

Works on the economic impact of modernization include Richard Weiner, *Race, Nation, and Market: Economic Culture in Porfirian Mexico* (Tucson: University of Arizona Press, 2004); Jürgen Buchenau, *Tools of Progress: A German Merchant Family in Mexico City, 1865–Present* (Albuquerque: University of New Mexico Press, 2004); William Schell Jr., *Integral Outsiders: The American Colony in Mexico City, 1876–1911* (Wilmington, Del.: Scholarly Resources, 2001); William Schell Jr., "Silver Symbiosis: ReOrienting Mexican Economic History," *Hispanic American Historical Review* 81.1 (2001): 89–133; Robert H. Holden, *Mexico and the Survey of Public Lands, 1876–1911: The Management of Modernization* (DeKalb: Northern Illinois University Press, 1994); Paul Vanderwood, *Disorder and Progress: Bandits, Police, and Mexican Development*, 2nd ed. (Wilmington, Del.: Scholarly Resources, 1992); Stephen Haber, *Industry and Underdevelopment: The Industrialization of Mexico, 1880–1940* (Stanford: Stanford University Press, 1989); Alex M. Saragoza, *The Monterrey Elite and the Mexican State* (Austin: University of Texas Press, 1988); Thomas Benjamin and William McNellie, eds., *Other Mexicos: Essays on Regional Mexican History, 1876–1910* (Albuquerque: University of New Mexico Press, 1984); Allen Wells, *Yucatán's Gilded Age: Haciendas, Henequen, and International Harvester, 1860–1915* (Albuquerque: University of New Mexico Press, 1985; and John Coatsworth, *Growth against Development: The Economic Impact of Railroads in Porfirian Mexico* (DeKalb: Northern Illinois University Press, 1981).

Porfirian society and culture have been analyzed in Robert Buffington and Pablo Piccato, eds., *True Stories of Crime in Modern Mexico* (Albuquerque: University of New Mexico Press, 2009); Teresa Miriam Van Hoy, *A Social History of Mexico's Railroads: Peons, Prisoners, and Priests* (Lanham, Md.: Rowman and Littlefield, 2008); Mark

Overmyer-Velázquez, *Visions of the Emerald City: Modernity, Tradition, and the Formation of Porfirian Oaxaca, Mexico* (Durham, N.C.: Duke University Press, 2006); Raymond B. Craib, "A Nationalist Metaphysics: State Fixations, National Maps, and the Geo-Historical Imagination in Nineteenth-Century Mexico," *Hispanic American Historical Review* 82.1 (2002): 33–68; Raymond B. Craib, *Cartographic Mexico: A History of State Fixations and Fugitive Landscapes* (Durham, N.C.: Duke University Press, 2004); Pablo Piccato, *City of Suspects: Crime in Mexico City, 1900–1931* (Durham, N.C.: Duke University Press, 2001); Pablo Piccato, "'El Chelaquera' or the Mexican Jack the Ripper: The Meanings of Sexual Violence in Turn-of-the-Century Mexico City," *Hispanic American Historical Review* 81.3 (2001): 623–52; Pablo Piccato, *The Tyranny of Opinion: Honor in the Mexican Public Sphere* (Durham, N.C.: Duke University Press, 2010); William E. French, "Imagining and the Cultural History of Nineteenth-Century Mexico," *Hispanic American Historical Review* 79.2 (1999): 249–67; Paul Vanderwood, *The Power of God against the Guns of Government: Religious Upheaval in Mexico at the Turn of the Nineteenth Century* (Stanford: Stanford University Press, 1998); Michael Johns, *The City of Mexico in the Age of Díaz* (Austin: University of Texas Press, 1997); William E. French, *A Peaceful and Working People: Manners, Morals, and Class Formation in Northern Mexico* (Albuquerque: University of New Mexico Press, 1996); and William Beezley, *Judas at the Jockey Club and Other Episodes of Porfirian Mexico* (Lincoln: University of Nebraska Press, 1987). On education, see Mary Kay Vaughan, *The State, Education, and Social Class in Mexico, 1880–1928* (DeKalb: Northern Illinois University Press, 1982).

Regarding the crisis of the Porfiriato, consult, among many other works, Paul Hart, *Bitter Harvest: The Social Transformation of Morelos, Mexico, and the Origins of the Zapatista Revolution, 1840–1910* (Albuquerque: University of New Mexico Press, 2005); Allen Wells and Gilbert M. Joseph, *Summer of Discontent, Seasons of Upheaval: Elite Politics and Rural Insurgency in Yucatán, 1876–1915* (Stanford: Stanford University Press, 1996); William K. Meyers, *Forge of Progress, Crucible of Revolt: The Origins of the Mexican Revolution in the Comarca Lagunera, 1880–1911* (Albuquerque: University of New Mexico Press, 1994); Jonathan C. Brown, "Foreign and Native-Born Workers in Porfirian Mexico," *American Historical Review* 98 (1993): 786–818; Ramón E. Ruiz, *The People of Sonora and Yankee Capitalists* (Tucson: University of Arizona Press, 1988); W. Dirk Raat, "The Diplomacy of Suppression: Los Revoltosos, Mexico, and the United States, 1906–1911," *Hispanic American Historical Review* 56 (1976): 529–60; and James D. Cockcroft, *Intellectual Precursors of the Mexican Revolution, 1900–1913* (Austin: University of Texas Press, 1968).

The literature on the Mexican Revolution is among the most extensive on any subject of Latin American history, and it has engendered several valuable syntheses: William H. Beezley and Colin M. MacLachlan, *Mexicans in Revolution, 1910–1946: An Introduction* (Lincoln: University of Nebraska Press, 2009); Michael J. Gonzales, *The Mexican Revolution, 1910–1940* (Albuquerque: University of New Mexico Press, 2002); Héctor Aguilar Camín and Lorenzo Meyer, *In the Shadow of the Mexican Revolution: Contemporary Mexican History, 1910–1989*, trans. Luis Alberto Fierro (Austin:

University of Texas Press, 1993); John M. Hart, *Revolutionary Mexico: The Coming and Process of the Mexican Revolution* (Berkeley: University of California Press, 1987); Alan Knight, *The Mexican Revolution*, 2 vols. (Cambridge, U.K.: Cambridge University Press, 1986); and Ramón Ruiz, *The Great Rebellion: Mexico, 1905–1924* (New York: W. W. Norton, 1982).

On the role of the United States and other foreign powers, see John J. Dwyer, *The Agrarian Dispute: The Expropriation of American-Owned Rural Land in Postrevolutionary Mexico* (Durham, N.C.: Duke University Press, 2008); Daniela Spenser, *The Impossible Triangle: Mexico, Soviet Russia, and the United States in the 1920s* (Durham, N.C.: Duke University Press, 1999); Linda B. Hall, *Oil, Banks, and Politics: The United States and Postrevolutionary Mexico* (Austin: University of Texas Press, 1995); Alan Knight, *U.S.-Mexican Relations 1910–1940: An Interpretation* (San Diego: Center for U.S.-Mexican Studies, University of California, 1987); Adolfo Gilly, *The Mexican Revolution* (London: New Left Books, 1983); Friedrich Katz, *The Secret War in Mexico: Europe, the United States, and the Mexican Revolution* (Chicago: University of Chicago Press, 1981); Mark T. Gilderhus, *Diplomacy and Revolution: U.S.-Mexican Relations under Wilson and Carranza* (Tucson: University of Arizona Press, 1977); Robert F. Smith, *The United States and Revolutionary Nationalism in Mexico, 1916–1932* (Chicago: University of Chicago Press, 1972); and Lorenzo Meyer, *Mexico and the United States in the Oil Controversy, 1917–1942*, trans. Lidia Lozano (Austin: University of Texas Press, 1972).

Regarding the myth of the revolution and how it evolved over time, see Thomas Benjamin, *La Revolución: Mexico's Great Revolution as Memory, Myth, and History* (Austin: University of Texas Press, 2000); Ilene V. O'Malley, *The Myth of the Revolution: Hero Cults and the Institutionalization of the Mexican State, 1920–1940* (New York: Greenwood Press, 1979); and Alan Knight, "The Myth of the Mexican Revolution," *Past and Present* 209 (Nov. 2010): 223–73, a state-of-the-art contribution on the occasion of the revolution's centennial.

Works on the principal protagonists of the revolution include the following: on the interim president Francisco León de la Barra, Peter V. N. Henderson, *In the Absence of Don Porfirio: Francisco León de la Barra and the Mexican Revolution* (Wilmington, Del.: Scholarly Resources, 2000); on Francisco I. Madero, William H. Beezley, "Madero, the 'Unknown' President and His Political Failure to Organize Rural Mexico," in *Essays on the Mexican Revolution: Revisionist Views of the Leaders*, ed. George Wolfskill and Douglas W. Richmond (Austin: University of Texas Press, 1979), 1–24; on Pancho Villa, Friedrich Katz, *The Life and Times of Pancho Villa* (Stanford: Stanford University Press, 1998); on Emiliano Zapata, Samuel Brunk, *Emiliano Zapata: Revolution and Betrayal in Mexico* (Albuquerque: University of New Mexico Press, 1995) and John Womack Jr., *Zapata and the Mexican Revolution* (New York: Knopf, 1968); on Venustiano Carranza, Douglas W. Richmond, *Venustiano Carranza's Nationalist Struggle, 1893–1920* (Lincoln: University of Nebraska Press, 1983); on Victoriano Huerta, Michael C. Meyer, *Huerta: A Political Portrait* (Lincoln: University of Nebraska Press, 1972); on Alvaro Obregón, Linda B. Hall, *Alvaro Obregón: Power and Revolution in Mexico, 1911–1920* (College Station: Texas A&M University Press, 1981) and Jürgen Buchenau, *The Last Caudillo: Alvaro Obregón and the Mexican Revolution* (Chichester, U.K.: Wiley Blackwell, 2011); on Plutarco Elías Calles, Jürgen Buchenau, *Plutarco Elías Calles and the Mexican Revolution* (Lanham, Md.: Rowman and Littlefield, 2007). A scholarly English-language biography of Lázaro Cárdenas has yet to be written, although William Cameron Townsend, *Lazaro Cardenas: Mexican Democrat* (Ann Arbor, Mich.: Wahr, 1952) remains helpful.

Much of the best scholarship on the Mexican Revolution is local or regional in character. The classic study of the revolutionary era (and before and after) at the village level is Luis González's magisterial study of his hometown, *San José de Gracia: Mexican Village in Transition*, trans. John Upton (Austin: University of Texas Press, 1944). Other subnational studies include Gilbert M. Joseph, *Revolution from Without: Yucatán, Mexico, and the United States, 1880–1924*, rev. ed. (Durham, N.C.: Duke University Press, 1988); Paul K. Eiss, *In the Name of El Pueblo: Place, Community, and the Politics of History in Yucatán* (Durham, N.C.: Duke University Press, 2010); Benjamin Smith, *Pistoleros and Popular Movements: The Politics of State Formation in Postrevolutionary Oaxaca* (Lincoln: University of Nebraska Press, 2009); Stephen Lewis, *The Ambivalent Revolution: Forging State and Nation in Chiapas, 1910–1945* (Albuquerque: University of New Mexico Press, 2005); Christopher R. Boyer, *Becoming Campesinos: Politics, Identity, and Agrarian Struggle in Postrevolutionary Michoacán, 1920–1935* (Stanford: Stanford University Press, 2003); John Lear, *Workers, Neighbors, and Citizens: The Revolution in Mexico City* (Lincoln: University of Nebraska Press, 2001); Timothy Henderson, *The Worm in the Wheat: Rosalie Evans and Agrarian Struggle in the Puebla-Tlaxcala Region of Mexico, 1906–1927* (Durham, N.C.: Duke University Press, 1998); Mark Wasserman, *Persistent Oligarchs: Elites and Politics in Chihuahua, Mexico, 1910–1940* (Durham, N.C.: Duke University Press, 1993); Heather Fowler Salamini, *Agrarian Radicalism in Veracruz, 1920–1938* (Lincoln: University of Nebraska Press, 1978); Gilbert M. Joseph, *Rediscovering the Past at Mexico's Periphery: Essays on the History of Modern Yucatán* (Tuscaloosa: University of Alabama Press, 1986); Jeffery T. Brannon and Gilbert M. Joseph, eds., *Land, Labor, and Capital in Modern Yucatán: Essays in Regional History and Political Economy* (Tuscaloosa: University of Alabama Press, 1991); Eric Van Young, ed., *Mexico's Regions: Comparative History and Development* (San Diego: Center for U.S.-Mexican Studies, 1992); and Edward D. Terry, Ben Fallaw, Gilbert M. Joseph, and Edward H. Moseley, eds., *Peripheral Visions: Politics, Society, and the Challenges of Modernity in Yucatán* (Tuscaloosa: University of Alabama Press, 2010). Anthologies that contrast the revolution in different regions include D. A. Brading, ed., *Caudillo and Peasant in the Mexican Revolution* (Cambridge, U.K.: Cambridge University Press, 1980); Jürgen Buchenau and William H. Beezley, eds., *State Governors in the Mexican Revolution: Portraits in Conflict, Courage, and Corruption* (Lanham, Md.: Rowman and Littlefield, 2009); Gilbert M. Joseph and Daniel Nugent, eds., *Everyday Forms of State Formation: Revolution and the Negotiation of Rule in Modern Mexico* (Durham, N.C.: Duke University Press, 1994); and Thomas Benjamin and Mark Wasserman, *Provinces of the Revolution: Essays on Regional Mexican History, 1910–1940* (Albuquerque: University of New Mexico Press, 1990).

A particular region (or group of regions) that has received burgeoning scholarly interest in recent years by historians of the revolution and its origins is the U.S.-Mexican borderlands. For a sampling of this literature, see Rachel St. John, *Line in the Sand: A History of the Western U.S.-Mexico Border* (Princeton: Princeton University Press, 2011); Samuel Truett and Elliott Young, eds., *Continental Crossroads: Remapping U.S.-Mexico Borderlands History* (Durham, N.C.: Duke University Press, 2004); Samuel Truett, *Fugitive Landscapes: The Forgotten History of the U.S.-Mexican Borderlands* (New Haven: Yale University Press, 2006); Benjamin Johnson and Andrew Graybill, eds., *Bridging National Borders in North America: Transnational and Comparative Histories* (Durham, N.C.: Duke University Press, 2010); Benjamin Johnson, *Revolution in Texas: How a Forgotten Rebellion and Its Bloody Suppression Turned Mexicans into Americans* (New Haven: Yale University Press, 2005); Charles H. Harris and Louis R. Sadler, *The Secret War in El Paso: Mexican Revolutionary Intrigue, 1906–1920* (Albuquerque: University of New Mexico Press, 2009); Elliott Young, *Catarino Garza's Revolution on the Texas-Mexico Border* (Durham, N.C.: Duke University Press, 2004); Paul J. Vanderwood and Frank Samponaro, *Border Fury: A Picture Postcard History of Mexico's Revolution and U.S. War Preparedness, 1910–1917* (Albuquerque: University of New Mexico Press, 1988); Joseph A. Stout, *Border Conflict: Villistas, Carrancistas, and the Punitive Expedition, 1915–1920* (Fort Worth: Texas Christian University, 1999); Linda B. Hall and Don M. Coerver, *Revolution on the Border: The United States and Mexico, 1910–1920* (Albuquerque: University of New Mexico Press, 1988); Neil Foley, *The White Scourge: Mexicans, Blacks, and Poor Whites in Texas Cotton Culture* (Berkeley: University of California Press, 1999); and Américo Paredes, *"With His Pistol in His Hand": A Border Ballad and Its Hero* (Austin: University of Texas Press, 1970).

On gender relations and their changing dynamics, see Ann S. Blum, "Speaking of Work and Family: Reciprocity, Child Labor, and Social Reproduction, Mexico City, 1920–1940," *Hispanic American Historical Review* 91.1 (2011): 63–95; Stephanie J. Smith, *Gender and the Mexican Revolution: Yucatán Women and the Realities of Patriarchy* (Chapel Hill: University of North Carolina Press, 2009); Jocelyn Olcott, *Revolutionary Women in Post-Revolutionary Mexico* (Durham, N.C.: Duke University Press, 2006); Jocelyn Olcott, Mary Kay Vaughan, and Gabriela Cano, eds., *Sex in Revolution: Gender, Politics, and Power in Modern Mexico* (Durham, N.C.: Duke University Press, 2006); Patience A. Schell and Stephanie Mitchell, eds., *The Women's Revolution: Mexico, 1900–1953* (Lanham, Md.: Rowman and Littlefield, 2007); Katherine E. Bliss, *Compromised Positions: Prostitution, Public Health, and Gender Politics in Revolutionary Mexico City* (University Park: Penn State University Press, 2001); Elizabeth Salas, *Soldaderas in the Mexican Military: Myth and History* (Austin: University of Texas Press, 1990); and Mathew C. Gutmann, *The Meanings of Macho: Being a Man in Mexico City*, rev. ed. (Berkeley: University of California Press, 2006).

There is still no overarching work on the turbulent 1920s and 1930s. John W. F. Dulles's *Yesterday in Mexico: A Chronicle of the Revolution, 1919–1936* (Austin: University of Texas Press, 1961) is still valuable for political history, as is Nora Hamilton, *The Limits of State Authority: Post-Revolutionary Mexico* (Princeton: Princeton University

Press, 1982), for issues of political economy. For a collection of essays examining the relationship between the revolutionary state and ordinary Mexicans, consult Mary Kay Vaughan and Stephen Lewis, eds., *The Eagle and the Virgin: Nation and Cultural Revolution in Mexico, 1920–1940* (Durham, N.C.: Duke University Press, 2005).

On society and culture in the 1920s and 1930s, see Alexander Dawson, *Indian and Nation in Revolutionary Mexico* (Tucson: University of Arizona Press, 2004); Rick López, *Crafting Mexico: Intellectuals, Artisans, and the State after the Revolution* (Durham, N.C.: Duke University Press, 2010); Andrae M. Marak, *From Many, One: Indians, Peasants, Borders, and Education in Callista Mexico, 1924–1935* (Calgary: University of Calgary Press, 2009); Patricia Elizabeth Olson, *Artifacts of Revolution: Architecture, Society, and Politics in Mexico City 1920–1940* (Lanham, Md.: Rowman and Littlefield, 2008); Mary Kay Vaughan, "Cultural Approaches to Peasant Politics in the Mexican Revolution," *Hispanic American Historical Review* 79.2 (1999): 269–305; Mary Kay Vaughan, *Cultural Politics in Revolution: Teachers, Peasants, and Schools, 1930–1940* (Tucson: University of Arizona Press, 1997); Andrew G. Wood, *Revolution in the Street: Women, Workers, and Urban Protest in Veracruz, 1870–1927* (Lanham, Md.: Rowman and Littlefield, 2001); Helen Delpar, *The Enormous Vogue of Things Mexican: Cultural Relations between the United States and Mexico, 1920–1935* (Tuscaloosa: University of Alabama Press, 1992); and John A. Britton, *Revolution and Ideology: The Image of the Mexican Revolution in the United States* (Lexington: University of Kentucky Press, 1995).

One of the enduring issues in historical scholarship is the relationship between the state and both the official and the popular church and, in particular, the Cristero Rebellion. See Matthew Butler, *Popular Piety and Political Identity in Mexico's Cristero Rebellion: Michoacán, 1927–1929* (Oxford, U.K.: Oxford University Press, 2004); Jennie Purnell, *Popular Movements and State Formation in Revolutionary Mexico: The Agraristas and Cristeros of Michoacán* (Durham, N.C.: Duke University Press, 1999); Jean Meyer, *The Cristero Rebellion: The Mexican People between Church and State, 1926–1929*, trans. Richard Southern (Cambridge, U.K.: Cambridge University Press, 1976); and David C. Bailey, *Viva Cristo Rey!: The Cristero Rebellion and the Church-State Conflict in Mexico* (Austin: University of Texas Press, 1974). For the multivalent relations of Protestant missionaries in revolutionary Mexico, see Todd Hartch, *Missionaries of the State: The Summer Institute of Linguistics, State Formation, and Indigenous Mexico, 1935–1985* (Tuscaloosa: University of Alabama Press, 2006).

Regarding the Cárdenas period, see Myrna I. Santiago, *The Ecology of Oil: Environment, Labor, and the Mexican Revolution 1900–1938* (Cambridge, U.K.: Cambridge University Press, 2006); Emily Wakild, *Revolutionary Parks: Conservation, Social Justice, and Mexico's National Parks* (Tucson: University of Arizona Press, 2011); Ben Fallaw, "The Life and Deaths of Felipa Poot: Women, Fiction, and Cardenismo in Postrevolutionary Mexico," *Hispanic American Historical Review* 82.4 (2002): 645–84; Ben Fallaw, *Cárdenas Compromised: The Failure of Reform in Postrevolutionary Yucatán* (Durham, N.C.: Duke University Press, 2001); Adrian A. Bantjes, *As If Jesus Walked on Earth: Cardenismo, Sonora, and the Mexican Revolution* (Wilmington, Del.: Scholarly

Resources, 1998); Jan Rus, "The 'Comunidad Revolucionaria Institucional': The Sub-version of Native Government in Highland Chiapas," in *Everyday Forms of State For-mation: Revolution and the Negotiation of Rule in Modern Mexico*, ed. Gilbert M. Joseph and Daniel Nugent (Durham, N.C.: Duke University Press, 1994), 265–300; Fried-rich E. Schuler, *Mexico between Hitler and Roosevelt: Mexican Foreign Relations in the Age of Lázaro Cárdenas, 1934–1940* (Albuquerque: University of New Mexico Press, 1998); Marjorie Becker, *Setting the Virgin on Fire: Lázaro Cárdenas, Michoacán Peas-ants, and the Redemption of the Mexican Revolution* (Berkeley: University of California Press, 1996); and Alan Knight, "Cardenismo: Juggernaut or Jalopy?" *Journal of Latin American Studies* 26 (1994): 73–107.

On Mexico during World War II, consult Monica A. Rankin, *Mexico, la patria: Propaganda and Production during World War II* (Lincoln: University of Nebraska Press, 2009); Daniel Newcomer, *Reconciling Modernity: Urban State Formation in the 1940s: León, Mexico* (Lincoln: University of Nebraska Press, 2004); Stephen R. Niblo, *Mexico in the 1940s: Modernity, Politics, and Corruption* (Wilmington, Del.: Scholarly Resources, 1999); María Emilia Paz, *Strategy, Security, and Spies: Mexico and the U.S. as Allies in World War Two* (University Park: Penn State University Press, 1997); and Stephen R. Niblo, *War, Diplomacy, and Development: The United States and Mexico, 1938–1954* (Wilmington, Del.: Scholarly Resources, 1995). On the Ávila Camacho period, see Alejandro Quintana, *Maximino Ávila Camacho and the One-Party State: The Taming of Caudillismo and Caciquismo in Post-Revolutionary Mexico* (Lanham, Md.: Rowman and Littlefield, 2010).

The post–World War II period is a new frontier of historical scholarship. Con-sult Jonathan Schlefer, *Palace Politics: How the Ruling Party Brought Crisis to Mexico* (Austin: University of Texas Press, 2008); Tanalís Padilla, *Rural Resistance in the Land of Zapata: The Jaramillista Movement and the Myth of the Pax Priísta, 1940–1962* (Durham, N.C.: Duke University Press, 2008); Donald C. Hodges and Daniel Ross Gandy, *Mexico: The End of the Revolution* (Westport, Conn.: Greenwood Press, 2002); Gilbert M. Joseph, Anne Rubenstein, and Eric Zolov, eds., *Fragments of a Golden Age: The Politics of Culture in Mexico since 1940* (Durham, N.C.: Duke University Press, 2001); Kevin J. Middlebrook, *The Paradox of Revolution: Labor, the State, and Authori-tarianism in Mexico* (Baltimore: Johns Hopkins University Press, 1995); and John W. Sherman, "The Mexican Miracle and Its Collapse," in *The Oxford History of Mexico*, ed. Michael C. Meyer and William H. Beezley (Oxford, U.K.: Oxford University Press, 2000), 575–98. Older studies include James M. Cypher, *State and Capital in Mexico* (Boulder, Colo.: Westview Press, 1990); Stanley R. Ross, *Is the Mexican Revolution Dead?* (New York: Knopf, 1966); Howard Cline, *Mexico: Revolution to Evolution* (New York: Oxford University Press, 1963); Raymond Vernon, *The Dilemma of Mexico's De-velopment: The Roles of the Private and Public Sectors* (Cambridge: Harvard University Press, 1963), and Paul Gillingham and Benjamin Smith, eds., *Dictablanda: Soft Authori-tarianism in Mexico, 1938–1968* (Durham, N.C.: Duke University Press, 2013).

Mexico's cultural history since World War II has seen a recent outburst of scholar-ship. For an overarching collection of essays, consult Gilbert M. Joseph, Anne Rubenstein, and Eric Zolov, eds., *Fragments of a Golden Age: The Politics of Culture in Mexico since 1940* (Durham, N.C.: Duke University Press, 2001). On the history of Mexican rock music, see Alejandro I. Madrid, *Sounds of the Modern Nation: Music, Culture and Ideas in Post-Revolutionary Mexico* (Philadelphia: Temple University Press, 2008); and Eric Zolov, *Refried Elvis: The Rise of the Mexican Counterculture* (Berkeley: University of California Press, 1999). Mexican visual culture is discussed in John Mraz, *Looking for Mexico: Modern Visual Culture and National Identity* (Durham, N.C.: Duke University Press, 2009); Roberto Tejada, *National Camera: Photography and Mexico's Image Environment* (Minneapolis: University of Minnesota Press, 2009); Jeffrey Pilcher, *Cantinflas and the Chaos of Mexican Modernity* (Wilmington, Del.: Scholarly Resources, 2001); Anne Rubenstein, *Bad Language, Naked Ladies, and Other Threats to the Nation: A Political History of Comic Books in Mexico* (Durham, N.C.: Duke University Press, 1998); Michael N. Miller, *Red, White, and Green: The Maturing of Mexicanidad* (El Paso: Texas Western Press, 1998); and Dina Berger and Andrew G. Wood, eds., *Holiday in Mexico: Critical Essays on Tourism and Tourist Encounters* (Durham, N.C.: Duke University Press, 2009).

Regarding the Cold War in Latin America, general treatments include Greg Grandin and Gilbert M. Joseph, eds., *A Century of Revolution: Insurgent and Counterinsurgent Violence during Latin America's Long Cold War* (Durham, N.C.: Duke University Press, 2010); Gilbert M. Joseph and Daniela Spenser, eds., *In from the Cold: Latin America's New Encounter with the Cold War* (Durham, N.C.: Duke University Press, 2008), which contains a section of essays on Mexico during the Cold War; and Rebecca M. Schreiber, *Cold War Exiles in Mexico: U.S. Dissidents and the Culture of Critical Resistance* (Minneapolis: University of Minnesota Press, 2008).

On the 1968 massacre, consult Elaine Carey, *Plaza of Sacrifices: Gender, Power, and Terror in 1968 Mexico* (Albuquerque: University of New Mexico Press, 2005); Paco Ignacio Taibo II, *68*, trans. Donald Nicholson-Smith (New York: Seven Stories Press, 2004); Lessie Jo Frazier and Deborah Cohen, "Defining the Space of Mexico '68: Heroic Masculinity in the Prison and Women in the Streets," *Hispanic American Historical Review* 83.4 (2003): 617–60; and Elena Poniatowska, *Massacre in Mexico*, trans. Helen R. Lane (Independence: University of Missouri Press, 1992). For studies on Mexico's Dirty War, see Alberto Ulloa Bornemann, *Surviving Mexico's Dirty War: A Political Prisoner's Memoir*, ed. and trans. Arthur Schmidt and Aurora Camacho (Philadelphia: Temple University Press, 2007).

On the neopopulist 1970s and early 1980s, see Amelia M. Kiddle and María L. O. Muñoz, eds., *Populism in 20th-Century Mexico: The Presidencies of Lázaro Cárdenas and Luis Echeverría* (Tucson: University of Arizona Press, 2010); Samuel Schmidt, *The Deterioration of the Mexican Presidency* (Tucson: University of Arizona Press, 1991); Yoram Shapira, *Mexican Foreign Policy under Echeverría* (Beverly Hills, Calif.: Sage, 1978); Stanley Ross, ed., *Views across the Border* (Albuquerque: University of New Mexico Press, 1978); and Susan Eckstein, *The Poverty of the Revolution: The State and the Urban Poor in Mexico* (Princeton: Princeton University Press 1977).

There is a rich literature concerning the economic crisis of 1982 and its aftermath as well as the process of globalization. See Stephen Haber, Herbert S. Klein, and Kevin J. Middlebrook, *Mexico Since 1980* (Cambridge, U.K.: Cambridge University Press, 2008); Dennis I. Gilbert, *Mexico's Middle Class in the Neoliberal Era* (Tucson: University of Arizona Press, 2007); Stephen D. Morris, *Corruption and Politics in Contemporary Mexico* (Tuscaloosa: University of Alabama Press, 1991); and Judith Adler Hellman, *Mexico in Crisis* (New York: Holmes and Meier, 1983). One particularly important protest and resistance movement is analyzed in Jeffrey Rubin, *Decentering the Regime: Ethnicity, Radicalism, and Democracy in Juchitán, Mexico* (Durham, N.C.: Duke University Press, 1997). On the 1985 earthquake in Mexico City, see Elena Poniatowska, *Nothing, Nobody: The Voices of the Mexico City Earthquake*, trans. Aurora Camacho de Schmidt and Arthur Schmidt (Philadelphia: Temple University Press, 1995).

On the Zapatista rebellion, see Adolfo Gilly, "Chiapas and the Rebellion of the Enchanted World," in *Rural Revolt in Mexico: U.S. Intervention and the Domain of Subaltern Politics*, ed. Daniel Nugent (Durham, N.C.: Duke University Press, 1998), 261–334; Nicholas P. Higgins, *Understanding the Chiapas Rebellion: Modernist Visions and the Invisible Indian* (Austin: University of Texas Press, 2004); Lynn Stephen, *Zapata Lives! History and Cultural Politics in Southern Mexico* (Berkeley: University of California Press, 2002); Shannan Mattiace, *To See with Two Eyes: Peasant Activism and Indian Autonomy in Chiapas* (Albuquerque: University of New Mexico Press, 2003); and Neil Harvey, *The Chiapas Rebellion: The Struggle for Land and Democracy* (Durham, N.C.: Duke University Press, 1998).

Among the studies of Mexico in the NAFTA era, see Kevin P. Gallagher, *Free Trade and the Environment: Mexico, NAFTA, and Beyond* (Stanford: Stanford University Press, 2004); Heather Williams, *Social Movements and Economic Transition: Markets and Distributive Conflict in Mexico* (New York: Cambridge University Press, 2001); Judith Adler Hellman, *Mexican Lives* (New York: New Press, 1995); Sarah Babb, *Managing Mexico: Economists from Nationalism to Neoliberalism* (Princeton: Princeton University Press, 2001); Susan Kaufman Purcell, *Mexico in Transition: Implications for U.S. Policy* (New York: Council on Foreign Relations, 1988); and Jorge G. Castañeda, *The Mexican Shock: Its Meaning for the United States* (New York: New Press, 1995).

Regarding democratization and the demise of the PRI as the ruling party, consult Julia Preston and Samuel Dillon, *Opening Mexico: The Making of a Democracy* (New York: Farrar, Straus and Giroux, 2005); George W. Grayson, *Mexico: Narco-Violence and a Failed State* (New York: Transaction, 2010); Louise Walker, "Economic Fault Lines and Middle-Class Fears: Tlatelolco, Mexico City 1985," in *Aftershocks: Earthquakes and Popular Politics in Latin America*, ed. Jürgen Buchenau and Lyman L. Johnson (Albuquerque: University of New Mexico Press, 2009); Daniel Levy and Kathleen Bruhn, *Mexico: The Struggle for Democratic Development*, 2nd ed. (Berkeley: University of California Press, 2006); Luis Rubio and Susan Kaufman Purcell, *Mexico under Fox* (Boulder, Colo.: Lynne Rienner, 2004); Kevin Middlebrook, ed., *Dilemmas of Political Change in Mexico* (San Diego: UCSD Center for Mexican Studies, 2004); Stephen D.

Morris, *Political Reformism in Mexico: An Overview of Contemporary Mexican Politics* (Boulder, Colo.: Lynne Rienner, 1995); Susan Kaufman Purcell and Luis Rubio, eds., *Mexico under Zedillo* (Boulder, Colo.: Lynne Rienner, 1998); and George W. Grayson, *Mexican Messiah: Andrés Manuel López Obrador* (University Park: Penn State University Press, 2007).